5/10

D0927857

2

ILLINOIS CENTRAL COLLEGE

A12901 775371

WITHDRAWN

I.C.C. LIBRARY

DEMCO

From BIRDWOMEN to SKYGIRLS

From BIRDWOMEN to SKYGIRLS

American Girls' Aviation Stories

by Fred Erisman

I.C.C. LIBRARY

TCU Press

Fort Worth, Texas

PS
374
.A37
E76
2009

Copyright © 2009 Fred Erisman

Library of Congress Cataloging-in-Publication Data

Erisman, Fred, 1937-
From birdwomen to skygirls : American girls' aviation stories / Fred
Erisman.
    p. cm.
Includes bibliographical references and index.
ISBN 978-0-87565-397-6 (cloth : alk. paper)
1. Aeronautics in literature. 2. American fiction--20th century--History
and criticism. 3. Children's stories, American--History and criticism. 4.
Young adult fiction, American--History and criticism. 5. Children's liter-
ature in series--History and criticism. 6. Women air pilots in literature.
7. Flight attendants in literature. 8. Women in aeronautics--United
States--History. 9. Sex role--United States--History--20th century. I.
Title.
PS374.A37E76 2009
813'.509356--dc22
                2009006782

TCU Press
P. O. Box 298300
Fort Worth, Texas 76129
817.257.7822
http://www.prs.tcu.edu

To order books: 800.826.8911

Designed by Barbara Whitehead

Cover illustration: *Linda Carlton's Ocean Flight,* (c) 1931.
(Author's collection).

3/10 B&T 29.95

FOR

PLE
JMacBA   LKH
JDS

Female role models par excellence

Contents

Illustrations

Illustration XI

Preface

L

egend tells us that the great names of aviation are male. Wilbur and Orville Wright, Glenn Curtiss and Charles A. Lindbergh, Jimmy Doolittle and Roscoe Turner, Chuck Yeager and Neil Armstrong—they make up an unbroken procession of men. Whether pioneering flight, crossing oceans, or achieving new levels of speed, distance, and altitude, men proudly carry the torch of aviation. Although journalistic coverage of their exploits would be enough to cement their mythic status, their legend has been reinforced by fictional dramatizations of their deeds aimed at air-minded American boys. These are the aviation series books that, from 1910 until well into the 1950s, provided adolescent and pre-adolescent American males with their notions of flight.

Embracing more than forty series and over three hundred volumes, the boys' books pick up on every technical or historical achievement in the realm of flight and show it to be the work of a male. Bill Bruce holds off the Boche during World War I; Ted Scott flies the Atlantic in 1927; Andy Lane pioneers rocket-powered flight and introduces the flying wing in 1931; Stan Wilson and "Lucky" Terrell confront the Axis powers of World War II and follow aviation into the early days of post-war expansion of commercial flight. One and all, the heroes are manly types, and their derring-do dramatizes, interprets, and romanticizes aviation lore for three generations of American boys.[1]

Legend notwithstanding, logic tells us that where there are men, there are women. No realm of exploration, no area of endeavor, has remained the exclusive preserve of men, and aviation is no exception. Almost from the beginning of powered flight, women were a notable presence in aviation. "Baroness" Raymonde de la

Roche and champion cyclist Hélène Dutrieu led the way among Continental fliers before World War I, and American women were not long in following suit. Ruth Law and Katherine and Marjorie Stinson before World War I; Amelia Earhart, Elinor Smith and Louise Thaden during the Depression years; Jacqueline Cochran and Patty Wagstaff in mid-century, "Jerrie" Cobb and Sally Ride in the last half of the twentieth century: they made their names in ways comparable to the men. Through speed and altitude records, long-distance and endurance flying, aerobatics and space flight, they, too, furthered the cause of aviation.

Women fliers' exploits, like those of the men, are echoed in a variety of books. These books, like the female fliers themselves, are a minority within the history of juvenile literature and aviation. Whereas boys had more than forty series to entertain and inform them, girls had a handful of free-standing books and barely a dozen series, fifty-some volumes extending from tales of plucky girls in the earliest days of flight to accounts of glamorous airline stewardesses in the era after World War II. Their small numbers notwithstanding, the girls' books consistently convey the message that the soaring world of flight offers young women a degree of independence, freedom, and responsibility unequaled by any earthbound technology. They also go on to acquaint their readers with the shifting nature of American attitudes toward social class, gender roles, and the larger place of women in a progressive society.

Boys' aviation books of every era stress historical continuity, technical authenticity, and responsible self-reliance. Those written for girls take a somewhat different tack. They echo, to be sure, the development of aviation. The earliest series invoke the Wright Brothers, Glenn H. Curtiss, Louis Blériot, Arch Hoxsey, and other notables of the era. Later books, following an eighteen-year hiatus spanning World War I and its aftermath, speak as readily of Charles and Anne Morrow Lindbergh, Amelia Earhart, the Britisher Amy Johnson, and others, noting their achievements and the advances they brought about. Neither do they stint on the technical side of flight. The books' heroines are comfortably at home with the theories of aeronautics and the diverse machinery that makes flight possible. To this extent, the girls' flying stories run generally parallel to those directed toward boys, with the added fillip that they imply that young American women are as knowledgeable about, and as interested in, the techniques and technology of flight as are young American boys.

The larger significance of the girls' stories lies in their differences from the boys' stories. In addition to calling upon the larger attributes of flight and the pilot's world, the books draw upon two powerful influences in modern women's history. One is the extent to which an up-to-date machine works to free women from social constraints. The other is the growing effort of modern women to be seen and evaluated as individuals rather than females. To the books' authors, almost exclusively women, the airplane was the latest and most advanced of a series of liberating machines embraced by women. First came the bicycle. As historian Stephen Kern points out, the bicycle provided women with a new kind of mobility and independence, one cutting across class lines and allowing them to acquire "confidence, employment, and strength."[2] The bicycle's association with women also began to influence fashions, leading to clothing that was freer and less formal than customary garb, yet as socially acceptable as the latter. Thus, in activity, outlook, and garb, the bicycle provided women with an accessible means of gaining independence, ultimately leading the ardent suffragist Susan B. Anthony to remark, "I think it [bicycling] has done more to emancipate women than anything else in the world."[3]

Close on the heels of the bicycle came the automobile, and women were quick to seize upon the opportunities that it offered. Although men's jokes about women drivers appeared as quickly as the drivers themselves, women pressed on, embracing the automobile as an agency of their growing independence and solidarity. Women's growing skills at the wheel by 1909 brought the grudging concession from the *New York Times* that "there are a number of prominent women drivers who can operate an auto as well as many of the best men pilots." Driving skills were paralleled by women's increasing comfort with the technology of their automobiles, and the ability of many to repair their machines as readily as any man. Embarking on a cross-country drive from New York City to San Francisco in 1910, Blanche Stuart Scott proclaimed that she had become "more or less independent by thoroughly familiarizing [herself] with the general mechanical principles and mechanism of [her] car," and pronounced herself "thoroughly competent" to deal with repairs along the way. Like the bicycle of an earlier time, the automobile became "an important cultural emblem of women's quest for autonomy and independence," embraced by feminist activists as both "transportation and an important sign of their modernity."[4]

The airplane speedily replaced the automobile as an emblem of modernity, with Blanche Stuart Scott announcing: "Automobiles are back numbers; It's a biplane I want now." Its very newness allowed women fliers to transcend "traditional social roles and assumptions about women's limited capabilities"[5] The ease with which women mastered the airplane's technology enabled them to compete more readily with men as equals. The skills required by flight were the same whether the operator was male or female, and role limitations imposed by society became less significant than the pilot's demonstrated skills. Moreover, like the automobile, the airplane introduced a whole new fashion of dress. Open cockpits were commonplace until well into the 1920s, and the blouses and skirts of everyday wear were wholly impractical for a woman pilot. Flying togs, usually incorporating jodhpur breeches, an open-collared tailored shirt, a leather jacket, and a snug-fitting helmet equipped with goggles, became acceptable in public overnight. The outfit revealed the wearer's modernity and her indifference to conventionality.

As women began to embrace aviation, the girls' books accompanied them. The earliest volumes record the days of air shows and public competitions, when a back-yard tinkerer could achieve notable advances and the mere sight of a flying machine was enough to gather a crowd. In these books, young women are active participants, equaling—and sometimes surpassing—the abilities of their male counterparts. Though the books pass over World War I without comment, they take on new vigor in the days following Charles A. Lindbergh's 1927 flight from New York to Paris. Now, like their male-oriented counterparts, the books record the empowerment provided by the airplane. Women fly oceans, reach new altitudes, or prove their skills at high-speed flight. The coming of World War II creates another hiatus. So far as the books are concerned, women have no place in military flying, and there is little mention of pre-war efforts to incorporate female fliers in public and military service or the wartime creation of the Women Air Service Pilots (WASP).[6]

The final iteration of the girls' flying stories is the stewardess story. In it, the coming of commercial aviation intersects with the growing presence of women in the workplace. Women early on began winning federal transport licenses, qualifying them to fly for pay. Yet, while women pilots struggled futilely to be accepted as airline pilots or co-pilots, the airlines had other ideas. They began to hire women to work as stewardesses, assisting passengers, and tending to other cabin duties. The young women of the stewardess stories, capable, intelligent, and as devoted to flight as their male and female antecedents, helped to establish commercial aviation as comfortable, reliable, safe, and modern.

In their earliest versions, the stewardesses are the last vestigial exponents of the individualistic spirit of flight among the series book heroines; they look upon flight with the same excitement as their literary forebears. Technology and society change, however, and the portrayal of the stewardess undergoes major alteration in the postwar years. Just as American attitudes toward women shifted dramatically in the years following World War II, so, too, does the implicit portrayal of the stewardess. Once an independent free spirit liberated by her work with an airline, the stewardess following

World War II emerges as a much more limited, societally shaped person. Aviation may well have offered liberation up to that date, but society continues to exert its power.

A final point needs to be made. The world of the girls' flying stories is not perfect. Like the times whence they sprang, the books accept and express views of class, race, and gender that twenty-first century readers often find repugnant. The heroines themselves are uniformly white, Protestant, and upper-middle-class, and live in a white, Protestant, and upper-middle-class society. Whatever their age, they speak of themselves—and are spoken of by others, female as well as male—as "girls," and take no offense at the label. Airline flight attendants refer to themselves as "stewardesses" or "hostesses," taking pride in the designation and all its implications. Other characters are less fortunate. New York clothiers shrug readily, gesticulate broadly, and speak with Yiddish inflections. Widows who take in boarders are quite often Irish and invariably comic. African Americans, when they appear at all, are shuffling, mush-mouthed, and servile. Foreigners in general are readily identifiable by outré dress, darker complexions, unkempt beards, and accented speech. Italian immigrants speak broken English, have large families, and green thumbs. Hispanics, initially comic menaces, become slightly more complex during the Second World War, appearing either as Nazi sympathizers or as persons to be catered to in accordance with the Good Neighbor Policy. Other stereotypes are as blatant.

The prejudices and stereotypes the books reflect are part of the times in which they were written and must be accepted as such; we cannot fully understand those times without understanding their beliefs and prejudices. We may deplore the usages, but to condemn them is folly, for we would be imposing the values of our time upon those of earlier times. These very stereotypes and succeeding generations' responses to them have led to the society that we enjoy. We need not applaud the unpalatable ideas of the past, but we should not condemn them out of hand. They are a part of our history.[7]

Notes

1. The fullest examination of boys' aviation series to date is Fred Erisman, *Boys' Books, Boys' Dreams, and the Mystique of Flight* (Fort Worth: TCU Press, 2006).

2. Stephen Kern, *The Culture of Time and Space 1880-1918* (Cambridge: Harvard University Press, 1983), 216-217.

3. "The World Awheel," *Munsey's Magazine* 15 (May 1896): 131-159; Susan B. Anthony, quoted in Pryor Dodge, *The Bicycle* (Paris: Flammarion, 1996), 130.

4. "Women Auto Drivers in Endurance Run," *New York Times,* 21 October 1909, S4; "Woman to Drive Auto to Frisco," *New York Times,* 15 May 1910, S4; Julie Wosk, *Women and the Machine: Representations from the Spinning Wheel to the Electronic Age* (Baltimore: Johns Hopkins University Press, 2001), 125. See also Deborah Clarke, *Driving Women: Fiction and Automobile Culture in Twentieth-Century America* (Baltimore: Johns Hopkins University Press, 2007).

5. "An American Bird-Woman," *Dallas Morning News,* 21 January 1912, 2; Wosk, *Women and the Machine,* 149.

6. A convenient overview of these efforts appears in Deborah G. Douglas, *American Women and Flight Since 1940* (Lexington: University Press of Kentucky, 2004).

7. See Roberta Seelinger Trites, *Disturbing the Universe: Power and Repression in Adolescent Literature* (Iowa City: University of Iowa Press, 2000), 31, for the importance of understanding a work's historical context.

Acknowledgments

The idea for this study arose during my 2002-2003 year as Charles A. Lindbergh Chair of Aerospace History at the National Air and Space Museum, Smithsonian Institution. My project at that time was focused on boys' aviation books, and my discovery of the analogous girls' stories was eye-opening. The Smithsonian year also provided the greater part of the technical materials offered here.

Research into the girls' books themselves was done principally at the Children's Literature Research Collections (CLRC), University of Minnesota, Minneapolis, and in the Special Collections section of the Mary Couts Burnet Library, Texas Christian University. Both depositories have impressive holdings, but the CLRC ranks among the best in the world.

For suggestions, encouragement, and general all-around help, I am indebted to these individuals:

—at the National Air and Space Museum: Dorothy Cochrane, Peter L. Jakab, Russ Lee, and Dominick A. Pisano of the Aeronautics Division; and Valerie Neal, Michael Neufeld, and David Devorkin of the Division of Space History.

—at the CLRC: Karen Nelson Hoyle, Curator, and her unfailingly professional staff.

—at Texas Christian University: Roger Rainwater, Head of Special Collections, Mary Couts Burnet Library; Kay Edmonson and the entire Interlibrary Loan staff; Judy Alter and Susan R. Petty of the TCU Press; and my colleague Linda K. Hughes, whose tutoring heightened my understanding of feminism and women's history.

—at home: my wife, Patricia L. Erisman. Despite having endured the gestation and birthing of one book, she encouraged me to pursue a second. She listened patiently and kept the coffee coming.

From BIRDWOMEN to SKYGIRLS

CHAPTER 1

Formula Stories and Young Readers:

1900-1930

Long before television, well before the coming of network radio, even before the widespread presence of motion-picture theaters, there was the formula story. Series book or free-standing volume, readily available and cheaply priced, these accounts provided entertainment, excitement, and information for four generations of American boys and girls. The books, called by some "a particularly American phenomenon," have their origins in 1835, when Jacob Abbott published the first of his "Rollo" books (which ultimately reached twenty-eight volumes), tales of a five–year-old boy who grew in age, worldly awareness, and morality as the series proceeded. Six years later, Abbott began the "Lucy" series, relating the adventures of Rollo's cousin, Lucy, who, like her forebear, experienced one adventure after another, all well-calculated to instill moral and factual lessons along with their excitement. The two series, combined with a third, Abbott's "Jonas" books, sold nearly a million-and-a-half copies by 1880.

Abbott established at least three continuing conventions of the formula genre. First was the highlighting of the protagonist's name in the title, as in *Rollo at Work*, of 1837. Second was the printing of the books in uniform format, enabling readers to identify them readily on the shelf. And third was the spinning off of a girls' series from an established boys' series, as the later "Motor Boys" books, begun in 1906, gave rise to "The Motor Girls" of 1910 and later. The formula story as a genre, however, did not come into its own until later in the nineteenth century, when the advent of the rotary press permitted mass publication and reduced per-copy costs, and the completion of the transcontinental railroad made easy national distribution of the books a reality.

The genre received a boost when Horatio Alger, Jr., began the "Ragged Dick" stories in 1867, making the "rags to riches" plot another convention of the series story. From that series and its successors came other conventions, as well. As Russel B. Nye points out, Alger throughout his career used his books to convey a distinctively American self-reliance. The basic Alger formula involved a searching vision of a new and evolving urban life and the conviction that solid, middle-class virtues and the corresponding social values undergirded every facet of American life. These values with little or no modification became staples of the twentieth century's formula books.[1]

For all the popularity of formula stories, their fullest development did not occur until 1906, when Edward Stratemeyer created the Stratemeyer Syndicate. Stratemeyer had already established himself as a prolific author of dime novels and series books; however, his ideas for stories quickly outstripped his ability to write them, and he conceived of the idea of outsourcing the plots to hired writers. These individuals, working from an outline of three to five typed pages, would generate a manuscript of two hundred pages and twenty-five chapters. Writing the text took anywhere from four to six weeks, and the author, in return for a flat fee of $50 to $100, waived all rights to any further recognition. The book would then be published with a Syndicate "house name" as its author, the name selected according to the series involved. These fictional authors quickly became household names, and took on a life of their own. "Laura Lee Hope" was known for the "Bobbsey Twins" books, "Lester Chadwick" the "Baseball Joe" stories, "Franklin W. Dixon" the "Hardy Boys" and "Ted Scott" adventures, and "Carolyn Keene" the "Nancy Drew" mysteries. All received quantities of fan mail, yet none existed in fact.[2]

The genre quickly spread world-wide, with young readers in Great Britain and Germany, in particular, reaping the benefits of stories set in their own national context. Nonetheless, the books remained singularly American in their nature, stressing American locations and American social values, and it was in the United States that they enjoyed their greatest dissemination. George T. Dunlap, head of the Grosset & Dunlap publishing firm, one of Stratemeyer's chief outlets, pointed to overall sales in the millions. The "Bobbsey Twins," for example, begun in 1904, had sold 5,619,129 copies by the end of 1936, while, in the same period, the "Tom Swift" technological books, a far smaller series begun in 1910, had sold 6,566,646 copies. Impressive though they are in their own right, these figures are not necessarily an entirely accurate reflection of the books' total readership. Volumes were routinely passed from hand to hand among young readers of both sexes and served as a convenient medium of exchange for childhood bartering. Their readership—and their influence—was thus far greater than the sales figures reflect.[3]

By the end of their first century (1835-1935), formula books were a substantial part of popular reading for young Americans. Whether one of a kind or part of a lengthy series, the books' popularity was due in great part to their authors' (and their publishers') sense of audience. Young readers of the time had ready access to writings by mainstream authors—such writers as William Cullen Bryant, Bret Harte, William Dean Howells, Rudyard Kipling, Lord Tennyson, Theodore Roosevelt, and Mark Twain—who freely directed many of their works to a youthful audience. Still, at a time when age discrimination by authors and publishers alike was much less prevalent in the trade than in the twenty-first century, formula works even more so than mainstream works anticipated the genre today known as "Young Adult" fiction. The appeal of their alternate view of reality extended from readers in their late teens downward to those in the pre-teen years. Girls' books, as a rule, were aimed at a readership ranging from eight to sixteen years of age. Boys' books, for their part, extended the range somewhat, speaking to an audience aged from ten to eighteen, and sometimes a bit older.[4]

The books soon developed a library of familiar topics. Boarding-school and high school stories gave an appealing picture of academic life to come. Sports stories told of victories on the gridiron and last-minute saves on the baseball diamond. Scouting tales appealed to both Boy and Girl Scouts, helping to reinforce their commitment to the organizations. Career stories offered glimpses of the coming adult life and suggested adventures to be found in even the most mundane occupation. Some series dealt with far-off locales, as in the "Bomba the Jungle Boy" books (1926-1938; twenty titles), set in an Africa that existed only in Stratemeyer's mind. Others focused on regions closer to home, as did "The X-Bar-X Boys" tales (1926-1942; twenty-one titles) of the American West. Hunting and fishing tales appealed to young male readers, while more general outdoor stories of camping and nature study were addressed to the girls; both outlined the possibilities of adventures in the Great Outdoors. Whatever their setting and story line, all of the series offered adventures suited to the particular locale and all offered attractive protagonists, female as well as male, who enjoyed singular freedom as they dealt with the contemporaneous world.

These books were not works of high literary quality. The stories, series or individual volumes, necessarily trafficked shamelessly in formulas and existing racial and ethnic stereotypes. This was, in part, a function of the way they were created. Individual Stratemeyer authors frequently produced eight or more books a year. Other authors were equally prolific: the two volumes of the "Girl Flyers" books (1932; two titles) and the four volumes of the "Dorothy Dixon" series (1933; four titles) were obviously written to permit publication within a single year. A basic formula enabled the series writer to generate speedy copy, with Stratemeyer's outlines stipulating characters, principal action, and even individual and social values. Mildred Wirt completed the first three volumes of the "Nancy Drew" series between October 1929 and April 1930. Leslie McFarlane wrote seven "Dave Fearless" books during 1926 and turned out the first three "Hardy Boys" stories between November 1929 and March 1930. Not surprisingly, then, stereotypes and a certain sameness would color each new book as authors strove to insert predetermined characters, predetermined values, and predetermined locales into the next thrilling installment.[5]

The series' literary sameness worked to readers' advantage as much as to the authors'. With each volume featuring the same characters, the same kind of dialogue and action, and even the same locales, young readers were assured of a reliable, predictable story that they could depend upon for excitement and entertainment. As Selma G. Lanes remarks in her examination of series books both cheap and mainstream, "The addicted reader opens book three or four or eleven in a given series and is thoroughly at home in the locale – its by now familiar native characters, the verbal shrubbery and the narrative floorboards that occasionally creak." For a young reader, therefore, series books could "always be relied upon for hours of pleasurable company." Such a revelation was nothing new to Stratemeyer, who took pride in the series' predictability. "We read a book of William Dean Howells because we hope to find it Howellsesque," he told an interviewer in 1917. "The young girl wants George Barr McCutcheon's every book to be like 'Graustark.' We feel cheated if we pick up a favorite author's new book and find it like nothing he ever wrote before."[6] The similarities among the books are as much a part of the formula as the characters and the dialogue, and, in very practical ways, formulaic writing served a necessary purpose for authors and readers alike.

Among the formula stories, one of the most timely was the technological story. Directed toward both female and male readers, these stories strove to present, explain, and interpret the marvels that twentieth-century technology was bringing about. The wonders of invention, generalized or specialized, became a principal topic. Railroad operations, wireless and radio construction, motion picture goings-on, and the possibilities of the automobile, the airship, and, ultimately, the airplane sprang from their pages. Francis Molson, in an essay surveying technological works created by the Stratemeyer Syndicate and other publishers, identifies four principal story types feeding the national interest in technology. These, he says, were "invention, radio, auto, and aviation." That is, the books tell of the creation of technical devices, then go on to demonstrate the applications of these same devices while addressing their social implications as the devices' influence spreads. All served to make technological stories a commonplace, and to stress technology's accessibility to all persons.[7]

The very success of the formula works available to American youth in the early twentieth century quickly created a backlash. Franklin K. Mathiews, Chief Librarian of the Boy Scouts of America, took the lead among the critics, in 1914 publishing an article entitled "Blowing Out the Boy's Brains." He readily acknowledged that teenaged boys craved excitement in their reading, and he saw no dangers in that craving. How it was to be satisfied, however, was another matter indeed. Looking at the full range of series books, he concluded: "I wish I could label each one of these books: 'Explosives! Guaranteed to Blow Your Boy's Brains Out.'" His contention was that the series books, which he lumped together as "the viler and cheaper sort, [which] by overstimulation, debauch and vitiate, as brain and body are debauched and destroyed by strong drink." So pernicious are these books, he concluded, that the steady reader, reaching maturity, will "be greatly handicapped in business, [and] the whole world of art in its every form almost is closed to him."[8] For Mathiews, the future of the country was at risk.

Some publishers took Mathiews's criticisms to heart, slanting their books to real-life concerns. Back-cover copy advertising the "Girl Aviators Series" (1911-1912; four titles) pointed out that "The great interest displayed in Aviation, with the knowledge that its

popularity is increasing among young women, prompts us in offering these excellent volumes. Absolutely clean and wholesome
throughout, these books will win favor with all girls who are fond
of adventure." Mathiews's criticisms seemed to carry weight even
two decades later, in Bess Moyer's "Girl Flyers" books. Back-cover
copy on the first volume, *Gypsies of the Air*, assured young readers'
parents that "Mothers who are deeply concerned for their children's
inner life will find this series a real boon. . . . Our policy is always to
publish good books for red-blooded boys and girls, without anything in the stories which may cause fright, suggest fear, or glorify
mischief."[9] That the stories contained in the books were not significantly different from those issued by Stratemeyer was of little con-
sequence; parents could pass the books to their children reassured
that their contents were clean, wholesome, and modern.

The Aeroplane Series

By JOHN LUTHER LANGWORTHY

1. The Aeroplane Boys; or, The Young Pilots First Air Voyage
2. The Aeroplane Boys on the Wing; or, Aeroplane Chums in the Tropics
3. The Aeroplane Boys Among the Clouds; or, Young Aviators in a Wreck
4. The Aeroplane Boys' Flights; or, A Hydroplane Round-up
5. The Aeroplane Boys on a Cattle Ranch

The Girl Aviator Series

By MARGARET BURNHAM

Just the type of books that delight and fascinate the wide awake Girls of the present day who are between the ages of eight and fourteen years. The great author of these books regards them as the best products of her pen. Printed from large clear type on a superior quality of paper; attractive multi-color jacket wrapper around each book. Bound in cloth.

1. The Girl Aviators and the Phantom Airship
2. The Girl Aviators on Golden Wings
3. The Girl Aviators' Sky Cruise
4. The Girl Aviators' Motor Butterfly.

For sale by all booksellers or sent postpaid on receipt of 75c.

M . A . D O N O H U E   &   C O M P A N Y
701-733 S. DEARBORN STREET   ::   CHICAGO

Books for Girls

• THE GIRL FLYER SERIES

By Bess Moyer

Dick Mapes, an airmail pilot and owner of a flying field, is the father of two high spirited and adventurous girls, Terry and Prim, who go in for all outdoor sports; especially flying.

Their adventures in the air, their experiences in helping to solve mysteries that are everyday occurrences of a modern flying field, will be extremely interesting to any real girl.

GYPSIES OF THE AIR
ON ADVENTURE ISLAND

• THE MADGE STERLING SERIES

By Ann Wirt

Madge Sterling is an out-of-doors girl with a keen, alert mind, who finds her talent for solving baffling mysteries put to test. Each story in this series is an exciting tale of adventure and mystery that will keep the reader guessing. The element of suspense is added to make the wholesome stories thoroughly enjoyable reading.

THE MISSING FORMULA
THE DESERTED YACHT
THE SECRET OF THE SUN DIAL

THE GOLDSMITH PUBLISHING COMPANY
New York, N. Y.

---

*Above left: M. A. Donohue advertisement (1911) for two early aviation series.
(Author's collection). Above right: Goldsmith Publishing Co. advertisement (1932)
linking the "Girl Flyer" books with a second girls' adventure series. .
(Author's collection).*

In the broadest sense, the formula, whether employed in a series or in a free-standing book, was designed to appeal to boys and girls alike. Though boys as a rule shunned "girls' books," girls happily read boys' books along with those intended for their own sex, absorbing the heroes' adventures and social views alongside those of their heroines. Whether intended for male or female readers, the basic story offered an attractive protagonist, male or female, generally aged between fifteen and twenty. These individuals, ethically upright, quietly competent, and utterly dependable, would explore their white, middle-class world by means of a machine—automobile, airplane, or what have you. At times, the machine would open the opportunity for a vocation and the protagonist would enter training for that job. At other times, it might serve merely to broaden the characters' world through travel. Accompanied by one or more intimate friends ("chums" in the parlance of the books) and unencumbered by adult interference, the protagonists would master the complexities of the machine, put their skills to good use in a series of exciting encounters, and look ahead to further adventures of the same sort. Fictional teenaged boys and girls roamed the world as photographers, automobilists, film-makers, pilots, or other workers, and their readers eagerly followed their activities.[10]

Formula writing served a social purpose as well. If a formula was to succeed, it had to appeal to the widest possible audience, engaging their immediate interests and concerns and embodying "the prevailing cultural vision of what a young person should do, be, and think." Here lies the real value of the series books: they offer their readers an interpretation of the contemporaneous world. John G. Cawelti, in *Adventure, Mystery, and Romance* (1976), speaks directly to this quality: formulas "successfully articulate a pattern of fantasy that is at least acceptable to if not preferred by the cultural groups who enjoy them. Formulas enable the members of a group to share the same fantasies." Thus, the formulas of series writing engage not only the individual reader but also an entire class or culture. They offer a way for boys and girls to live out the fantasies that are shared by their peers *and* endorsed by their elders, making both the fantasy world and the mundane world seem more appealing and attainable.[11]

From this general premise, Cawelti develops several specific postulates. First, he argues, "Formula stories affirm existing interests and attitudes by presenting an imaginary world that is aligned with these interests and attitudes. . . . By confirming existing definitions of the world, literary formulas help to maintain a culture's ongoing consensus about the nature of reality and morality."[12] Formula stories, that is to say, build upon generally held public attitudes toward society and social interaction. They tap into their time's beliefs toward morality, behavior, and work. In so doing, they enhance the centrality of those attitudes in real life, confirming and illuminating the part that the attitudes play in the culture's day-to-day life. Thus, for example, the "Motor Girls" stories reflect and reinforce generalized popular attitudes toward the roles of young women. The girl protagonists may well enjoy an uncommon degree of liberation in their thinking and personal actions, but they still live by the mores of their day. They are honest, capable, moral, and open-minded, reflecting attributes the time esteems in its women.

Next is Cawelti's argument that "Formulas resolve tensions and ambiguities resulting from the conflicting interests of different groups within the culture or from ambiguous attitudes toward particular values." If a society has mixed feelings concerning a particular development or a particular behavior, a widely read popular formula can help to reconcile those feelings among the larger group. The "Tom Swift" stories, for example, on the one hand celebrate the versatility and ingenuity of the American inventor, and on the other reassure readers who might be unsettled by the ongoing course of technological development. Tom's technical and financial successes with his newest creation reflect both the inevitable advancement of technology and the sense that that advance will be valuable to the workings of the larger society.[13]

Third among Cawelti's premises is the proposition that "Formulas enable the audience to explore in fantasy the boundary between the permitted and the forbidden and to experience in a carefully controlled way the possibility of stepping across this boundary." The books present a world in which the fantasies of the future are realized. Adolescents over the years have longed for the independence of adult life, when they can take part in activities currently forbidden them by age or sex. At the back of their minds, young readers know it is highly unlikely that as adults they will single-handedly fly the Atlantic, blithely tour the United States in their own airplane, or regularly round up miscreants and bring them to justice. Even so, they enjoy speculating about what just *might* be possible. The readers identify with the series characters and their achievements and come to see the differences between the practical, real world in which they live and the realistic yet fantasy world in which the characters live. They vicariously revel for the moment in the unfettered freedom enjoyed by the series characters, and come away more comfortable with their own situation in the future.[14] If only in their minds, they are savoring the liberation that *might* be theirs.

The final premise contends that "literary formulas assist in the process of assimilating changes in values to traditional imaginative constructs." How is one to deal with new and socially influential devices such as the electric locomotive, the radio transmitter and receiver, the television set or the automobile? How should one look upon the rapidly expanding job market, with its new opportunities for women as well as men, its new occupations that require new skills and new education, and the possibility of its putting previously minimized and unempowered individuals into positions of responsibility or authority? Formula stories suggest a number of ways that these concerns might be incorporated into the coming society. The books show, if not *the* way, at least *a* way of compatibly merging new developments with older ways of looking at life. Their circumstances present the kind of world that embracing technological changes may bring, and demonstrate how society may well be changed. Even so, ties to the older ways of life will still be apparent and young readers will take away a sense of the accretive, constructive nature of progress.[15]

From the formula stories, therefore, come what Selma Lanes calls "primers of life": books that "are practical handbooks for getting along successfully in the workaday world." The books' vision may be limited, constrained by the strictures imposed by outline or by haste. Yet the vision they portray is one of young persons getting along, even triumphing, in ways that clearly conform to, are acceptable to, and are rewarded by the larger adult world the readers are facing. No matter how fanciful or improbable the settings and circumstances, the formula shows the importance of education, of competence, of dependability, and of integrity. A book's protagonists may well soar into the skies, travel the world, or plumb the ocean depths in ways that lesser souls can only imagine, but "each action-packed adventure . . . rests on the bedrock of conventional practicality and sensible rules of day-to-day behavior which surely would rate general grownup approval." Behind the special skills or circumstances of the formula heroes or heroines lies a solid foundation of realistic virtues and common-sensical attitudes, a grounding that will well serve young readers in the world to come.[16]

As both Cawelti and Lanes point out, the formula story, be it a volume in a series or a free-standing book, introduces and reinforces compelling cultural views. Whether directed toward boys or girls, the stories stress the importance of individual action, the value—*and* responsibilities—of personal freedom, the manner in which competence will always overcome incompetence and ineptitude, and the overwhelming necessity for absolute personal integrity in one's dealings with individuals or the larger society. These views appear in various combinations throughout the series and formula stories, whether Stratemeyer-created or not, and they give to their young *male* readers a subtle yet sound sense of what may lie ahead in the adult world they are preparing to enter.

For young *female* readers, however, there is another dimension. The values that resonate throughout the girls' books are in most respects identical to those that permeate the boys' books. In and of themselves, they are as vital to young girls' societal maturation as they are to young boys'. Yet whereas the boys' books reflect the values as national cultural norms central to the boys' emerging roles as movers and shapers of society, the girls' books embed those values in a matrix of shifting American attitudes toward the place of women in the greater society. The female characters must balance the fantasy world's ideals and opportunities for freedom with the socially dictated reality about them. What might they as young women *like* to do, what are they as young women *expected* to do, and how can the two desires be balanced? Whereas the boys' books tacitly imply that their heroes will take their places as entrepreneurs, technological celebrities, or leaders of industry, the girls' books must address such matters as the inherent intelligence (or lack thereof) of women, the kinds of activities and occupations that are suitable for women, and the compatibility of career and domesticity. From the suffragettes and "New Women" of the *fin de siècle* through the forthright heroines of the 1930s to the women caught up in the post-World War II backlash, the girls' books' formulas provide a young person's guide into how women were seen and how they saw themselves as the twentieth century proceeded.

Notes

1. Gillian Avery, *Behold the Child: American Children and Their Books 1621-1922* (Baltimore: Johns Hopkins University Press, 1994), 89, 190; Deidre Johnson, "From Abbott to Animorphs, from Godly Books to Goosebumps: The Nineteenth-Century Origins of Modern Series," In *Scorned Literature: Essays on the History and Criticism of Popular Mass-Produced Fiction in America,*ed. Lydia Cushman Schurman and Deidre Johnson (Westport, CT: Greenwood Press, 2002), 147-148,

150, 158; Russel B. Nye, *The Unembarrassed Muse: The Popular Arts in America* (New York: Dial Press, 1970), 63, 65-66.

2. Carol Billman, *The Secret of the Stratemeyer Syndicate* (New York: Ungar Publishing Co., 1986), 21-23; Deidre Johnson, ed., *Stratemeyer Pseudonyms and Series Books* (Westport, CT: Greenwood Press, 1982), 144, 76, 97-98, 170; Peter Stoneley, *Consumerism and American Girls' Literature 1860-1940* (Cambridge, UK: Cambridge University Press, 2003), 91-92.

3. George T. Dunlap, *The Fleeting Years: A Memoir* (New York: privately printed, 1937), 193; Melanie Rehak, *Girl Sleuth: Nancy Drew and the Women Who Created Her* (Orlando, FL: Harcourt, 2005), 99-100.

4. Nye, *Unembarrassed Muse*, 77; "For It Was Indeed He," *Fortune* 9 (April 1934): 86; Henry Steele Commager, "When Majors Wrote for Minors," *Saturday Review* 35 (10 May 1952): 10-11, 44-46; Roberta Seelinger Trites, *Disturbing the Universe: Power and Repression in Adolescent Literature* (Iowa City: University of Iowa Press, 2000), 7.

5. Rehak, *Girl Sleuth*, 114-116; Marilyn S. Greenwald, *The Secret of the Hardy Boys: Leslie McFarland and the Stratemeyer Syndicate* (Athens: Ohio University Press, 2004), 44-45, 49-50, 61-62.

6. Selma G. Lanes, *Down the Rabbit Hole* (New York: Atheneum, 1971), 128; [Josephine Lawrence], "The Newarker Whose Name Is Best Known," *Newark Sunday Call,* 9 December 1917, 1.

7. Francis J. Molson, "American Technological Fiction for Youth: 1900-1940," In *Young Adult Science Fiction,* ed. C.W. Sullivan, III (Westport, CT: Greenwood Press, 1999), 9.

8. Franklin K. Mathiews, "Blowing Out the Boy's Brains," *Outlook* 108 (11 November 1914): 653.

9. "Girl Aviators Series" back dust jacket advertisement, Margaret Burnham, *The Girl Aviators' Motor Butterfly* (New York: Hurst & Co., 1912), unpaged; Goldsmith Publishing Co. back dust jacket advertisement, Bess Moyer, *Gypsies of the Air* (Chicago: Goldsmith Publishing Co., 1932). (Although the "Girl Aviators Series" ran only from 1911 to 1912, the copy cited is dated 1914 in a parental flyleaf inscription.)

10. Rehak, *Girl Sleuth*, 155-156.

11. Peter A. Soderbergh, "Edward Stratemeyer and the Juvenile Ethic, 1894-1930," *International Review of History and Political Science* 11 (February 1974): 62-63; John G. Cawelti, *Adventure, Mystery, and Romance: Formula Stories as Art and Popular Culture* (Chicago: University of Chicago Press, 1976), 34.

12. Cawelti, *Adventure, Mystery, and Romance,* 35.

13. Ibid.

14. Ibid. Lanes, *Down the Rabbit Hole,* 133, 140-142, discusses the adolescent desire for independence at some length. Gillian Avery, *Behold the Child: American Children and Their Books 1621-1922* (Baltimore: Johns Hopkins University Press, 1994), 200-209, treats the motif as part of the American story of the "Good Bad Boy," while Trites, *Disturbing the Universe* 2-3, remarks on adolescents using literature to understand the power relationships that adulthood will necessitate. Alison Lurie, in "Reading at Escape Velocity," *New York Times Book Review,* 17 May 1998, 51, touches upon modern youths' preference for stories replacing adult guidance with youthful independence. Kathleen Chamberlain, "'Wise Censorship': Cultural Authority and the Scorning of Juvenile Series Books, 1890-1940," in Schurman and Johnson, *Scorned Literature,* 189, 206-207, presents literature's fostering of adolescents' dreams of freedom as a necessary and desirable part of youngsters' transition to adulthood.

15. Schurman and Johnson, *Scorned Literature,* 36.

16. Lanes, *Down the Rabbit Hole,* 130, 134.

CHAPTER 2

Birdwomen Take to the Air:

1905-1915

T he summer of 1911 found Margaret Burnham and Edith Van Dyne testing the winds of flying fiction for girls. Their pioneering books, *The Girl Aviators and the Phantom Airship* and *The Flying Girl*, respectively, both published in September 1911, were partly opportunistic and commercial, partly idealistic and forward-looking. By the time the two put pen to paper, the United States was in a frenzy of aeronautical enthusiasm. Burnham's and Van Dyne's stories were intended to capitalize not only upon that enthusiasm, but also upon the burgeoning popularity of two aviation series written for boys: H.L. Sayler's "Airship Boys" books (1909-1913; eight titles) and Ashton B. Lamar's "Aeroplane Boys" tales (1910-1913; seven titles). These two series created the aviation genre in the United States and established a format for similar works that continued until the advent of the First World War.

Burnham and Van Dyne proposed to do for girls what Sayler and "Lamar" (Sayler writing under a pseudonym) were doing for boys—preach the gospel of aviation. They had, however, other intentions as well. The two recognized the social and educational limitations placed upon young women in the 1910-1913 period, yet they also saw evidence that attitudes were changing. In their books, they suggest that young women, given the opportunity, could acquit themselves admirably in fields not normally associated with female interests. Their accounts of teenaged girls' taking to the air, the first "pure" aviation stories written for girls, capture the spirit of the times, tacitly speaking out in support of the progressively minded woman and demonstrating that the air held as much promise for women as for men.

Called the *fin de siècle* in Europe and England and the Progressive Era in the United States, the thirty years from 1890 to 1920 were marked by sweeping changes in public attitudes toward government, social theory, and religion. Among the changes in the United States was an increase in public activism. Their concerns manifested in such organizations as the Women's Christian Temperance Union (1873), New York's National Consumers' League (1891), Chicago's Municipal Voters' League (1895), and the General Federation of Women's Clubs (1904), citizens both male and female set themselves the mission of correcting abuses in politics, the workplace, and the home. Not the least of their efforts was an intensifying of the push for women's suffrage and an expansion of women's rights, leading at last to the ratification of the Nineteenth Amendment to the Constitution in 1920.[1] Another was an explosion of progress in technology and the public's consciousness of that technology. Social activism and the emergence of a new sense of womanhood combined with the coming of the automobile, the wireless, the cinema, and the airplane to give the era a pervasive sense of vital, progressive change, a sense that a truly modern United States was just around the corner.[2] Yet two still larger changes were to come that would shape the course of American society *and* aviation.

One was the growing feminine interest in airplane and aviation technology. American national interest in the airplane, spurred by well-publicized achievements emanating from England and France, came to life in 1908, when Orville and Wilbur Wright published their first extensive account of their flights in *The Century Magazine*. Perhaps the leading upper-middle-brow magazine of its time, *The Century* was an ideal forum for the Wrights' revelation, presenting their achievements to the educated upper-middle class of the United States. This was followed by even greater excitement when motorcycle champion and engine-designer Glenn H. Curtiss took part in the world's first international aviation competition, the *Grand Semaine de l'Aviation de la Champagne*, held in Rheims, France, in August 1909. There, before an audience totaling more than a half-million onlookers, Curtiss captured the Gordon Bennett International Trophy, besting French favorite Louis Blériot in a twenty-kilometer race against time, and the *Prix de la Vitesse*, achieving a speed of 47.73 miles per hour along a thirty-kilometer course. He returned home a celebrity, and the American public discovered the airplane.[3]

The financial success and the accompanying publicity of the Rheims competition were not lost on American promoters. Recognizing a way to feed public curiosity about the airplane and profit from it at the same time, they quickly mounted a series of comparable domestic meets. Well-funded and widely attended, these meets capitalized upon the novelty of the "flying machine." For the audiences, the mere sight of a man-made, heavier-than-air machine in flight was excitement enough. When competitions for substantial cash prizes were added and the machines began to do rudimentary "stunts" to show off their pilots' skills, the public appeal became almost irresistible. While the meets provided useful occasions to test and publicize new aircraft designs, they also served a valuable educational purpose—to familiarize and tantalize the American public with powered flight and its possibilities.

The first such meet to be held in the United States was the Dominguez Meet held outside Los Angeles, California, in January 1910. Reported in newspapers and magazines across the country, it introduced several individuals who would become central figures in the history of American flight: Louis Paulhan, a French flier who thrilled the crowd with his airborne swoops and dives; Glenn Curtiss, already known for his victory at Rheims; and Charles F.

Willard, Charles K. Hamilton, and Lincoln Beachey, pilots who would win individual prominence in subsequent meets. Following the Dominguez meet was the Harvard-Boston Aviation Meet of September 1910. It was notable for the presence of British fliers Claude Grahame-White and A.V. Roe, along with Americans Glenn Curtiss, Charles F. Willard, Clifford B. Harmon, Walter Brookins, and Ralph Johnstone.[4]

The final major meet of 1910, the International Aviation Meet at Belmont Park, New York, in October, featured Grahame-White, Brookins, Johnstone, and Willard, and introduced two new names: Arch Hoxsey and John B. Moisant. Hoxsey was known as a skilled daredevil and speed flier, Moisant as a designer, entrepreneur, and long-distance flier. Ironically, both would be killed in separate crashes on the same day, 31 December 1910. Crashes notwithstanding, these meets served to feed and heighten the American fascination with the airplane. Writing of the Dominguez meet, the *Los Angeles Times* praised it for establishing the reality of flight for the "native sons [who] were skeptical of its accomplishment until they actually set eyes on the performance." Other publications echoed this point, one remarking that "the American public . . . was hungry to put to ocular proof the much-discussed flying machines," and another hailing "the moment for which the faith of a world grown used to material conquests has waited, apparently baffled—it is the dream of centuries come true."[5]

The commercial potential of the air meets quickly led to the creation of professional exhibition teams. The first of these was the Wright Exhibition Company, featuring Wright aircraft designs; its fliers included Walter Brookins, Arch Hoxsey, and Ralph Johnstone, who made their first appearance at the Indianapolis Motor Speedway in June 1910. Close behind was the Curtiss Exhibition Company, with Curtiss designs flown by Eugene Ely (first person to land an airplane on, and take off from, a warship), Augustus Post, and Charles F. Willard (who coined the expression "holes in the air" following a bumpy flight at the Dominguez meeting). Their first outing was at the Sheepshead Bay Racetrack in Brooklyn, New York, in August 1910. Last came the Moisant International Aviators, established in November 1910. Its pilots included not only Roland Garros, who had competed for France at Rheims and went on to still greater fame as a World War I "ace," and the designer John Moisant himself, but also two women: journalist Harriet Quimby and Moisant's sister, Matilde Moisant.[6]

The presence of Quimby and Matilde Moisant on the Moisant team signals a surprising facet of early aviation history: the prominence of women in the enterprise. Women were a visible part of early flight virtually from the outset. Much of the early attention went to two Continental women, the self-styled "Baroness" Raymonde de Laroche of France and Hélène Dutrieu of Belgium. Laroche made her first actual flight on 22 October 1909, becoming the first woman in history to pilot an airplane, and received her license from the *Fédération Aéronautique Internationale* (FAI) on 8 March 1910, making her the first woman in the world to be licensed as a pilot. Close behind her was the Belgian cycling champion and performer, Hélène Dutrieu. Working with the Farman brothers of France, Dutrieu set a number of women's flying records—among them those for altitude, distance, and duration. Her most publicized flight was from Blankenberge, Belgium, to Bruges in September 1910, when she drew attention by circling the towers of the Bruges cathedral in the process. In 1911 she was invited to take part in the Nassau International Aviation Meet, held in late September on Long Island, New York, where she flew in the company of Harriet Quimby and Matilde Moisant and took the American women's record for duration from Moisant.[7]

Responding to the publicity given women fliers from abroad, progressively-minded American women also began to explore aviation. Among the first was Blanche Stuart Scott, who already had made a national name for herself through her cross-country automobile trip in 1910. When she was approached by the Curtiss Exhibition Company to join their ranks, she accepted, learning to fly from Glenn Curtiss himself. Her solo flight, the first by an American woman, took place on 2 September 1910, and she began flying with the Curtiss team in October of that year. She never won a formal license, but, as "The Tomboy of the Air," gained national prominence for her spectacular flying "stunts." She also appeared at the Nassau meet of September 1911, listed in an advertisement in the technical press with Dutrieu, Quimby, and Matilde Moisant as among "30 of the greatest aviators," and continued to fly until 1916.[8]

For her part, Matilde Moisant began flying lessons in 1911 at her brother's school, winning her FAI license on 17 August 1911. She began exhibition flying immediately, taking part in the Nassau meet of 1911, where she edged out Harriet Quimby and Hélène Dutrieu for the Rodman Wanamaker Trophy for altitude. She then flew with the Moisant International Aviators at exhibitions in Mexico and the United States. She had begun to talk of retirement by early 1912, and, after surviving a fiery crash on 14 April 1912 in Wichita Falls, Texas, made her retirement effective on the spot.[9] Other women fliers followed in her tracks, however, and quickly confirmed the female presence in early aviation in the United States.

The other notable change of the Progressive Era in many ways made the first possible. This was the appearance of the so-called "New Woman," a liberally-minded individual who held new and vigorous views concerning her place and her role in society. Her origins were in the nineteenth century, drawing upon the new vigor of European women in the *fin de siècle* era and the earlier Seneca Falls, New York, convention of 1848. This meeting, one of the earliest concerted expressions of the American interest in women's rights, introduced such feminist leaders as Elizabeth Cady Stanton, Lucretia Mott, Carrie Chapman Catt, and Susan B. Anthony. All would figure significantly in the growing campaign for the vote and a general liberalizing of woman's place in the larger culture.[10]

The American New Woman of the early twentieth century

Hélène Dutrieu at the Nassau (NY) International Air Tournament,
September 1911. National Air and Space Museum,
Smithsonian Institution (SI 73-4023).

broadened her interests and brought an activist's energy to everyday affairs as well. As historian Nancy Woloch remarks of the New
Woman: "Vigorous and energetic, she was involved in institutions
beyond the family—in college, club, settlement, or profession." She
was, in many ways, already her own woman. Although entirely willing to marry, she saw no stigma in remaining single. Although
ready to take on many of the traditional homemaker's obligations,
she saw no stigma in supporting herself with employment outside
the home. A largely urban person possessing a higher level of education than the run of most women, she was of the middle class, or
even the upper class. She possessed the knowledge, skills, and energy
to step forward and, each person in her own way, make her contribution to American life.[11]

Although attitudes and priorities obviously varied from person to person, the New Woman, as part of a discrete subculture, can generally be said to hold to three principal tenets. The first is a belief, not so much in the idea of sex equality, but rather in "opposition to sex hierarchy." She did not want to be judged automatically as a woman and therefore inferior. Instead, she strove to establish her capabilities by meeting criteria comparable to those used to rank men, letting her be objectively judged up or down by her accomplishments. Second, she believed that "women's condition is socially constructed, that is, historically shaped by human social usage rather than simply predestined by God or nature." What had been perceived as the shortcomings of women in earlier generations, she saw as attributes imposed by the society rather than the accident of sex. What society had established, therefore, society could amend, and the New Woman made it her mission to speed that amending. Third, and finally, she believed that her individual actions reflected upon all womankind—she possessed, i.e., the "awareness that one's experience reflects and affects the whole." Whatever the realm, each woman's visible achievement and visible success served to heighten the place of all women. Conversely, failure or inappropriate actions would unfairly blacken the female sex in general, and so the New Woman had a particular incentive to succeed.[12]

All of these tenets appeared, in various proportions, in the actions of the New Woman. She was, obviously, a person for whom political activism was appealing. Women led various national movements for the vote, temperance, and social reform. Women's activism gave rise to the National American Woman Suffrage Association (1890), an organization principally concerned with attaining the suffrage, that by 1917 evolved into the National Woman's Party, an organization with interests ranging from anti-war protests to overt birth-control advocacy and similar concerns. She was also a person of deep social engagement. As historian George E. Mowry notes, "the influence of the reform-minded woman in the progressive period is self-evident in such matters as woman's rights, suffrage, the protection of minors, and in such moral crusades as those against liquor and prostitution." The Women's Christian Temperance Union dates from 1873. Jane Addams's 1889 establishing of Hull House marks the start of the settlement-house movement and women's growing agitation for improved schools, purer food and drugs, and improved conditions for children in the workplace. The Women's Trade Union League of 1903 pressed for the unionization of women in the workplace and an associated improvement in work conditions.[13] In these ways, and others, women strove to demonstrate their intellectual and cultural concerns, proving that they, as much as men, could operate effectively in the modern world.

Not everyone, to be sure, viewed the coming of the New Woman as desirable. Many men, and even some women, recoiled at the vision of an activist woman, and in many circles suffragettes, protestors, social workers, and other female "do-gooders" became objects of ridicule. The larger response, though, was positive, as more and more individuals became conscious of the tangible achievements that women were bringing about. The social critic Randolph Bourne summed up the positive view in 1913. New Women, he wrote:

> have an amazing combination of wisdom and youthfulness, of humor and ability, and innocence and self-reliance, which absolutely belies everything you will read in the story-books. . . . They are of course all self-supporting and independent, and they enjoy the adventure of life; the full, reliant, audacious way in which they go about makes you wonder if the new woman isn't to be a very splendid sort of person.[14]

The energies and audacity fostered by socio-political activism among women soon found their way to aviation. Women already had seized upon the bicycle and the automobile as technological means of attaining a new degree of independence and freedom. The advent of the airplane offered a still more exhilarating way for women to seek and express their mechanical capabilities and to embrace the freedom that it offered. It gave them a means of exercising "a welcome feeling of power and control, a way to transcend the boundaries of traditional social roles and assumptions about women's limited capabilities." Like the bicycle and the automobile before it, the airplane encouraged a new freedom in dress. Hélène Dutrieu set critics a-twitter when she admitted to flying without a corset, flexibility of movement being more important to her than social propriety. For her part, Matilde Moisant regularly donned "knickerbockers in one piece, with severely plain shirt. High laced boots, gauntlets, a cap to cover curls and the nape of her neck. . . , and a pair of disfiguring goggles." She also favored a belted, closely fitting pants suit of heavy tweed, which is generally credited with saving her from burns in her final crash. Flying togs for women quickly became commonplace, and an aviatrix in trousers occasioned little if any comment.[15]

The airplane also proved to be a device allowing women to proclaim their parity with men. Again and again, notable women fliers commented upon the relationship of their feats to those of men fliers. As early as 1911, Hélène Dutrieu predicted that "within a short time women will be flying from city to city as well as men." In 1913, the aviation journalist Henry Woodhouse opened an essay on "Pioneer Women of the Air" with the comment, "the women of the air have shown that they are as good as men in handling the aerial ponies." Nineteen-year-old Katherine Stinson, having dazzled audiences in 1916 by flying night-time loops with magnesium flares burning beneath her wings, announced that "Now that I have equaled the greatest efforts of the male flyers I am going to go ahead and evolve a new stunt or two that will put woman ahead of man at the most difficult of all sciences."

Matilde Moisant in her tweed flying togs. National Air and Space Museum, Smithsonian Institution (SI 73-3564).

Later in 1916, Ruth Law set a distance record on 20 November by flying solo from New York to Chicago, and, the following day, returning non-stop to New York. She used both occasions to make a plea for equality of judgment. Of the first flight she said: "It was the only distance flight I ever tried and I did better than the man who tried it. But I don't mean that the fact that I am a woman makes any difference to speak of. I suppose I ought to say that I am in favor of woman suffrage—but what has that got to do with it?" Following the return flight, when a reporter asked whether she had made the longest flight ever made by a woman, she retorted: "'I have made the longest flight an American ever made. . . ,' leaving no doubt that she wished to be known as an aviator rather than an aviatrice."[16] Be it Dutrieu, Stinson, Law, or any of a host of other female fliers, the airplane provided women an opportunity to challenge men in their own milieu on their own terms. It was a major step forward.

Few public figures in aviation so personified the melding of New Woman and female flier in the public eye than did Harriet Quimby. Quimby, a journalist working principally for *Leslie's Illustrated Weekly* and the first American woman to win a pilot's license, embodied the best qualities of both the female flier and the New Woman, providing her readers and those who read about her in the press with an object lesson in independence, audacity, and freedom. Although her flying career spanned barely a year, she quickly became a public icon and "the darling of her day," giving almost daily evidence that "women were serious about flying as a career and were not in it just for the novelty or the fun of it."[17] Her prominence was increased by photographs in the popular and technical press, publicity given her participation in air shows, and the form-fitting, vivid purple flying suit that soon became her trademark. For much of the American public, she was *the* personification of the New Woman as flier.

Quimby was born in 1875 in rural Michigan, but soon moved with her family to California. There she passed through the public schools and, in 1900, began working as a journalist with several California newspapers. (She later disguised her origins, moving her birthdate to 1884 and claiming the benefits of an extensive private education in Europe.) She moved to New York in 1902, initially working as a free-lance writer, then, in 1903, becoming a regular staff member of *Leslie's Illustrated Weekly*. Her employment with *Leslie's* was fortuitous. A weekly magazine with a circulation nearing 400,000, the journal was known for its mix of lavishly illustrated articles on sports, politics, automobiles, and the theater. The journal presented the articles in easy-going language, making it, as a later historian called it, "a kind of tired business man's weekly" that gave the reader "the satisfaction of thinking he was improving himself, while he was being mildly entertained and amused." For Quimby, it was an outlet well-suited to her aviation writings and an entrée to the homes of middle-class America that would prove of considerable value.[18]

Quimby's interest in aviation was awakened when she attended the Los Angeles aviation meet of 1910, and later covered the Belmont Park meet of November 1910. In May 1911, she enrolled in the Moisant School of Aviation on Long Island, beginning a three-month course of training that ended with her receiving her flying license on 1 August 1911. Her presence at the Moisant field quickly caused comment. The *New York Times* for 11 May 1911 published an article headed "Woman In Trousers Daring Aviator," and quoted her as saying, "There are already several French women aviators. Why shouldn't we have some good American air pilots?" Other mentions followed, as she became the first American woman, and the second woman world-wide, to be licensed as a pilot.[19]

Quimby continued her work at *Leslie's*, where she had risen to the post of theater editor, but also joined the Moisant International Aviators, flying with them at events throughout the region and accompanying them in early 1912 on their demonstration trip to Mexico. All of these activities she reported in *Leslie's*. By late 1911 her flights were already attracting reporters and newsreel photogra-

Matilde 1.1. M.A. Donohue advertisement (1911) for two early aviation series. (Author's Moisant (standing, left) and Harriet Quimby (standing, right) with class-mates at the Moisant School of Aviation. National Air and Space Museum, Smithsonian Institution (SI 78-14184).

phers, spreading her activities to the nation.[20] She gained her greatest prominence in April 1912, however, when she became the first woman to fly solo across the English Channel, flying from England to France in slightly more than half an hour. Her achievement was temporarily eclipsed by the same-day sinking of the ocean liner *Titanic,* but soon was recognized as a significant accomplishment.

Her growing celebrity led to her taking part in other air shows, and, in June 1912, she was invited to take part in the Harvard-Boston Aviation Meet of June-July 1912, to fly alongside Lincoln Beachey, Glenn Curtiss, and Blanche Scott. Disaster struck on 1 July as she was flying a trial circuit between the meet's landing field and the Boston Light across the bay. For the flight, she took as a passenger William A. P. Willard, father of the demonstration flier Charles F. Willard. Preparing to land, she briefly lost control of her ship and she and Willard were thrown from the aircraft, falling to their deaths before a horror-struck audience. Her airplane landed itself with only minor damage. News of her death made headlines from coast to coast, with accounts hailing her as "America's best-known aviatress" and praising her "for her remarkable courage in demonstrating her faith in the science of aviation."[21]

Quimby patently embodies the New Woman. Single, attractive, and free-thinking, she had no quarrel with the traditional trappings of femininity. She was conscious of her clothing yet independent in her thought, embracing both familiar women's garb and the more radical garb of the aviator. A 1911 photograph taken at the Moisant Aviation School shows her with Matilde Moisant, the two of them wearing elbow-length gloves, elaborate hats, and trimly tailored dresses with ankle-length skirts. Conversely, she let practicality rather than fashion dictate her flying togs. She flatly stated that "the woman who resolves to be a flyer must . . . abandon skirts and don a knickerbocker uniform." Her own suit she described as "fashioned all in one piece, including the hood, and, by a most ingenious contrivance, can be almost immediately converted into a quite conventional-appearing walking skirt when not used in its knickerbocker form." Distinctive as the outfit was, she made it even more striking by having the outer layer constructed of brilliant purple satin.[22]

Quimby's kinship with the New Woman appeared even more overtly in her writings, for she was an adventurous and socially concerned author. She wrote of child care among the Chinese of New York, gave advice to young mothers on prudent grocery shopping, visited various ethnic neighborhoods of the city and detailed their distinctive characteristics, and cautioned young women of the perils of white slavery. At *Leslie's* expense she traveled to the Caribbean and to Europe, writing of her experiences as she traveled. She showed an intimate familiarity with the automobile, driving her own machine and writing of the exhilaration she experienced during a hundred-mile-an-hour ride in a racing car. Yet, throughout her writings, she disclaimed being an active feminist, laughingly

Matilde Moisant (l) and Harriet Quimby, ca. 1911. National Air and Space Museum, Smithsonian Institution (SI 2002-23707).

refusing feminists' insistence that she name her airplane the "Pankhurst" or the "Catt." While she was aware of the women's movement and its leaders, she preferred to say only that her exploits showed that any woman "can do the same—if she really wants to," and that, overall, women "are as adaptable as men" in whatever endeavor they choose to undertake.[23]

Although Quimby never presented herself as an overt spokesperson for American feminism, she did not hesitate to speak out as an advocate for aviation. Eleven of her last thirty-eight articles for *Leslie's*, published between May 1911 and June 1912, dealt with the subject, and she wrote at least two articles for other periodicals, *The World* magazine and the women's magazine *Good Housekeeping*. Her fundamental premise throughout these writings was that any woman could master the airplane and the art of flying, if only she had the desire. In developing her thesis, Quimby spoke of practicalities—matters of cost, requirements for maintenance of an airplane, necessary clothing, etc.—as well as intangibles. She became, for a moment, the public voice of aviation, and her writings crossed the nation.

Several of her articles in *Leslie's* dealt with the simple process of learning how to fly. In three essays, "How a Woman Learns to Fly" (25 May 1911), "How a Woman Learns to Fly, Part 2" (17 August 1911), and "How I Won My Aviator's License" (24 August 1911), she detailed the progress of her lessons at the Moisant School, then traced the various tests required by the Aero Club of America to certify her as a licensed pilot. Three other articles took up the hazards inherent in flying: "Exploring Air Lanes" (22 June 1911) and "Dangers of Flying: How to Avoid Them" (31 August 1911), and "In the World of People Who Fly" (18 January 1912). In them she stressed the importance of meticulous care of the aircraft and in its pre-flight inspection, augmented by prudence on the part of the pilot in avoiding foolhardy tricks and obviously dangerous weather.[24]

Two more articles, "With the Intrepid Flyers" (1 February 1912) and "An American Girl's Daring Exploit" (16 May 1912), reported her flights in Mexico and across the English Channel. "Flyers and Flying" (27 June 1912) talked of the cost of learning to fly and the opportunities for employment in aviation, with a particular emphasis on women's possibilities. The final two, "New Things in the Aviation World" (6 June 1912) and "Lost in the Sky!," a manuscript found among her papers and published posthumously on 28 November 1912, were ruminations upon national pride, aviation's role in the present day, and thoughts that occurred while flying. Taken as a group, the essays provide a thoughtful, substantial introduction to general aviation as it existed in 1911 and 1912—an enterprise well worth undertaking, for "the real achievement is to master the air as proof of human progress."[25]

Harriet Quimby boarding her Bleriot XI, 1912.
National Air and Space Museum, Smithsonian Institution (SI 84-18035).

For all her concern with practicalities, however, Quimby was convinced of the opportunity that aviation offered women. Again and again, she looked beyond the wire-and-canvas aircraft of her day to a time when national aviation would be a commercial as well as sporting enterprise, and women could take their place in it as equals to men. To Quimby, flight was a liberation: "I felt like a bird cleaving the air with my out-stretched wings. There was no thought of obstruction and obstacle." And from that liberation will come great progress. "The time is coming when we shall find the means of transportation by bird-like flights as safe and satisfactory by steamship or locomotive and with still greater speed." And women will be a part of the undertaking: "There is no reason why a woman flyer could not do this work [commercial flying] if she so chooses."[26] In Quimby's vision of the future, men and women alike had equal access to, and equal opportunity in, the world of aviation. They also had the freedom to make the choice.

The fullest statement of her hopes for flight came not in a *Leslie's* piece, but, significantly, in a well-established women's magazine aimed at the American homemaker. "American Bird Women: Aviation as a Feminine Sport," published posthumously in *Good Housekeeping,* explicitly sums up Quimby's confidence in the future for women. After pooh-poohing her achievement in crossing the Channel ("Within a few months, perhaps weeks, some other woman probably will make the same flight, or even achieve some greater undertaking."), she went on to make an assured prediction: "There is no reason why the aeroplane should not open up a fruitful occupation for women. I see no reason why they cannot realize handsome incomes by carrying passengers between adjacent towns, why they cannot derive incomes from parcel delivery, from taking photographs from above, or from conducting schools of flying."[27] For Quimby, women are as capable of carrying out commercial flight as they are of sport flight, and their participation will not be long in coming.

The aviation stories for American girls quickly embraced Quimby as a model. Her independence, her obvious commitment to aviation, her articulate writings on the subject, and her personification of the progressive outlook of the New Woman made her an attractive choice, and the books that appeared, although not mentioning her explicitly, made clear their authors' awareness of her celebrity and her skill. Thus, while the widespread popularity of the flying meets stimulated the creation of the boys' aviation series, the growing prominence of American women in the activity prompted the creation of the girls' series, and the books were not long in reaching the public.

The first such books, Margaret Burnham's "Girl Aviators" books (1911-1912; four titles), appeared in September 1911, close on the heels of the notable meets of 1910 and contemporaneous with the Nassau meet of 1911. "Burnham," a previously unknown writer, seems to have been a "house name" for the publishers, Hurst & Co. She published no other books under that name, and nothing is known of her identity. The initial book of the series, *The Girl Aviators and the Phantom Airship* (1911), sets the scene. Teenaged Roy and Peggy Prescott, orphaned children of a largely unsuccessful inventor, live with their aunt, Sally Prescott, and their pet bulldog, Monsieur Blériot, on Long Island, New York. Their ambition is to complete the Prescott Airplane, a craft designed by their late father. The machine promises to be superior to all other aircraft then flying, and will enable them to pay off the mortgage threatening the Prescott property.

With the help of their schoolmates and best chums, Jess Bancroft and her brother James (Jimsy), members of a wealthy family living nearby, they bring the airplane project to fruition. During their flights, they befriend an eccentric hermit, Peter Bell, and reunite him with his long-lost brother, millionaire mine-owner Jim Bell. Meanwhile, Peggy, substituting for the absent Roy and flying the Prescott Airplane, wins $5,000 at the locally-sponsored Acatonick Meet, pays off the mortgage, and thwarts the designs of an unscrupulous banker, Simon Harding, and his foppish son, Fanning. Impressed by seeing the Prescotts fly Jess and Jimsy to catch a train and Peggy's expertise in the meet, Jim Bell commissions a fleet of Prescott aircraft to fly ore out of his Nevada gold mine, providing Peggy and Roy with a secure future.

The second volume, *The Girl Aviators on Golden Wings* (1911), takes Peggy, Roy, Jess, Jimsy, and Aunt Sally to Nevada, where they assemble two monoplanes to fly between their base camp and Jim Bell's mine. As events unfold, the little party encounters bandits led by "Red Bill" Summers, meets a group of chivalric cowboys, and takes up with the eccentric medicine-show proprietor, "Wandering William," who proves to be Secret Service agent Sam Kelly on the trail of Red Bill. When Bell's claim papers are stolen by one of the bandits, Peggy and Kelly make an epic flight to Monument Rocks to file their claim ahead of the thief, while Red Bill and the other miscreants are rounded up by Bell's cowboy friends. In the third volume, *The Girl Aviators' Sky Cruise* (1911), Peggy and Roy find themselves once again in competition with Simon Harding, who is seeking to beat them out of a naval aviation contract by funding a craft designed by inventor Eugene Mortlake. Despite several setbacks, including the arrest of Roy, who's falsely accused of espionage, the Prescotts reunite the glamorous Regina Mortlake with her true father, Pierce Budd, and take part in a public fly-off to decide the winner of the naval competition. They handily defeat the Mortlake aircraft, and win a substantial contract to manufacture airplanes for the United States Navy.

The final volume, *The Girl Aviators' Motor Butterfly* (1912), sees Peggy, Roy, Jess, and Jimsy, again with Aunt Sally, embark on a cross-country aerial cruise to North Carolina, accompanied by flying chum Bess Marshall. En route they survive a mid-air fire and rescue a small girl, known only as "Wren," who has been kidnapped by gypsies. They also run afoul of a small-town politician and encounter a group of professional exhibition fliers, the United Aviators' Exhibition Company. When they join an air meet spon-

*Peggy Prescott and Jess Bancroft see off the
Prescott Airplane as Aunt Sally looks on.
(Author's collection).*

sored by the town of Millbrook, they find themselves competing
with the United Aviators' pilots, and, most notably, the star, Pepita
Le Roy, "the Cuban Skylark, the Only Woman Flyer in the World."
By book's end, Peggy, Roy, and Jimsy reunite Wren with her griev-
ing mother and prevail over the professional fliers, thanks to the
superior engineering of the Prescott Airplane.

Throughout the series, Burnham combines familiar formula-
story materials (the grasping banker, the wealthy but democratic

family, and the poor-but-honest family who are the focus of the stories) with a useful portrayal of the earliest days of aviation. The books supply glimpses of the public excitement engendered by the mere appearance of an airplane and the appeal of itinerant air shows, and they convey a good sense of the technical side of aircraft development and flight. They capture, despite their series-book trappings, a microcosm of the aviation world, and they present it to their young female readers as a world that is plausibly within reach.

The American public's fascination with the novelty of the "flying machine" is a consistent motif throughout the "Girl Aviators" series. The first pages of *The Girl Aviators and the Phantom Aircraft* record Peggy's and Roy's excitement over the announcement of a meet sponsored by a local nabob, offering ten thousand dollars in prize money for various achievements, including the "most carefully constructed machine" and the aircraft "bearing the most ingenious devices for perfecting the art of flying." When it finally takes place, the Acatonick Meet includes entries from the Agassiz High School in New York, Philadelphia Polytechnic, and Boston Tech; its contestants, "rising into the still air almost in a body, like a flock of birds," create "a spectacle never to be forgotten, and the crowd appreciated it to the full."[28]

Later books only reinforce the reader's sense of the public's fascination with flight. The competition for the naval contract in *The Girl Aviators' Sky Cruise,* which includes "monoplanes, bi-planes, machines of the helicopter type, and a few devices based on the parachute principle," takes place in the full glare of eager publicity. "Reporters darted here and there followed by panting photographers bearing elephantine cameras and bulging boxes of plates, for the metropolitan press was 'playing up' the tests." Meanwhile, the throng of onlookers "wandered about the grounds gazing open-mouthed at the freak types." A brief landing in *The Girl Aviators' Motor Butterfly* proves to be the first sighting ever of an airplane in a small Pennsylvania town, and creates "commensurate excitement," while the arrival of the little group's aircraft provides the town of Meadville with "the greatest excitement of its career. People rushed out of stores and houses as the 'flock' of aëroplanes came into sight." Later, as the group sets out for the flying field in Millbrook, where they will fly against the United Aviators' Exhibition professionals, "everyone who saw the aëroplanes start made up his or her mind to pay a visit to the park to see some more extended flights."[29]

Even as the books evoke some of the public fascination that flight creates, they go on to reflect several of the problems faced by the early aviators. Early airplanes were fragile things. Frequently home-built without the benefit of engineering studies or designs, they were constructions of wood, fabric, and wire, powered by cranky, unreliable engines.[30] Even Peggy and Roy's craft suffer these weaknesses. In the first book alone, a slack spring threatens a test flight, a broken rod compels Peggy to make an unplanned landing, and a maladjusted spark plug forces a flight's delay. Matters have not significantly improved in the later volumes; a leaky radiator line brings down Peggy in *The Girl Aviators on Golden Wings* and a leaking fuel line causes the in-flight fire that threatens Peggy and Jess in *The Girl Aviators' Golden Butterfly.*[31]

More important even than construction was the problem of stability. To be practical, an airplane must be controllable. It must go where it is directed without unnecessary deviation from its intended flight path. Yet an airplane must also be able to operate freely wherever the pilot directs it along any of three spatial axes: roll (rotation around a fore-and-aft axis), pitch (up-and-down movement around a side-to-side axis), and yaw (horizontal rotation around a vertical axis). Without this capacity, it is unmanageable. Methods of achieving the necessary combination of stability and maneuverability quickly separated experimenters into two camps. One group, championed by the Wrights, favored an inherently *unstable* aircraft, whose control depended "entirely upon the skill of the aeronaut." The other, promoted by French fliers such as Henri Farman and Charles and Gabriel Voisin, argued for a machine that "should be automatically and inherently stable."[32] Each method had its virtues and defects. The Wright system created a nimble, maneuverable craft, but required a highly trained pilot; the French system produced an aircraft that was easy to fly and placed few demands upon the pilot, but one that lacked a high degree of in-flight agility.

The stability issue was not resolved until the invention of the Sperry gyroscopic stabilizer in early 1914. Meanwhile, in recognition of the demands of their design, the Wright Brothers patented an "automatic stabilizing system" of their own design in 1909 and 1910, while Grover Cleveland Loening, a rising young aeronautical engineer who would go on to be a notable designer in the 1930s, offered a survey of other proposed stabilizing devices in an article published in 1911.[33] None of these devices, the Wrights' or anyone else's, proved to be wholly satisfactory, and the issue of aircraft stability remained a prime topic throughout the early days of flight.

How to attain in-flight stability is a consistent problem throughout the "Girl Aviators" series. Their father's dream had been to build "a non-capsizable aeroplane of great power," and Peggy and Roy at last achieve the goal. Giving navy lieutenant Bradbury a demonstration of the Prescott Airplane, Peggy throws it into a violent maneuver: "Suddenly the airplane slanted to one side, as if it must turn over. Peggy had banked it on a sharp aerial curve. The young officer, in spite of himself, in defiance of his training, gave a gasp." There is, however, nothing to fear: "The words had hardly left his lips before the aeroplane was on a level keel once more. At the same time a rasping, sliding sound was heard."[34] The Prescott stabilizing device has proved its worth.

Flight stability comes in for even greater attention as Peggy, Roy, and their friends take on the United Aviators' Exhibition Company. Early on, the professional fliers realize that the amateurs' craft have an edge. "They are equipped with a balancing device that makes them much more reliable than ours," says the group's manager. "I read an account of it in an aviation paper; but the description was too sketchy for me to see how the thing was worked." The device comes to the fore as the competition unfolds. Jimsy wins an altitude contest by employing a smooth, spiraling ascent; his opponents rise "in curious zigzags. This was because their machines were not equipped with the stability device." In even more dramatic fashion, Peggy outflies Pepita Le Roy, passing her in a quick turn; "the monoplane flown by the Cuban aviatrix could not negotiate it with as sharp an angle as Peggy's machine, owing to its not being equipped with an equalizing, or stability device."[35]

Whatever else they may contribute to the early days of aviation history, the "Girl Aviators" books achieve two noteworthy ends: they acquaint their young readers with a sense of the excitement of flying, and they acquaint those same readers with some knowledge of the technical problems faced by the airmen and airwomen of the day. They do so in a spirit of modernity. For all their femininity, Peggy and Jess are embodiments of the progressive spirit, and Roy and Jimsy accept their activism unhesitatingly. Here, they imply, is the coming wave of the future, and girls as well as boys would do well to appreciate it. Its requirements are complex, but they can be mastered by all.

Close on the heels of Burnham's "Girl Aviators" series came the "Flying Girl" books of Edith Van Dyne (1911-1912; two titles). These were actually written by L. Frank Baum, author of the well-known Oz books. Baum's "Van Dyne" *persona* was already well-established, for he had used it since 1906 for his on-going series of "Aunt Jane's Nieces" books (1906-1918; eleven titles), relating the adventures of three free-spirited girl cousins and their wealthy Uncle John. The series numbered six volumes by 1911, and would continue until Baum's death in 1918. By 1911, however, Baum was ready to explore new topics. He had ended the Oz series, of which he had grown tired, with *The Emerald City of Oz* (1910), placing the wonderland under a shield of invisibility to prevent its being discovered by that new-fangled invention, the airplane. A move from the Chicago area to California with his family was complete and he had a pressing need for money. Finding himself in Los Angeles at the height of the city's aeronautical enthusiasm, a flying series seemed an ideal way to go, and he threw himself into the project with enthusiasm.

The first volume, *The Flying Girl* (1911), introduces Orissa Kane and her Cornell-educated brother, Stephen, who live in a suburb of Los Angeles with their blind, widowed mother. Orissa works as secretary to real-estate speculator George Burthon, while Stephen, unable to find work as an engineer, is earning a substantial reputation as a capable airplane mechanic, starting with his mending a craft owned by exhibition flier Charles F. Willard. In their off-hours, the two work on Stephen's own design for a flying machine, the Kane Aircraft. Financed by Mr. Cumberford, a crusty but warm-hearted businessman, they finish a workable aircraft and enter it in the second Dominguez International Aviation Meet, an actual event scheduled for late December and early January, 1910-1911.

Orissa's employer, Cumberford's brother-in-law and a ruthless business rival, attempts to overshadow the Kane Aircraft's flight by sponsoring a rival airplane. Anticipating such skullduggery, Cumberford launches a volley of advance publicity, bringing the Kane Aircraft to the public's notice before Burthon's ship is ready. Frustrated by this ploy, Burthon sabotages the Kane ship, and Stephen's triumphant inaugural flight ends in a crash that breaks his leg. Despite the crash, Cumberford insists that the Kane Aircraft be kept in the entries for the Dominguez meet. Orissa then takes the controls of the repaired aircraft. Flying spectacularly before the thousands of spectators, she replicates the feats of several actual aviators, returning to earth and wide-spread acclaim as "The Flying Girl."

The second volume, *The Flying Girl and Her Chum* (1912), picks up shortly after the events of the first book. Orissa, now a nationally-known flier much in demand for air shows, travels to San Diego with Sybil Cumberford, Cumberford's free-thinking daughter and her closest friend. There she plans to fly in a sched-

Orissa Kane takes to the air on the cover of Edith Van Dyne's The
Flying Girl *(1911). (Author's collection).*

uled air show demonstrating Stephen's newly designed hydroplane,
an amphibious craft capable of flying from, and landing on, either
land or water. (Stephen's San Diego experiments with a hydroplane
parallel the contemporaneous ones of Glenn Curtiss, also conducted in San Diego).[36] En route she befriends wealthy young Madeline
Dentry and her party, who are headed to San Diego for a cruise on
Madeline's yacht. When Orissa takes Sybil aloft on her first demon-

Orissa Kane rescues a falling birdman.
(Author's collection).

stration flight, a glitch in the steering system causes the hydroplane to run away. Although Orissa is at last able to land the craft safely, she and Sybil are stranded on an island well off the California coast.

Madeline offers her yacht to Cumberford and Stephen for a rescue mission and the combined parties set out. After a series of rambunctious adventures, including the stranding of the yacht, the capture of the Dentry group by a renegade Mexican bank robber, a perilous flight to the mainland in the repaired and refueled hydroplane, and the timely intervention of the United States Navy, Orissa and Sybil are retrieved and both groups set out for a holiday in Hawaii aboard the yacht, looking forward to further adventures. Both books maintain the usual high standard of story-telling found in Baum's non-fantasy works, combining adventure with a plausibly drawn background, and both take up timely and newsworthy topics.

From the outset, Baum attempts to evoke the excitement and adventure of the days when air shows fed the public hunger for sights and news of the flying machine. His "Foreword" to *The Flying Girl* remarks that "The world is agog with wonder at what has been accomplished [in aviation]; even now it is anticipating the time when vehicles of the air will be more numerous than are automobiles to-day." He goes on to describe the first Dominguez Field meet (1910) as "destined to be an epoch in the history of aviation." Stephen and Orissa, who take time off from work to attend, are as affected as the general public: "The enthusiasm of the Kanes rose to fever heat in witnessing this exhibition, at the time the most remarkable ever held in the annals of aviation," and Stephen resigns his mechanic's job to work full-time on his design.[37]

Public enthusiasm has diminished not a whit when the second Dominguez meet opens. The field's lots are crowded with automobiles, its stands filled with gaily dressed men and women, and its events well-planned to "arouse the interest of a people just awakened to the possibilities of aerial navigation." Aviators from throughout the country have joined the meet, drawn by the fifty thousand dollars in gold offered as prize money. As Baum notes, "It is little wonder public interest was excited and every aviator determined to do his best. Many thronged the hangars, asking innumerable questions of the good-natured attendants, who recognized the popular ignorance of modern flying devices and were tolerant and communicative." The public interest is amply repaid. Orissa gives a spectacular performance, and, when she lands, "Men shouted until they were hoarse; women wept, laughed hysterically and waved their handkerchiefs; everyone stood up to applaud; [and] thousands crowded the field about Orissa."[38] It is a day of excitement for everyone.

For all his emphasis on the allure of the flying meets, Baum if anything gives even more attention to the technicalities of flight than does Burnham. He inserts substantial technical information into the stories, and, even when his speculations become fanciful, they have their counterparts in the technology of the day. Baum's "Foreword" to *The Flying Girl* sets the scene, thanking Glenn Curtiss and Wilbur Wright for their assistance with the manuscript; their expertise, by implication, is reflected in the book. There is no evidence that Baum actually consulted the two, but their names confer a degree of authenticity to the subsequent events. Other names enter as well. Stephen early on encounters Charles F. Willard; he and Orissa sit next to Arch Hoxsey (who soon "would become the greatest aviator in all the world") at the first Dominguez meet; and the two eagerly look forward to their association at the climactic meet "with such famous aviators . . . as the Wright Brothers, Glenn Curtiss, Hubert Latham, Arch Hoxsey, their old friend Willard, [Philip] Parmalee, [Eugene] Ely, [Walter] Brookins, [James] Radley and many others." Orissa and Stephen are shoulder-to-shoulder with the greats of early aviation, and the point would not be lost on Baum's readers.[39]

Adding to the technical authenticity of the stories is Stephen's assimilation of current aeronautical research and developments. He says he has "bought all the books on aviation [he] can find, and [has] been reading of Professor Montgomery's discovery of the laws of air currents and his theories concerning them." Stephen refers here to the Californian John J. Montgomery, who began experimenting with gliders in the mid-1880s, presented his theoretical findings at an aeronautical conference held at the 1893 Chicago World's Fair, and conducted a series of highly publicized glider flights in 1905. He was, ironically, killed in the crash of one of his gliders on 31 October 1910, shortly before the events of which Baum writes.[40] One of the earliest experimenters with gliders, Montgomery was hailed by aviation writer Victor Lougheed as a progenitor of powered flight, though he never made any attempt to equip his gliders with an engine.

The Kane Aircraft itself is a biplane, distinguished by having its upper wing mounted at right angles (i.e., longitudinally) to the lower wing. This arrangement "as a duplex balance . . . , with the swinging wing-ends, comprised the safety device that the inventor believed made his aeroplane superior to any other." Bizarre as the design sounds to the modern reader, these and other equally absurd designs flourished as experimenters felt their way into the realm of aeronautic theory. More telling, however, is the mention of "swinging wing-ends," which refers to a method of control originated by Octave Chanute and described by Victor Lougheed in his *Vehicles of the Air* (1910). Since Lougheed's book was published by Reilly & Britton, publishers of Baum's Oz books and the "Flying Girl" volumes, and Baum uses the expression "vehicles of the air" in his "Foreword," it is conceivable that he used the volume for much of his technical detail.[41]

Baum presents in the "Flying Girl" stories two books conveying a substantial amount of technical detail. In fact, the first book was recognized in the aeronautical press, being reviewed in *Fly Magazine* alongside Waldemar Kaempffert's *The New Art of Flying* ("another alluring digest of the new science which is arousing every wide-awake nation in the world") and William Duane Ennis's *Flying Machines Today*. The anonymous reviewer described the book as "a clean and wholesome novel in which the heroine flies a type [*sic*] airship, the actual perfection of which would make aviation safer than automobiling." It notes Baum's invoking of Curtiss and the Wrights, and goes on to remark that "the names of several of the world's greatest aviators are cleverly woven into the story." The review speaks well of the air of authenticity that the book carries, and concludes that "it is just the book to arouse in the boy or girl a wholesome interest in the art of aviation."[42] Better even than their predecessors, the "Girl Aviators" books, the "Flying Girl" stories carry on the task of educating American girls in the wonders of aviation.

For all their emphasis upon the air-meet scene and their conveying of technical details, the two series are bound together by a third theme. This theme, central to both series, is the exploration of the place of the New Woman in aviation and a consideration of what aviation offers to women. That the books deliberately intend to address these issues is certain. An advertisement for the "Girl Aviators" books describes them as "Just the type of books that delight and fascinate the wide awake girls of the present day who are between the ages of eight and fourteen years," while the "Foreword" to *The Flying Girl* is even more direct. There Baum writes:

> The American youth has been no more interested in the development of the science of aviation than the American girl; she is in evidence at every meet where aëroplanes congregate, and already recognizes her competence to operate successfully any aircraft that a man can manage . . . . There are twenty women aviators in Europe; in America are thousands of girls ambitious to become aviators.[43]

Both authors present themselves as female spokespersons for women in aviation, and set out to make their case with detail and enthusiasm.

The two series show their heroines to be well-versed in the achievements of women in aviation. In the opening pages of *The Girl Aviators and the Phantom Airship*, Peggy frets that the prizes for girls offered at the pending air show are smaller than those offered boys, then points out to Roy that "It's discrimination, that's what it is. Don't you read every day in the papers about girls and women making almost as good flights as the men? Didn't a—a Mademoiselle somebody-or-other make a flight around the bell tower at Bruges the other day . . . ?" In *The Flying Girl,* Mr. Cumberford tells Orissa that "In Europe—especially in France—a score of women have made successful flights," while Orissa's initial conversation with Madeline Dentry in *The Flying Girl and Her Chum* invokes the names of Blanche Scott and Matilde Moisant— who are, Madeline declares, only "imitators of Orissa Kane!"[44] Not content merely to tout their heroines as exemplars of aviation, both series establish that women at home and abroad are making their mark in aviation.

They make that mark through their heroines' ready mastery of the skills and knowledge required by flight. Peggy Prescott proclaims that she "can run the Butterfly [the Prescott Airplane] almost as well as Roy. . . . I could run an auto before. I learned on the one that Jess had at school, so it really wasn't hard to get to understand the engine." Her later actions bear out her confidence; aping Blanche Scott's "Death Dive," she plunges downward until, "within a few feet of the ground, just when it seemed they must dash against the surface of the earth with crushing force, Peggy set the planes on a rising angle and the Golden Eagle settled to earth as gracefully as a tired bird." Her expertise amazes Lieutenant Bradbury: he discovers her whiling away a leisure afternoon with "a treatise on aeronautics," only then realizing that she is "Miss Margaret Prescott, the girl aviator I have read so much about in the technical publications." And those skills only improve as the series progresses, until she can easily outfly the professional Pepita LeRoy in the final volume.[45]

Orissa Kane is equally competent. She has, Baum observes, "made herself familiar with the latest modern improvements in aeroplanes and had personally examined several of the best devices." She takes to the air at the Dominguez meet, demonstrating that "her control of the aëroplane was really wonderful. . . . She shot up into the air, rising to the height of half a mile and then performing the hazardous evolution known to aviators as the 'spiral dip'. . . . It was a bewildering and hair-raising performance, and no one but Walter Brookins had ever before undertaken it." Even her brother concedes that she is his superior at the controls: "I'll never be able to run the thing as you can, Ris," he says, and the book ends with the two looking forward to a dazzling succession of appearances at air shows at home and abroad. In the second volume, Baum speaks explicitly to Orissa's knowledge and skills required of flight: "The remarkable success of her aerial performances was due to an exact knowledge of every part of her aeroplane. . . . And aside from this knowledge she had that prime quality known as 'the aviator's instinct'—the intuition what to do in emergencies, and the coolness to do it promptly."[46] By training and by nature, she is as skilled a flier as any other person, female *or* male, in the air.

Also noteworthy is the degree to which both series present the airplane and flying as liberating elements in the lives of young women. The heroines of both series, to be sure, are wholly up-to-date, familiar with the automobile and comfortable at its wheel. The airplane, however, provides them with something entirely different. Peggy's demonstration flight with Lieutenant Bradbury fills her with "a wild, reckless feeling, born of the thrilling sensation of aerial riding," and she "buzzes" the Mortlake aircraft plant to show off the qualities of her airplane and herself. Bradbury, for his part, can only say, "This is the twentieth century with a vengeance." Later, as she prepares for the naval competition, Peggy prophesies that "I dare say women as aviators will be as common as men. . . . Ten years ago a woman who ran an automobile would have been laughed at, if not insulted. But now, why lots of women run their own cars and nobody thinks of even turning his head." Jimsy Bancroft, who has been listening in, applauds her remarks, saying "I declare I feel like a lone man at a suffragette meeting."[47] Personal and social independence, already conveyed by the automobile and by feminist urgings, has an ally in the airplane and its properties.

Baum's remarks in the "Flying Girl" books are as progressive as

Orissa Kane consoles her brother as Mr. Cumberford and Sybil look on.
(Author's collection).

Burnham's, and wholly in keeping with his own views toward women. He was no stranger to feminist thought. His wife's mother, Matilda Joslyn Gage, was a founder of the National Woman Suffrage Association, and editor, with Susan B. Anthony and Elizabeth Cady Stanton, of the *History of Woman Suffrage* (1881 ff.). As a newspaper editor in the South Dakota Territory during the 1890s, he consistently supported suffrage and other expressions of feminine independence, arguing that American women were an oppressed and underappreciated population. He echoed this outlook in his fiction for young readers. Almost three-quarters of the Oz books feature female protagonists, and from Dorothy Gale and Glinda the Good to Princess Ozma and Scraps the Patchwork Girl, Baum's heroines radiate capability, courage, independence, and resourcefulness, all qualities "that patriarchs restricted to men."[48]

The women of *The Flying Girl* books continue that vigor. When Stephen Kane observes that "The most successful aviators of the future . . . are bound to be women," Sybil Cumberford expands upon his theme. "I have discovered my future vocation," she says. "I shall aviate parties of atmospheric tourists. When the passenger airships are introduced I'll become the original sky motoress, and so win fame and fortune. . . . I'll . . . become a free lance in the sky, roaming where I will." Orissa is just as receptive to the allure of flight. As she ascends before the crowd at Dominguez Field, "She began to realize her control of the craft and her dominance of the air. A masterful desire crept over her to accomplish great deeds in aviation." She returns to this outlook in *The Flying Girl and Her Chum*, telling Madeline Dentry and her friends that flying "grows on one until its fascinations are irresistible. I have the most glorious sense of freedom when I'm in the air—way up, where I love best to be."[49] Flight provides a greater liberation than any earthbound activity, and both young women are ready to grasp it. They are, indeed, spokespersons for the "New Woman" of the times.

For all their timeliness and contemporary appeal, the girls' aviation series ended as abruptly as they began. Burnham's "Girl

Aviators" saw its last volume appear in October 1912, while Baum's "Flying Girl" books, even though he had received a go-ahead to begin a third volume, *The Flying Girl's Brave Venture,* came to a halt in July 1912. There is evidence that poor sales contributed to the demise of both series; however, the poor sales are more likely related to current events than to any diminishing of girls' interest in aviation.[50] The very timeliness that gave the series their appeal also worked to bring about their departure.

The termination of the two girls' series seems closely linked to the death of Harriet Quimby and a sudden drop in the public visibility of women aviators. Quimby's popular image can be inferred from two references in the "Girl Aviators" series. Pepita LeRoy ("a handsome woman, in a foreign way, with large, dark eyes and an abundance of raven black hair") has the same dark good looks possessed by Quimby, echoing an interviewer's comment in 1911 that Quimby "looks more Spanish than the wholly American girl she declares herself to be." Moreover, Burnham twice refers to Regina Mortlake in language that evokes Quimby. Regina's eyes "were black as sloes, and flashed like smoldering fires. A great mass of hair of the same color was piled on the top of her head," and she was clad in "a gown of magenta hue"—a color repeated in her "rubicund aviation costume."[51] Quimby's beauty was as much a part of her public *persona* as her purple satin flying suit, and Burnham could count on the public's awareness of both.

Chronology also points to the reverberations of Quimby's death. *The Girl Aviators and the Phantom Airship* was logged by the Library of Congress on 6 September 1911, and *The Flying Girl* on 22 September 1911, well after the first two Los Angeles meets but before Harriet Quimby had received widespread publicity. Conversely, *The Flying Girl and Her Chum* was registered on 31 July 1912, less than a month after Quimby's death, while *The Girl Aviators' Motor Butterfly* was logged on 4 October 1912. *The Flying Girl and Her Chum* ends with Orissa, Sybil, and Madeline looking forward to their holiday in Hawaii, implying a third volume to come. In contrast, *The Girl Aviators' Motor Butterfly*, three months later, brings the series to a satisfying end. The final paragraph has Aunt Sally reflecting on the achievements of Peggy, Roy, Jess, and Jimsy, seeing the four as "fulfilling the bright phophecies [*sic*] of the present. She saw them stronger because of adversity, braver because of success, and ennobled by all their experiences; and she deemed herself happy in her capacity of chaperon to the Girl Aviators." Female and male acting as equals, the four young persons proceed confidently into a freer, more uplifting future.[52]

Women, to be sure, continued to work and advance in aviation following Quimby's death. Ruth Law and the sisters Katherine and Marjorie Stinson achieved prominence as record-setters, advocates of aviation and the military, accomplished stunt fliers, and flight instructors. Henry Woodhouse's "Pioneer Women of the Air" (1913) made the point that "the women of the air have shown that they are as good as men in handling the aerial ponies, and their number has increased from one, in 1910, to about two scores," but focused principally on already well-known names in the United States and abroad. Muck-raking journalist Ida M. Tarbell also took up the cause of women in aviation, making her first flight in November 1913 and writing of her adventures in *Flying*.[53] None, however, commanded the degree of public attention stirred by Quimby during her brief career. The sensational coverage given Moisant's fiery last flight and Quimby's horrific death no doubt made the idea of girls' flying unpalatable to many of the adults who tended to buy the girls' books, and a corresponding drop in sales was quick to follow. No other girls' flying series would appear for almost two decades, the genre lying silent until the early 1930s.

Whatever the causes for their demise—the lack of suitable public role models, the onset of World War I and its use of the airplane as a killing machine, or a simple failure of sales—the two early series of girls' aviation stories offer a sound introduction to the spirit and technology of flying as it existed in the Progressive Era. They establish that up-to-date young women can have an interest in flight and all that it entails without losing their feminine identities, and, even more to the point, that these same young persons, younger editions of the time's "New Woman," have the intelligence, skill, and emotional wherewithal to master flight. Women, the books say, can competently deal with this most advanced expression of modern technology, and can do so on a par with their male counterparts. The books send an eloquent message to their young readers. Women of all ages are competent to act as fully involved, up-to-date American citizens, and the stories make their statement a full decade before the Nineteenth Amendment to the Constitution made that citizenship a statutory fact.

Notes

1. Arthur S. Link and William B. Catton, *American Epoch: A History of the United States Since the 1890's,* 3rd ed. (New York: Alfred A. Knopf, 1967), 17-45. Although dated in its treatment of some specific issues, notably the rise of the women's movement, Link's study remains an accessible, comprehensive, and sound overview of the Progressive Era and its aftermath.

2. Nancy Woloch, *Women and the American Experience: A Concise History,* 2nd ed. (New York: McGraw-Hill, 2002), 198-200, 207-211; Link and Catton, *American Epoch,* 36-38; Nancy F. Cott, *The Grounding of Modern Feminism* (New Haven: Yale University Press, 1987), 22.

3. Orville and Wilbur Wright, "The Wright Brothers' Aëroplane," *The Century Magazine* 76 (September 1908): 641-650; "Termination of the Rheims Aviation Meeting," *Scientific American* 101 (11 September 1909): 180-181. See also Robert Wohl, *A Passion for Wings: Aviation and the Western Imagination 1908-1918* (New Haven: Yale University Press, 1994), 102-109.

4. Cleve T. Shaffer, "The Los Angeles Aviation Meet," *Scientific American Supplement* 69 (5 February 1910): 90-91; "The Harvard Aviation Meeting," *Scientific American* 103 (12 September 1910): 216-217, 227.

5. "Glenn Curtiss Flies Over Aviation Park," *Los Angeles Times,* 10 January 1910; Samuel Travers Clover, "First Meet of the Man-Birds in America," *Outing Magazine* 55 (March 1910): 750, 763; Charles K. Field, "On the Wings of To-day," *Sunset* 24 (March 1910): 248-249.

6. Tom Crouch, *The Bishop's Boys: A Life of Wilbur and Orville Wright* (New York: Norton, 1989), 426-428; C. R. Roseberry, *Glenn Curtiss: Pioneer of Flight* (Syracuse, NY: Syracuse University Press, 1991), 286-287; Glenn H. Curtiss and Augustus Post, *The Curtiss Aviation Book* (New York: Frederick A. Stokes, 1912), 87-89; Doris L. Rich, *The Magnificent Moisants: Champions of Early Flight* (Washington, DC: Smithsonian Institution Press, 1991), 74-77.

7. Eileen F. Lebow, *Before Amelia: Women Pilots in the Early Days of Aviation* (Washington, DC: Brassey's, 2002), 10-16, 21-28; "Autour du beffroi de Bruges," *L'Aerophile* 8 (1 October 1910): 435.

8. Claudia M. Oakes, *United States Women in Aviation through World War I.* Smithsonian Studies in Air and Space, Vol.2 (Washington, DC: Smithsonian Institution Press, 1978), 17-19; International Aviation Meet Advertisement, *Fly Magazine* 3 (October 1911): back cover.

9. Rich, *Magnificent Moisants,* 74-77, 114-122; "Woman's Monoplane Wrecked and Burned," *Dallas Morning News,* 15 April 1912, 1.

10. Woloch, *Women and the American Experience,* 133-134.

11. Ibid., 180-181.

12. Cott, *Grounding of Modern Feminism,* 4-5.

13. George E. Mowry, *The Era of Theodore Roosevelt, 1900-1912* (New York: Harper & Brothers, 1958), 36; Cott, *Grounding of Modern Feminism,* 53-60; Woloch, *Women and the American Experience,* 207-211.

14. Randolph Bourne, quoted in Cott, *Grounding of American Feminism,* 34-35.

15. Wosk, *Women and the Machine,* 149; Lebow, *Before Amelia,* 28-29; "Lady Monoplanist Arrives in City," *Dallas Morning News,* 20 March 1912, 6; Oakes, *United States Women in Aviation through World War I,* 30. See also Edith Brown Kirkwood, "With Milady of the Skies," *Aerial Age* 1 (June 1912): 5-6.

16. "French Aviatrice Here," *New York Times,* 24 September 1911, C5; Henry Woodhouse, "Pioneer Women of the Air," *Flying* 2 (June 1913), 22; "Miss Katherine Stinson's Looping at Night," *Aerial Age Weekly* 2 (17 January 1916): 424; Ruth Law, "Miss Law Tells of Her Record Flight; To Try Non-Stop New York Trip Next," *New York Times,* 20 November 1916, 4; "Ruth Law Lands Here from Chicago in Record Flight," *New York Times,* 21 November 1916, 1, 3.

17. Oakes, *United States Women in Aviation through World War I,* 25.

18. All biographical details concerning Quimby are taken from Ed. Y. Hall, *Harriet Quimby: America's First Lady of the Air* (Spartanburg, SC: Honoribus Press, 1997). Although not entirely satisfactory, Hall's book is the only extended biography of Quimby to date. Frank Luther Mott, *A History of American Magazines, 1850-1865* (Cambridge: Harvard University Press, 1938), 464.

19. "Woman in Trousers Daring Aviator," *New York Times,* 11 May 1911, 6.

20. "Miss Quimby Flies English Channel," *New York Times,* 17 April 1912, 15.

21. "The Fatal Aeroplane Accident at Boston," *Scientific American* 107 (13 July 1912): 27; "The Quimby Monument Fund," *Fly Magazine* 4 (September 1912): 16.

22. Oakes, *American Women in Aviation through World War I,* 29; Elizabeth Anna Semple, "Harriet Quimby, America's First Woman Aviator," *Overland Monthly* 58 (December 1911): 530.

23. Hall, *Harriet Quimby,* 161-173; Semple, "Harriet Quimby," 531-532; Bonnie R. Ginger, "Here's the Airgirl! A Talk with Harriet Quimby," *World Magazine,* 27 August 1911, 3.

24. Harriet Quimby, "In the World of People Who Fly," quoted in Hall, *Harriet Quimby,* 94.

25. Harriet Quimby, "The Dangers of Flying And How to Avoid Them," *Leslie's Weekly,* 31 August 1911, 249.

26. Harriet Quimby, "How I Won My Aviator's License," *Leslie's Weekly,* 24 August 1911, 221; Quimby, "The Dangers of Flying And How to Avoid Them," 249; Harriet Quimby, "Flyers and Flying," *Leslie's Illustrated Weekly Newspaper,* 27 June 1912, 735.

27. Harriet Quimby, "American Bird Women: Aviation as a Feminine Sport," *Good Housekeeping Magazine* 55 (September 1912): 315.

28. Margaret Burnham, *The Girl Aviators and the Phantom Airship* (Chicago: M.A. Donohue, 1911), 7-8, 207-208, 235.

29. Margaret Burnham, *The Girl Aviators' Sky Cruise* (Chicago: M.A. Donohue, 1911), 214-215, 245; Margaret Burnham, *The Girl Aviators' Motor Butterfly* (New York: Hurst, 1912), 73-74, 89, 201.

30. An Aeroplane Blue Print Company advertisement in the *Scientific American* for 29 October 1910 (p. 352) offered plans for Curtiss, Blériot, and Farman airplanes, while aeronautical historian Victor Lougheed published a how-to-do-it manual, *Aeroplane Designing for Amateurs* (Chicago: Reilly & Britton, 1912), speaking overtly to experimenters throughout the country.

31. Burnham, *Girl Aviators and the Phantom Airship,* 26-27, 96, 112; Margaret Burnham, *The Girl Aviators on Golden Wings* (Chicago: M.A. Donohue, 1911), 258; Burnham, *Girl Aviators' Motor Butterfly,* 88.

32. "The Wright and Voisin (Farman) Flying Machines Compared," *Scientific American* 100 (9 January 1909): 18.

33. Richard P. Hallion, *Taking Flight: Inventing the Aerial Age from Antiquity through the First World War* (New York: Oxford University Press, 2003), 326-327; "Automatic Stabilizing System of the Wright Brothers," *Scientific American*

Supplement, no. 1828 (14 January 1911): 20-21; Grover Cleveland Loening, "Automatic Stability of Aeroplanes," *Scientific American* 104 (13 May 1911): 470-471, 488.

34. Burnham, *Girl Aviators' Sky Cruise,* 27.

35. Burnham, *Girl Aviators' Motor Butterfly,* 213, 232, 246.

36. Roseberry, *Glenn Curtiss: Pioneer of Flight,* 338-339.

37. Edith Van Dyne [L. Frank Baum], *The Flying Girl* (Chicago: Reilly & Britton, 1911), 11, 29, 33.

38. Ibid., 184-185, 198.

39. Ibid., 32, 139.

40. Ibid., 28; Lougheed, *Aeroplane Designing for Amateurs,* 20; "John J. Montgomery Falls to Death in Glider," *Fly Magazine* 4 (December 1911): 19.

41. Van Dyne, *Flying Girl,* 141; Victor Lougheed, *Vehicles of the Air: A Popular Exposition of Modern Aeronautics with Working Drawings,* 3rd ed. (Chicago: Reilly & Britton, 1911), 219. Stephen's design is no more outlandish than many others of the time; even so experienced a designer as Louis Blériot experimented at one point with a cylindrical wing. For other contemporaneous aeronautical oddities, see Marius C. Krarup, "A Chamber of Horrors: Wild Designs in Flying Machines," *Scientific American* 105 (14 October 1911): 338-339.

42. "New Books for the Aeronautical Library," *Fly Magazine* 4 (April 1912): 26.

43. Back matter, Burnham, *Girl Aviators on Golden Wings,* unpaged; Van Dyne, "Foreword," *The Flying Girl,* 11-12.

44. Burnham, *Girl Aviators and the Phantom Airship,* 9; Van Dyne, *The Flying Girl,* 11-12, 161; L. Frank Baum, *The Flying Girl and Her Chum,* 1912 (Bloomfield, NJ: Hungry Tiger Press, 1997), 3. Peggy refers to Hélène Dutrieu's record-setting flight of September 1910.

45. Burnham, *Girl Aviators and the Phantom Airship,* 43; Burnham, *Girl Aviators' Sky Cruise,* 25-26.

46. Van Dyne, *Flying Girl,* 30, 190-191, 230; Baum, *Flying Girl and Her Chum,* 11.

47. Burnham, *Girl Aviators' Sky Cruise,* 34, 36, 218.

48. Woloch, *Women and the American Experience,* 229; Katherine M. Rogers, *L. Frank Baum: Creator of Oz* (New York: St. Martin's Press, 2002), 29-30, 247.

49. Van Dyne, *Flying Girl,* 161-162, 189; Baum, *Flying Girl and Her Chum,* 6.

50. James E. Haff, "Bibliographia Pseudonymiana," *Baum Bugle* 18 (Spring 1974): 4-5.

51. Semple, "Harriet Quimby," 531; Burnham, *Girl Aviators' Sky Cruise,* 118-119, 178.

52. Burnham, *Girl Aviators' Motor Butterfly*, 307. See also Dean Jaros, *Heroes Without Legacy: American Airwomen, 1912-1914* (Niwot: University Press of Colorado, 1993), 107-109.

53. Henry Woodhouse, "Pioneer Women of the Air," 22; Ida M. Tarbell, "Flying – A Dream Come True," *Flying* 2 (November 1913): 20-22.

CHAPTER 3

The Earhart Era:

1925-1940

U ndeterred by the onset of World War I, boys' aviation stories absorbed its events and soldiered on through- out the war years and the dozen years following. Young American fliers contested the Germans from 1915 (Horace Porter, "Our Young Aeroplane Scouts," 1915-1919; twelve titles) through 1932 (Eustace Adams and Thomson Burtis, "Air Combat Series," 1932-1937; seven titles), oblivious to the social and techno- logical changes that were swirling about them. In one forward step the genre began making more frequent references to the air mail (Lewis Theiss's "Air Mail Series," 1927-1932; six titles), but not until Charles A. Lindbergh's New York-Paris flight of May 1927, did the aviation genre as a whole pick up new energy, with girls' stories as well as boys' getting a new lease on life. Between 1927 and 1939, boys saw twenty-four new aviation series appear, comprising near- ly one hundred and fifty volumes.

Girls' stories, single-volume or series, lay fallow from 1912 until 1930, their development in great part inhibited by the post-war cult of the "ace." From the war years until well into the 1930s, champion World War I-era fighter pilots (the "aces"—e.g., Eddie Rickenbacker and Frank Luke for the United States, Manfred von Richthofen for Germany, Roland Garros and Georges Guynemer for France) were held up as exemplars of skill, courage, and chivalry for young males. "Ace" flyers dominated the boys' series until 1927, when the Lindbergh flight pushed them from the stage. For the purposes of the girls' stories, however, the "aces" proved problematic role models, for they were a company exclusively male whose celebrity came from killing other males, principally by shooting them in the back. Not surprisingly, the authors of girls' flying stories were unable or unwilling to combine girls and combat in any plausible manner.[1]

Not until the excitement of the post-Lindbergh years did girls' aviation stories resume, but they resumed with renewed progressivism. When Dorothy Verrill, Harrison Bardwell, and Mildred Wirt published, respectively, *The Sky Girl* (1930), *Roberta's Flying Courage* (1930), and *Ruth Darrow Wins Her Wings* (1930), they ushered in a new vision of how young American women might embrace, participate in, and profit from aviation. Other manifestations of feminine air-mindedness were quick to follow, giving young women five "pure" flying series comprising nineteen volumes and at least three free-standing tales to spur their interests.

Systematic efforts to stimulate a national consciousness of aviation began as early as 1920. In April of that year, the Aero Club of America proposed "a huge movement to popularize civilian aeronautics." Arguing that "America's leadership in aeronautics depends on starting a great movement to create national civilian interest in aeronautics," the club proposed a national assembly, its representatives taken from the sixty or more local flying clubs spread across the country along with delegates from cities, universities, and other sporting clubs to plan ways of publicizing aviation to the general public.[2] The Aero Club's efforts were enhanced by a sudden ready access to airplanes. As the military rid itself of its aircraft in the months following World War I, airplanes of all descriptions, often unflown and still crated, became available to the public at fire-sale prices.

Demobilized military pilots found themselves in need of work. Many turned to aviation. Barnstormers, free-wheeling pilots flying hand-me-down trainers or decommissioned military craft, crisscrossed the country, thrilling audiences with hair-raising stunts and selling airplane rides to anyone with the desire and the price of admission. Other pilots strove to make a living operating small airfields and giving flying lessons.³ These activities helped to heighten public interest and to introduce the capabilities possessed by aircraft. The press did its part, romanticizing the government air mail pilots, who began flying the mail throughout the country in 1918. Rough-and-ready sorts who quickly became known for their disregard of danger and their determination that the mail "get through," mail pilots acquired an air of romance that turned many of them into folk heroes.⁴ It was, though, not until Lindbergh's flight in 1927 captured public attention and catalyzed a boom in national enthusiasm that popular aviation truly came into its own.

A one-time barnstormer and air mail pilot himself, Charles Lindbergh knew the appeal, hazards, and possibilities of aviation as it stood in 1927. He was a well-read if largely self-taught student of aeronautics and aircraft, able to extrapolate and articulate what aviation might mean to the country. Using his celebrity as a timely bully pulpit, he set out to "sell" aviation to the United States. In the last of several newspaper columns published under his name in the days immediately following his flight, he called for an increased public involvement in aviation, offering himself as a means of achieving that involvement: "Please regard me as a medium for having concentrated attention upon the subject of transatlantic flying in particular and aviation in general and do all you can to encourage aeronautics. I am convinced that aviation will soon take its place among the big activities of the United States." He returned to this theme later in the same year, as he reported on his good-will flight to Mexico: "The next generation will fly as naturally as the last drove automobiles." The time was ripe, he believed, for a national system of aviation, commercial *and* general.⁵

He continued his campaign in a series of weekly columns published in the *New York Times* and syndicated throughout the country, beginning in August 1928. The first of these, "Lindbergh Writes of Aviation's Advance," stated bluntly: "The airplane has now become a vital part of our life." Subsequent columns took up the topic of general aviation. "Differing Types of Planes Now Built to Serve Special Uses" (18 November 1928) surveyed aircraft suitable for private owners, noting that open-cockpit craft could be had for $3,000 to $5,000, while small cabin planes, with an enclosed cockpit and carrying three to five passengers, could cost up to $15,000—costly, but still within the reach of an affluent citizen. The following week, in "Aircraft for Private Owners and How to Choose One," he talked of the dramatic increases in airplane comfort and engine reliability, compared the virtues of monoplanes and biplanes, and spoke confidently of the ease of flying that modern designs made possible.[6]

Lindbergh's advocacy highlighted the significant advances in aircraft technology that had occurred since the 1914-1918 war. Recognizing the shortcomings of reconditioned military craft and responding to the potential of a new, civilian market, aircraft manufacturers in the years following World War I increasingly turned their attention to designs suitable for the amateur flier. In May 1927, the very month of Lindbergh's flight, *Aero Digest* published an overview of typical airplanes "intended for production and to be available to the general public." The article, illustrated with photographs of twelve biplanes equipped with water-cooled engines, another twelve powered by radial, air-cooled engines, and thirteen monoplanes, both single- and multi-engined, observed that "copies of the old war type planes have practically disappeared from the market and designers have supplanted them with modern types designed and built purely for commercial purposes." Later articles, such as Alexander Klemin's "Planes for Private Flying" (1929) and "The Evolution of the Private Plane" (1935), only whetted the public appetite for new, advanced, and accessible aircraft.[7] The possibilities of these aircraft, moreover, were emphasized by a number of highly publicized, record-setting flights that, in their way, drew as much public attention as the air shows of the pre-World War I era.

One of these, obviously, was Lindbergh's flight, which created a national frenzy unlike any other. He became, overnight, a national hero and authority on aviation, and the press sought his opinions on every topic. Others, however, soon captured their own share of attention. Clarence Chamberlin and Charles Levine, flying a Bellanca WB-2, surpassed Lindbergh in June 1927 by flying non-stop from New York to Eisleben, Germany, a distance of 3,905 miles. Commander Richard E. Byrd, flying in a Fokker F.VII trimotor, followed soon after, crossing the Atlantic from New York to France in July 1927. Meanwhile, army lieutenants Lester Maitland and Albert Hegenberger, in a Fokker C-2, made the first nonstop flight from California to Hawaii in June 1927. None of these other accomplishments, however, so captured the public eye as did the June 1928 transatlantic flight of Amelia Earhart.

Earhart's flight was funded by Amy Phillips Guest, a wealthy matron determined to sponsor the first trans-Atlantic flight by a woman. She herself was unable to make the trip, but commissioned George Palmer Putnam, publicist for the undertaking, to locate "an American girl who would measure up to adequate standards of American womanhood." Earhart at this time was employed as a social worker at a settlement house in the tenement district of Boston. A licensed pilot who had accumulated some 500 hours in the air, she flew for recreation and had off-handedly set a women's record for altitude in 1920. Her license and her clean-cut looks attracted Putnam and others, and she was selected for the flight. To her dismay, she was not allowed to share piloting duties in the aircraft, a float-equipped Fokker tri-motor named *Friendship*, telling a friend upon her return that "All I did was lie on my tummy and take pictures of the clouds. . . . I was just baggage, like a sack of potatoes."[8] In other interviews she readily gave full credit for the flight to pilot Wilmer Stutz and navigator Louis ("Slim") Gordon. Nonetheless, when she stepped from the airplane in Burry Port, South Wales, she was a celebrity. As column after column of praise followed her activities in 1928 and afterward, she became the aviation heroine of the decade.

Earhart's instant fame was catalyzed by several changes in American society. These were the result of the opening of new occupations for women and the growth of national mass media. Whereas the New Woman of the turn-of-the-century period had been a person principally involved with socio-political issues, the 1920s and after were populated by women of diverse minds. Some women sought greater roles in the professional and business worlds; some continued the feminists' push for full economic independence and legal assimilation; others looked upon marriage with liberated ideas about the relationship of male and female. The majority of them were young and single, characterized by "energy, spunk, and sportive esprit" and a desire to question conventional rules and practices.[9] Their efforts helped to change the face of the surrounding culture.

Evidence of women's new independence came in the increase of women in the workplace. The growth of urbanized business brought about a new need for office workers, sales personnel, and others. Jobs such as typist, stenographer, and file clerk quickly became known as "women's jobs." Work in settlement houses continued to be attractive to the socially concerned, while new occupations such as cosmetics, real estate, advertising, journalism, and banking saw increasing numbers of women in their ranks. By 1930, close to 20 percent of the female workforce was dedicated to office work, while the percentage of women joining the professions (law, medicine, etc.) increased from just under 12 percent to more than 14 percent. These numbers only increased after the onset of the 1929 Depression. More and more married women entered the workplace, with working women overall increasing their numbers by 25 percent.[10] Where once the "working girl" had been somewhat of an oddity, she now became almost a commonplace.

Much of the popular conception of the twentieth-century woman came from the mass media, and especially from motion pictures. Almost without exception, women in motion pictures were portrayed as assertive and independent, exuding "vitality [and appearing] dynamic, aggressive, even flamboyant." They were women who not only could do things, but did them, living by their wits and in numerous ways competing successfully with men. Some of the assertive roles, to be sure, were less than desirable—heroines who were sly, selfish, and scheming. The most appealing, however, appeared as dedicated career women, "competent, confident, and full of ambition." Stars like Joan Crawford, Bette Davis, Katherine Hepburn, and Rosalind Russell played reporters, political workers, middle-level executives, and government agents in a host of films. They were slim, athletic, attractive, and capable women offering to the movie-going public a view of womanhood that definitively established the image of the independent woman of the era.[11]

Yet another sign of independence appeared in the growing visibility of women in aviation. As more and more American women began to take part in aviation, their numbers caught the attention of the popular press as well as the technical press. *Vogue* magazine published "Madame, the Aeroplane Waits" in 1920, talking up the accessibility and affordability of private flight and concluding that "One must have a ship of one's own." Howard Mingos, offering "The Ladies Take the Air" in the *Ladies' Home Journal* for May 1928, reviewed the careers of a dozen or more women pilots, making reference to Harriet Quimby, Hélène Dutrieu, and Matilde Moisant, then going on to point out the more recent achievements of Thea Rasche in Germany, Hilda Hewlett in England, and, among others, Katherine Stinson, Ruth Law, Ruth Nichols, and Phoebe Omlie of the United States.[12]

Later, Alicia Patterson announced that "I Want to Be a Transport Pilot" (the highest license rating) in *Liberty* magazine, identifying Ruth Nichols, Louise Thaden, Amelia Earhart, Phoebe Omlie, and Bobbi Trout as among those holding "the highest recognition the Department of Commerce can give to an aviator." Hugh Amick, with "The *Fimmale* Wing" in *U.S. Air Services*, concluded that women fliers had legitimately become "a power in masculine enterprise." Still later, Ruth Nichols spoke out concerning "Aviation for

You and for Me" in *Ladies' Home Journal,* supporting her campaign for a national network of flying clubs, and G. K. Spencer, writing in *Sportsman Pilot,* a periodical intended for the well-off amateur flier, in 1930 linked women's flying to the earlier New Woman:

> There has not been a single step in aviation's development in which the student woman, the woman of action or the woman of derring-do has not played an important role.... The subtle influence of fashion and the electric tension of our post-war world seem perpetually to invite achievement by women, [and] since the war ... there are none but 'new women'.[13]

Already a "presence" in earth-bound society, the American New Woman was taking to the air.

Later in 1930, Margery Brown, a journalist-pilot specializing in aviation matters, published "Flying is Changing Women" in the *Pictorial Review.* Brown in particular singled out the individualistic and societal opportunities for women that aviation held: "Flying is a symbol of freedom from limitation.... Flying inculcates a marked self-reliance, [and] it is creating a bond among women, knitting womankind into a better understanding of their common problems." Two months later, in the *New York Times,* T. J. C. Martyn concluded that "it would be temeritous for any one to assert that women do not make every bit as good pilots as men. They do, and in many cases they make better pilots." These and numerous other comparable articles established that women were embracing the air, their activities quietly establishing them as what historian Susan Ware calls "liberal feminists." These, says Ware, are women who are "advancing [their] personal and professional interests at the same time [they hope their] achievements will benefit women as a group." Each of the extant women fliers, in her own way, was making a visible statement of all women's abilities.[14]

Women fliers won a prominent place in the public eye with the National Women's Air Derby of 1929. Dubbed "The Powder Puff Derby" by humorist Will Rogers, the race was a cross-country flight against time from Santa Monica, California, to Cleveland, Ohio. Contestants took off in sequence, and their in-flight times were recorded at each of the intermediate landing fields used during the week-long race. The Derby drew twenty of the most notable women fliers of the time, including Amelia Earhart, Ruth Elder, Jessie ("Chubbie") Keith-Miller, Ruth Nichols, Phoebe Omlie, Louise Thaden, and Evelyn ("Bobbi") Trout. All were record-holders or soon-to-be record holders. Of the twenty, sixteen finished, with Louise Thaden winning, Gladys O'Donnell placing second, and Amelia Earhart third. One contestant, Marvel Crosson, was killed in a crash on the second day, but the race continued at the insistence of the other pilots. The Derby achieved its purpose, winning Will Rogers's sincere respect for women fliers and providing visible, public proof of the flying skills of women. They had publicly matched their abilities and capabilities against those of their male counterparts.[15]

Given the confluence of the evolving role of women in the workplace, their increasing and visible presence in aviation, and the national excitement over Charles Lindbergh, it comes as no surprise that the iconic female flier of the era was Amelia Earhart.[16] Born in 1897 in Acheson, Kansas, Earhart passed through a series of public schools and the private Ogontz School in Pennsylvania. She put in a term of service with the Canadian Red Cross in 1918 as a V.A.D. nurse's aide, then began a series of enrollments of various lengths at Columbia University (where she began a pre-medical course), the University of California, and the University of Massachusetts. During this time she supported herself by working as a truck driver, a photographer, and a telephone company clerk, beginning her social work at Denison House in Boston in 1926.

When her interest in flying was piqued by a California air show in 1920, she began flying lessons, receiving her National Aeronautic

Participants in the 1929 Women's Air Derby (Powder Puff Derby).
(l-r): Louise Thaden, Bobbi Trout, Patty Willis, Marvel Crosson,
Blanche Noyes, Vera Dawn Walker, Amelia Earhart,

Association flying license in 1921 and a license from the *Fédération Aéronautique Internationale* in 1923. She continued her training even after her trans-Atlantic flight of 1928, winning her transport pilot's license in 1929. The acclaim from her 1928 flight, meanwhile, made her a public figure. Like Lindbergh, she wrote a series of newspaper accounts of the flight, combining them into a book, *20 Hrs., 40 Min.: Our Flight in the Friendship*, that was published in September 1928. She joined the staff of *Cosmopolitan* magazine as "Aviation Editor" in November 1928, writing a series of columns that continued, off and on, until September 1932.

Marjorie Crawford, Ruth Elder, and Pancho Barnes. Louise McPhetridge Thaden Collection, National Air and Space Museum, Smithsonian Institution (SI-83-2144).

Earhart married publisher George Palmer Putnam in 1931, keeping her own name for her writings and activities, although newspapers at times spoke of her as "Mrs. Putnam." With Putnam working as her publicist and manager, she became the first woman to solo in an autogiro (a precursor of the helicopter), making the flight in April 1931 and two days later setting an altitude record for the craft. This flight established the pattern for her subsequent endeavors, as she sought one aeronautical record or another, then wrote of her flights for the public media. In May 1932, on the fifth anniversary of Lindbergh's flight, she made a solo flight across the

Atlantic, the first woman and second person to do so, and followed the flight with a second book, *The Fun of It* (1932). She received the National Geographic Society's Special Gold Medal for the flight, the first woman to be so recognized, and wrote of her activities for the *National Geographic Magazine* and numerous other periodicals. Her prominence increased still further when it became known that she was a personal friend of President and Mrs. Franklin D. Roosevelt, and was a welcome visitor at the White House.

Despite a certain slackening of public interest in record-setting flights as the steady increase in domestic and international commercial aviation made aviation more commonplace, Earhart continued to seek new undertakings.[17] In January 1935, she made a non-stop solo flight from Hawaii to California, the first woman to fly the route and the first person to fly it alone, then followed this exploit in May with a non-stop solo flight from Mexico City to Newark. These flights, too, she described in several articles. What she announced would be her final public flight came in 1937, when she began plans for a west-to-east around-the-world flight at the Equator. Her first attempt failed when her aircraft, a twin-engined Lockheed Electra 10-E, cracked up in Hawaii. She returned to the mainland, planning a second attempt, this time east-to-west, for later in the year. This flight began with her take-off from Miami, Florida, on 1 June 1937, and ended with her disappearance somewhere over the Pacific in early July. The mystery surrounding her fate only assured her place as the most newsworthy woman flier of the times.

Throughout her career, media accounts of Earhart portrayed her as a progressive, individualistic, modern woman. If accounts at times referred to her as a "girl" (she was 30 at the time of the 1928 flight), dubbed her "Lady Lindy," and dwelt on her slim figure, her unruly hair, and her penchant for wearing trousers, they also pointedly stressed all that she was accomplishing *as a woman*. Initially unmarried, gainfully employed, and amusing herself with the most modern of hobbies, she personified all that was progressive in 1920s

Amelia Earhart in the cockpit of her Lockheed 10-E Electra, August 1936.
Rudy Arnold Photo Collection, National Air and Space Museum,
Smithsonian Institution (SI 2007-12883).

womanhood. Even before the 1928 flight took off, newspapers were referring to her as "the greatest woman aviator in the country." A citation presented to her upon her return by the city of New York praised her for having "glorified the name of American woman-hood," and spoke of her progressive work in business and at Denison House. *The Literary Digest* quoted the Baltimore *Sun* as saying: "She seems to represent American women at their best— quiet, capable, intense in purpose, versatile, and self-reliant. She is womanly, she is intelligent."[18]

In an essay welcoming her to the staff of *Cosmopolitan,* O. O. McIntyre announced that Earhart "has become a symbol of new womanhood." In a reinforcement of that "new womanhood,"

Cosmopolitan surrounded her first article, "Try Flying Yourself," with photographs showing her sporting a fashionable but informal dress, clad in flying togs, attired for tennis and horseback riding, and comfortably wearing slacks, a white shirt and a masculine necktie.[19] Although journalists nationwide may not yet have decided precisely how to treat her, Earhart already was becoming a model of the modern American woman, whose personal achievements reflected on all womanhood.

The response to her 1932 solo trans-Atlantic flight only continued the adulation. A telegram from President Herbert Hoover on the day of her arrival in Great Britain praised her for demonstrating "the capacity of women to match the skill of men in carrying through the most difficult feats of high adventure." Charles L. Lawrance, inventor of the Whirlwind engine that had powered *The Spirit of St. Louis* and *The Friendship* of 1928, pointed out that "Miss Earhart has always felt that women should be afforded the same opportunity as men in the field of aviation," while George S. Wheat, an executive of United Aircraft and Transport Corporation, parent company of United Air Lines, affirmed that the flight "proves that the emancipation of women, already established in the domestic and the commercial fields, is extending to that of strenuous pioneering."[20]

Trade and specialized journals as well as the popular press picked up on the theme of Earhart's individualism and what her work meant for women. The *National Aeronautic Magazine*, official journal of the National Aeronautic Association, which oversaw licensing and other concerns, credited her with having "given further dramatic proof of feminine ability in flying." *National Geographic Magazine* subsequently reprinted President Hoover's remarks when he awarded her the Society's Special Gold Medal. Earhart, the president said, was motivated in her flight "by a wish also to enlarge those opportunities by expanding the powers of women as well as men to their ever-widening limits." Her image of modernity followed her to as late as 1937, bare months before the

Three flying notables of the 1930s. (l-r) Laura Ingalls, Amelia Earhart, and Col. Roscoe Turner with Ingalls' Lockheed Model 9-D Orion. National Air and Space Museum, Smithsonian Institution (SI 89-19607).

start of her round-the-world flight, when an interviewer for *Better Homes & Gardens* magazine alluded to her as "a very modern young woman with a man's career and a man's courage."[21] In the mind of the public, she stood for all that women might, and could, accomplish, whether in flight or in other endeavors.

Earhart initially had no plans for making a career in aviation. Describing herself as "a social service worker on a bat or a vacation," she followed her return from Europe with a six weeks' recreational flight to the West Coast and back. Her book, *20 Hours, 40 Minutes,* appeared in September 1928, and, when she returned from her holiday in mid-October, she took up the offer from *Cosmopolitan.* She considered the magazine "progressively air-minded." In taking the job, she stated openly that she "was casting [her] lot permanently with aviation," and her first article, "Try Flying Yourself," appeared in November 1928.[22] With that essay, Earhart began a ten-year career of writing in which she established herself as an outspoken advocate of flying *and* of women's concerns.

As an author, Earhart presented the American public with three propositions concerning aviation. The first contended that aviation was a progressive enterprise that would soon find an integral place in society. Costs will come down, facilities will expand, and "the family car of today will be the family plane of tomorrow." She spoke of the young persons of 1929 as the "Flying Generation," who would think of flying as a normal adjunct to life. After her solo trans-Atlantic flight, she told her *Cosmopolitan* readers that "Flying is Fun!," and in her second book, she concurred with Anne Morrow Lindbergh's belief that "aviation is one of the most progress-bring-ing occupations today. . . [and] is an important part of living."[23] Aviation is a reality, she argued, and the United States should embrace it wholeheartedly.

Earhart's second proposition grows from the first: the United States will benefit from an expansion of commercial aviation. The infrastructure is present. Nine thousand miles of navigational bea-cons allow "the most extensive night-flying service in the world," major cities are developing well-equipped, up-to-date passenger terminals, and "three transcontinental trunks are building a sturdy backbone to aerial service in this country." Safety should not be an issue. Air travel in 1929 was at least as safe as auto travel and improved equipment was making it still safer. To advance this cause, she took on publicity work as a vice-president of Transcontinental Air Transport, which utilized a combination of rail and air service between New York and Los Angeles, and later did the same as vice-president of the Ludington Line, a company offer-ing hourly air service linking New York, Philadelphia, and Washington, DC. In 1931 the National Aeronautic Association acknowledged her concern for commercial flight, noting that she had "taken an active part in the development of scheduled passenger air transportation in the United States." Even her 1935 flight from Hawaii she presented as "marking a little more plainly the pathway over which the inevitable air service of the future will fly." Commercial aviation was a reality; the public must be educated as to its possibilities and benefits if both were to benefit.[24]

Her third proposition is perhaps the broadest of all, for it held that aviation, be it amateur or commercial, was a liberating, exhilarating force within American society. Earhart's second *Cosmopolitan* article conceded that "there are tribulations in air vagabonding. But the fun of it far outbalances them. There is joy in exploring a new country in new ways." The next year, she remarked that "as flying enters into everyday life, the dreams of centuries become actualities," and she concluded in 1932, avowing that "There are other worlds to conquer. Open to all, the world of the air may make an explorer of anyone who wishes . . . It is the newest of the uncharted ways." She expanded this view during an article in *American Magazine*, linking her 1932 Atlantic flight to the challenges faced by all. She flew the Atlantic, she said, "Because I wanted to." One's individualistic desires, if sincere, are more potent than the whims of society: "To want in one's heart to do a thing, for its own sake; to enjoy doing it; to concentrate all one's energies upon it—that is not only the surest guarantee of its success. It is also being true to oneself." By enabling participants to face the challenges of the air, aviation equips them to face the greater challenges of life. They become the open-minded, individualistic persons who test the easy shibboleths of society. As Earhart notes, "Everyone has his own Atlantics to fly. Whatever you want very much to do, against the opposition of tradition, neighborhood opinion, and so-called 'common sense'—that is an Atlantic."[25] Freedom, joy, and integrity are essentials to every existence; that aviation nurtures them is important.

Her aeronautical writings may have established her prominence as a determined spokesperson for contemporary aviation in general, but Earhart's writings concerning women, both within aviation and outside of it, show another realm of concern. Throughout her career, she denied being a feminist in any overt sense. On the other hand, she was consistently emphatic about her belief in the need for women to challenge and move beyond the stereotypes applied to them. In 1927, more than a year before her first Atlantic flight, she wrote to Ruth Nichols, a pilot widely known for her support of amateur aviation, suggesting a professional organization for women affiliated with flying. She closed the letter saying: "I can not claim to be a feminist but do rather enjoy seeing women tackling all kinds of new problems—new to them, that is." Earhart continued pressing for such an association, and helped to establish the "Ninety-Nines" following the Powder Puff Derby of 1929. In later years, she lent her name and celebrity to organizations such as Zonta International, the Society of Women Geographers, and the National Woman's Party.[26] She did not, however, alter her fundamental call to arms: women must test the assumptions and conventions that surround every part of their lives.

Earhart maintained first of all that women were no more and no less able than men in any undertaking not requiring raw bulk and strength. "There is," she said in an address at Columbia University, "no cause inherent in her nature which would make a woman inferior to a man as an air pilot." She echoed this belief in 1932, following her solo trans-Atlantic flight: "Women can do most things that men can do. . . . What I contend is that women, in any job that requires intelligence, coördination, spirit, coolness, and will power (without too heavy muscular strength) are able to meet men on their own ground." And she repeated it yet again in *Last Flight*, a collection of previously unpublished writings published posthumously in 1937. The day will come, she says, "when women will know no restrictions because of sex but will be individuals free to live their lives as men are free."[27] Women, in short, can—and should—do virtually everything they choose to turn their efforts to.

Earhart's next contention addresses the issue of *why* women seem so willing to be overshadowed by men. The reason, she says, is societally-shaped education and training. She dedicated an entire *Cosmopolitan* essay, "Why are Women Afraid to Fly?," to the topic: "Some girls do enter the shops in the public schools. More often such instruction is barred, and they are shunted into cooking and sewing classes without a choice. . . . A man has mechanics thrown at him from the cradle, at least in America. Women haven't." She makes an even more sweeping charge in *20 Hrs., 40 Min.*, pointing out that "inheritance, training and environment seem to make women less aggressive than men, although in real courage I think they are equals." Becoming more vehement as she progresses, she notes in *The Fun of It* that "I know many boys who should, I am sure, be making pies and girls who are much better fitted for manual training than domestic science. Too often little attention is paid to individual talent. Instead, education goes on dividing people according to their sex, and putting them in little feminine or masculine pigeonholes." Her vehemence she acknowledges in "Women and Courage," published in *Cosmopolitan:* "Doubtless by now I am running the risk of becoming a heavy-handed feminist. In a measure, I'm guilty, as I do become increasingly weary of male superiority unquestioned."[28] Feminist or not, she recognized that "femaleness" was a socially, rather than biologically, determined quality, and she argued against the conventions that limited its opportunities.

A possible solution to the problem of female conditioning occupied Earhart's third argument. First, women must be recognized for what they achieve *as women*. Second, when women and men compete on equal terms, their achievements must be judged on equal terms. The first of these matters concerned her in "Why Are Women Afraid to Fly?," where she took up the issue of the criteria for judging women's achievements in flight: "Inasmuch as women haven't traveled so far as man aeronautically, I [feel] a much keener interest would result if they could be properly credited with what efforts they can make at the present times." Then, once women have established their abilities, they can confront men on their own terms: "Such regulation does not mean that when a woman is capable she cannot compete with men on equal terms. I'd like to see men's and women's records *and* a sexless thing called a world's record in all activities, flying being no exception."[29]

She expanded upon this notion in *20 Hrs., 40 Min.*, writing that "It is ability, not sex, which counts, in the final analysis. There should be no line between men and women, so far as piloting is concerned." Earhart's belief in the importance of equity even took her to the White House. As part of a delegation from the National Woman's Party, she spoke to President Hoover on behalf of women who had experienced discrimination:

> I know from practical experience of the discriminations which confront women when they enter an occupation where men have priority in opportunity, advancement and protection. . . . In aviation the Department of Commerce recognizes no legal differences between men and women licensed to fly. I feel that similar equality should be carried into all fields of endeavor, so that men and women may achieve without handicap because of sex.

Her views continued to resonate even after her death. Early in *Last Flight*, Earhart spoke of her "conviction that there is so much women can do in the modern world and should be permitted to do irrespective of their sex." Throughout her advocacy of the cause of women, she acknowledged that it was "the accident of sex" in 1928 that had given her the opportunity to speak out.[30] She meant to see that other women's voices were not heard by accident.

Less than two years after Amelia Earhart's first trans-Atlantic flight, girls' aviation books began to appear in bookstores, echoing Earhart's advocacy of aviation and her insistence that women take a greater role in all aspects of contemporary flying. These were *The Sky Girl* by Dorothy Verrill (1930), two free-standing books and the "Ruth Darrow" books by Mildred A. Wirt (1930-1931; four titles), and the "Airplane Girl" books by Harrison Bardwell (1930-1931; four titles). Each cluster presents an independent-minded young woman who casts her lot with aviation. Each also presents a different mode of access to aviation, and each captures the feminist optimism engendered by Earhart and her writings. The first is a single-volume story of sport flying and the simple joy of flight, with a hint at commercial applications to come. The second, although containing a degree of mystery-melodrama, explores the possibilities of aviation as a sport, presenting it as a means of broadening one's experiences. The third, for all its secret-service-story overtones, is a career series. It presents aviation as a profession in which women can serve alongside men, make their way in a mercantile world, assimilate the requirements of flying, and achieve recognition and distinction that might not otherwise have come their way. Four of the books' heroines fly principally for their own entertainment. Affluent enough to own and maintain their own airplanes, they live easily within the culture of their class, enjoying the privileges and social contacts available to an upper-middle-class young woman. The fifth demonstrates how a woman might make her way in the business of aviation by flying as a vocation. Altogether, the several books present a substantial dramatization of women's response to modern aviation and the enterprise's appropriateness for a female enthusiast.

Dorothy Verrill's *The Sky Girl* was published by the Century Company, a well-established New York publisher having a long-standing association with juvenile literature. Originally the Scribner firm, Century launched the children's periodical *St. Nicholas* in 1873. The magazine, originally edited by Mary Mapes Dodge, soon became the most distinguished publication for American youth of the turn-of-the-century period. Among the works it introduced were Louisa May Alcott's *Eight Cousins* and *Jack and Jill*, Rudyard Kipling's *The Jungle Book*, Frances Hodgson Burnett's *Little Lord Fauntleroy*, and Mark Twain's *Tom Sawyer Abroad*. Its stories embraced modern times as readily as medieval, and its articles (often written by public figures of the day) offered a wide range of information on topics extending from government to technology. The magazine appeared regularly until 1936, when the Depression made it no longer profitable.[31]

The Sky Girl fits the pattern of modernity established by *St. Nicholas*. Fifteen-year-old Susan Thompson comes from a flying family. Her mother took flying lessons, but was disqualified because of eye problems; her father is an ex-World War I ace and owner of the International Aircraft Corporation. International's holdings extend nation-wide, and he routinely makes business trips in the company's Ford tri-motor, often taking Susan and her mother along. Susan and best chum Patty Carlisle, junior students at Midford High School in New England, save the day when they persuade a company pilot to fly them and boxes of pep-squad pennants to the Midford-Newton football game, the Big Game of the season. Susan asks her father for flying lessons. He refuses, but arranges for a company pilot to fly her and a party of friends to the Harvard-Yale football game. She then surreptitiously begins ground school training at the International flight school, and, upon turning sixteen, again asks for flying lessons. Her father relents, Susan wins her license, meets the British aviatrix Lady Mary Heath, and receives an Avian airplane from her father as a graduation present.

Susan's story is a straightforward one, imbued with the ambiance of autumn in New England and the aura of the Ivy League. It nonetheless introduces several themes that will resonate throughout the girls' aviation stories of the 1930s. One acknowledges the opposition that female fliers are likely to meet. Susan's father initially refuses to let her take lessons, saying "My dear little girl, you're so young—much too young to fly. . . . And you're my only daughter, bless you!" Youth and femininity are *de facto* obstacles to any young woman seeking to fly, and the individual must make a special effort to overcome them. Another is the chum who yearns to be a pilot, yet is somehow inferior to the heroine; Patty is disqualified from flying lessons because of an incipient heart condition.[32]

Still another theme asserts that women are capable of mastering flight technology while retaining conventional femininity. Susan easily absorbs books on aerodynamics, "and understood more about what made it possible to fly than Patty had ever heard." Once she begins her flight lessons, theory becomes fact and she revels in "really seeing flying-surfaces, and angles of incidence and dihedrals and other things in aërodynamics actually at work." Her easy mastery of the principles and skills of flight, however, does nothing to diminish her "girl's" attributes. She has "a weakness for . . . housekeeping [and] could prepare a meal if necessary and enjoyed baking almost as much as she did sports. But the setting and decorating of the table was her particular hobby." She is delighted to receive "a lovely new evening frock of pale yellow taffeta and tulle" for her sixteenth birthday, and makes a mental note that Lady Mary Heath's leopard-skin coat and helmet were "attractive for winter flying."[33] Be they aspiring female flier or skeptical male observer, the citizenry need not fear that flying will create a generation of mannish women hostile to conventional values.

Finally, *The Sky Girl* presents aviation and the act of flying as progressive, emotionally elevating enterprises that affect men and women alike. Early on, readers learn that Susan feels sorry for the majority of her friends because "their fathers only walked, or rode, to tiresome business on the earth, while her father soared through the sky." Later, taking an extended interstate joyride with her father, she thinks, "We take the skyways instead of the highways." She and Patty are struck by the glory of the upper air, feeling that they "were engulfed in a magic world. It seemed almost too beautiful to be real, and the strange, disembodied sensation of the flight through this peaceful and colorful atmosphere made it all the more lovely." The last word, though, goes to the chief pilot for the International works. As he prepares Susan for a final check flight before her official solo, he exclaims: "There's nothing like it . . . ! Gosh, what did the world do before there was flying!"[34] Aviation, whether commercial or sport, offers insights and attitudes gained from no other occupation.

The "Ruth Darrow" series (1930-1931; four titles) written by Mildred A. Wirt introduces the premise that sport flying can lead to numerous unconventional opportunities for women pilots. The series takes on an unusual resonance among the girls' aviation stories for Wirt, as "Carolyn Keene," was simultaneously working as principal writer of the "Nancy Drew" series (1930-1981; 64 titles) for the Stratemeyer Syndicate. Edward Stratemeyer, noting the success of the "Hardy Boys" books (1927-1981; 71 volumes), decided to offer a comparable series for girls; the Syndicate's offerings, he remarked to a potential publisher, were "weak on girls books with a single heroine." When Grosset & Dunlap accepted the series for publication, Stratemeyer turned initially to Wirt, who had been contributing to the earlier "Ruth Fielding" series. The first of the Drew volumes appeared on 28 April 1930—barely a month after the publication of the first of the "Ruth Darrow" books. Wirt was proficient at creating stories of independent, intelligent girls, and she did so under both her own name and that of Carolyn Keene.[35] Ruth and Nancy not surprisingly share several characteristics, but each remains her own woman, with her own priorities and her own goals.

Ruth Darrow is the air-minded daughter of widower Colonel F. H. Darrow, the "Flying Colonel" famed for his achievements in early aviation. In the first volume, *Ruth Darrow in the Air Derby or, Recovering the Silver Trophy* (1930), Ruth and her best chum Jean Harrington are taking flying lessons at the Brighton, California, airport from instructor Sandy Marland, an established pilot who is respected by all. Jean has difficulty mastering the controls, but Ruth solos readily. After her solo, Ruth's father gives her a monoplane, the *Silver Moth,* and the two girls go on to win transport licenses. Colonel Darrow thereupon proposes an all-woman, California-to-

Ohio air race to publicize the presence of women in aviation. The race is sponsored by investors in California and Ohio, and offers a silver trophy to the winner. After a series of setbacks including the bitter rivalry of another female pilot, the crash of the *Silver Moth*, and the last-minute theft of the race's trophy, Ruth and Jean enter the race as pilot and navigator, respectively. Their flight is tense, but they win by seconds with their last drops of fuel.

Volume two, *Ruth Darrow in the Fire Patrol or, Capturing the Redwood Thieves* (1930), takes Ruth and Jean to a northern California forest ranger camp where Colonel Darrow and Sandy Marland are working on detached duty. The two girls fly to the camp in the *Silver Moth*, experiencing a forced landing in the desert while on the way but easily effecting repairs after an overnight delay. At the camp, they learn the ropes of fire patrol flying, spot some fires on their own, and discover that Colonel Darrow is trying to track down a gang of timber thieves. The girls' lives are threatened when they make a flight in one of the camp's "Fire Eagles" and have to parachute to safety when the aircraft suffers a structural failure. The accident uncovers the machinations of corrupt ranger Webb Randall, who proves to be the mastermind of the thieves' ring. When his complicity is revealed, Randall sets a forest fire to draw off pursuit, putting Colonel Darrow and Sandy in mortal danger. The two men take shelter in an abandoned silver mine, only to find that the thieves' ringleaders *and* a rescue party including Ruth and Jean are waiting out the fire in the same site. Sandy gives Ruth a "brotherly" kiss, the ringleaders are arrested, and Ruth and Jean return to Brighton relishing the praise of the entire camp.

Ruth Darrow in Yucatan (1931), third in the series, lets Ruth show off her flying skills by landing the *Silver Moth* on the deck of the aircraft carrier *Saratoga* as Colonel Darrow is preparing for a flying expedition to Yucatan. Ruth yearns to join the venture, and she and Jean master the intricacies of flying seaplanes to show their determination. Impressed by their ability, the naval officer sponsoring the expedition permits the two to go along, with Ruth flying the

Ruth Darrow and Jean Harrington come to the rescue of Sandy Marland.
The background airplane resembles a Lockheed Vega. (Author's collection).

smaller of the group's two seaplanes and Jean accompanying as a passenger. Although Darrel Vandervort, the resident archeologist who joins the party in Panama, opposes the girls' presence, both Colonel Darrow and Sandy Marland support them and they proceed with their travels. In Yucatan, the party discovers previously unknown Mayan ruins and retrieves a Mayan *codex* likely to prove valuable to scholars deciphering the Mayan language. After the codex disappears, the girls and Sandy survive a forced landing when

Ruth Darrow hits the silk as her Fire Eagle plunges to its doom.
(Author's collection).

Vandervort sabotages their airplane, then rescue Colonel Darrow, who's been stranded on the shores of a jungle lake. Their safe return to camp breaks Vandervort's spirit. He confesses to the sabotage and the theft of the codex and the party returns to the United States and renown.

In the final volume, *Ruth Darrow in the Coast Guard* (1931), Ruth joins Jean and her family in vacationing at the upscale seaside resort of Orville Beach. When they discover that Sandy Marland is attached to the nearby Coast Guard station, they become regular visitors and learn that the Guard is attempting to break up a ring smuggling Chinese immigrants into the United States. During a weekend air show there, Ruth rescues a small girl from an aircraft accident and receives a seaplane as a thank-you gift from the child's father, owner of the Airway Aviation Corporation. Naming the seaplane *Sea Gull*, Ruth and Jean fly up and down the coast, and rescue an older girl from a boating accident. They become increasingly interested in the smuggling story and begin poking about a nearby lighthouse. There they are captured by ne'er-do-wells and locked into an upper room of the lighthouse, which is the nerve center of the smuggling operation. Ruth uses the lighthouse radio set to send an SOS to the Coast Guard, she and Jean are rescued, the smugglers are trapped, and the book ends with a hint of pending romance for both girls.

In 1935, with the "Nancy Drew" series well under way and the "Ruth Darrow" series completed, Wirt returned to aviation, broadening her presentation of women in the enterprise. Her focus this time was on the national phenomenon of professional air-racing, which had grown in prominence after 1930.[36] *The Sky Racers* features Jane Grant, the teenaged daughter of Midwestern aircraft manufacturer Samuel Grant. Although she's long been air-minded, has completed ground school, and is well-informed concerning aeronautical theory, Jane's widower father refuses to let her take flying lessons. He relents, however, after Jane, with the assistance of second-string test pilot Ralph Erwing, saves him from crashing. Jane and best chum Helen Wright start lessons with the company's top pilot, Jerry Barnes, and Jane quickly emerges as a "natural" flier. Both girls win their licenses and go on to achieve transport licenses without incident. Meanwhile, Grant is vying with rival manufacturer J. K. Fletcher to win the Reilly Cup, a national racing award that promises substantial prize money and lucrative contracts. The Grant racer crashes on its maiden flight, forcing Jane and Jerry to parachute to safety, but a new craft is quickly produced and entered in the Reilly race. When Jerry is disabled by a broken arm, Jane steps in, flies the race, and handily defeats rival girl flier Gloria Fletcher as well as her male opponents. The book ends with the hint of sequels to come.

Those sequels never materialized. Instead, Wirt continued her work with the "Nancy Drew" books, began the "Kay Tracey" series (1935-1942; eighteen titles) as "Frances K. Judd" for the Stratemeyer Syndicate, and set out on her own "Mildred A. Wirt Mystery Stories" (1936-1939; seven titles). Then, in 1937, she turned again to aviation, publishing *Courageous Wings,* a book evoking the "barnstorming" years when itinerant fliers criss-crossed the country giving stunt demonstrations and selling rides. Fixed-base operators Jim Sherman and Shorty Dawes come to the aid of Cleo Bowman, motherless seventeen-year-old daughter of failed aircraft manufacturer Martin Bowman. Bowman has resorted to barnstorming to earn money, but faces a second failure until Jim and Shorty join him to form the Bowman Flying Circus. Cleo, her interest in flying stirred, takes flying lessons but apprehensively delays a solo flight. Then, when her father is endangered during one of his routines, she flies to his rescue in Jim and Shorty's craft. Solo accomplished, she becomes an alternate pilot with the group. A well-off joy-rider, Herman Hodgson, impressed by Cleo's flying skills, stakes Bowman to a new venture, a flying operation allowing him to work on a revolutionary new engine. The latter wins the promise of a major contract if its durability can be proven, where-upon Jim and Shorty undertake a six-week-long endurance flight. Cleo flies the refueling ship and the flight nears completion, only to have her and her father held hostage by Randall Marcus, a disgruntled ex-employee. Bowman's estranged partner, Sam Efflinger, who has previously striven to force him out of business but who has had his eyes opened by Cleo, intervenes and frees the two. Cleo refuels the endurance ship in time, Jim and Shorty set a new record, and land to great acclaim and prosperity for all.

All six books make their heroines' privileged status evident from the outset. Ruth and Jean are members of the Brighton

Country Club, playing regular rounds of golf, and traveling briskly throughout the region in Ruth's blue roadster. At home, Ruth is comfortably at ease in the social world appropriate to a high-ranking officer in the army. She retains a "woman's eye" for decor, scanning the Darrow dining room prior to her birthday dinner "with the eye of a critical hostess," making sure that "the gleaming silver, the linen, the candles and the centerpiece of roses were as they should be." Her feminine side comes out, as well, as she and Jean prepare for the Orville Beach vacation with "a glorious week of shopping. There were sports clothes to be purchased, party dresses and odds and ends almost without number. The girls did not forget to include bathing suits, tennis racquets, and golf clubs in their luggage."[37]

Wirt gives comparable status to Jane Grant and Cleo Bowman. Jane's father is an affluent aircraft manufacturer and bank director, able to maintain a gated estate and giving Jane her own sedan and personal airplane. Although the collapse of her father's business has reduced the Bowmans to near-pennilessness, Cleo until then has enjoyed comparable luxury. An early part of the action in *Courageous Wings* takes place at the Bowman country estate, "a large, rambling white Colonial house" with extensive gardens and its own private landing strip. Like Ruth and Jean, Jane and Cleo take privilege for granted; the Grants' family estate has its own gardener, while Cleo's Chinese cook, the only servant retained from more prosperous times, is a constant admirer and source of comic relief. All four of Wirt's heroines cheerfully accept the conventions of their sex and their class and enjoy the perquisites of both.[38]

Wirt's young women may be conventional in a social sense, but they readily embrace the details and discipline of aviation. Even before they first sit in an airplane, Ruth and Jean "had studied the theory of aviation and had crammed facts about engines, air currents, aircraft construction and the elements of meteorology." Jane, for her part, "understood the theory of flying for . . . she had read every available book on the subject." Before soloing, Ruth and Jean complete "their necessary ten hours of dual instruction and [learn] a great deal about taxiing, straight flying, turns, take-offs, spirals and landings." Ruth easily masters the seaplane, having "to exercise keen judgment and caution as the ship moved with increasing speed through the water," and throughout the series handles occasional forced landings with practiced skill.[39]

For all their emphasis upon aviation skills, Wirt's books are even stronger in their advocacy of independence for women. Using aviation as the context and pretext, the books consistently show an intelligent, capable, and determined young woman who wants to make her mark on her own. Colonel Darrow introduces the theme when he proposes the Derby: "It would be a fine thing for the cause of aviation if only there were more opportunity for competition— especially more women flyers. It seems to me that more girls and women would be interested in aviation if only there were some special goal; a derby race, for instance." Sandy Marland, who already recognizes Ruth's flying abilities, seconds him, murmuring that the race "will be a great thing for aviation. . . . It should interest more women in flying." Ruth's entering the race is a foregone conclusion, and her victory comes about solely through her flying skills. Jane Grant, still later, "is never more annoyed than when singled out for special attention because of her father's position," and goes on to win the Reilly Cup race, a grueling closed-course race flown in laps around three pylons, ahead of a host of experienced male fliers. Both heroines have taken a step for women.[40]

The question of women's activity and men's opposition appears explicitly as well. In *Ruth Darrow in the Fire Patrol*, after teasingly suggesting that Ruth might be drafted into the patrol, Sandy tells her, ruefully, "It's against the rules to have women in the fire patrol." Ruth's response is blunt: "Rules make me tired anyway," and Sandy acknowledges that "Maybe we can make some new ones." In *Ruth Darrow in Yucatan*, Jean frets over women's inability to join the navy, telling Ruth that her ambition to fly a navy seaplane "will go unfulfilled unless the navy lets down the bars and invites the members of our fair sex to see the world." Ruth demurs and, when Commodore Williams visits with Colonel Darrow, expresses her interest in naval aviation. Her interest and subsequent proof of her flying skill win the Commodore's respect and a relaxing of naval rules. Six years later, Cleo Bowman reinforces Wirt's point, challenging her father's prohibition on her taking flying lessons: "You won't let me fly or anything. I'm tired of being protected!"[41] Here and elsewhere in the books, Wirt captures the frustration of a forward-thinking young woman who is confined by traditional yet untested rules, and makes clear her determination to force a rethinking of those rules through her own particular achievements. Wirt, like Verrill, offers flight as a means of achieving independence and progress, and uses her books to present her case at length.

Another perspective on women in aviation comes in the "Airplane Girl" stories. Although published as by "Harrison Bardwell," the series was written by Edith Janice Craine, one of the few women authors to write aviation stories for both boys and girls. Little is known of her background, although as "E. J. Craine" she wrote the contemporaneous "Airplane Boys" books (1930-1932; eight titles). These relate the adventures of two young New Englanders who fly first into Canada, then into the American Southwest, and at last into Central America. The boys' doings are considerably more dramatic than those in the "Airplane Girl" books, for the boys quickly encounter a secret society of super-scientists whose members identify each other by the ornate emerald ring each wears. The boys are initiated into the society, presented with rings, and go on to become active participants in the group's world-wide enterprises.

The "Airplane Girl" stories, although carrying their own share of melodrama, are more realistic and down-to-earth. Volume one, *Roberta's Flying Courage* (1930) introduces sixteen-year-old Roberta Langwell, newly graduated from a Long Island high school business course and in need of a job. She wins a secretarial position at the Lurtiss airplane factory, where her conscientiousness and reli-

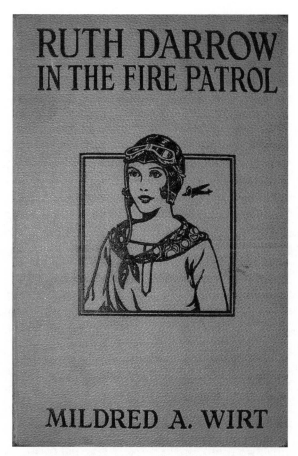

Cover drawing of Ruth Darrow in the Fire Patrol *(1930),
showing Ruth in flying togs and the silk scarf popularized
by Amelia Earhart. (Author's collection).*

ability as a stenographer bring her increasingly complex assignments. After she is assigned to transcribe a series of aeronautical training lectures for publication, she becomes interested in actual flying. The company, recognizing her interest, gives her flying lessons and she wins her pilot's license. When a company executive and his wife need to make a lengthy inspection tour throughout the Midwest and Canada, Roberta is tapped to pilot them, removed from the secretarial pool and put on the pilots' payroll. During the tour she parachutes to safety from a crippled experimental ship and later successfully lands a privately-owned amphibian after its pilot is taken ill. The Lurtiss officials, proud of her achievements, present her with one of their newest aircraft, and offer her full-time work as a member of their flying staff. She christens her airplane *Nike,* and eagerly looks forward to her new job.

The second volume, *The Lurtiss Field Mystery* (1930), finds Roberta a full-fledged test pilot for the Lurtiss works. After hearing reports of a mysterious air pirate at work, company officials decide to put an end to his depredations and assign Roberta to the task. She is sent to fly a series of seemingly random flights, her *Nike* equipped with a special radio device that allows authorities to locate her position should she encounter the pirate. Her flights prove eventful. She saves two small boys from drowning, makes an emergency flight to deliver serum to a distant hospital, is gassed by the pirate but lands safely, survives an arson fire at the plant, and discovers the pirate's camouflaged base hidden in the hills. The Secret Service is brought in and, with the help of the military, shuts down the pirate's activity. Roberta meets with the Lurtiss executives and Secret Service Inspector Howe, who offers her the opportunity for further investigative work. She agrees, but stipulates that the Lurtiss Company has first call on her flying expertise.

The final two volumes, *The Airplane Girl and the Mystery of Seal Islands* and *The Airplane Girl and the Mystery Ship* (both 1931), make up a single extended story. In the first pages of the initial volume, Roberta is summarily discharged from the Lurtiss organization, part of a staff reduction forced by the Depression. Heart-broken but still spunky, she takes a job as private pilot for the mysterious Mrs. Pollzoff, widow of a furrier, who has taken flying lessons but has never won a license. When Roberta's growing suspicions of her employer's activities prompt her to resign the job, Mrs. Pollzoff drugs her and flies the two nonstop, using in-flight refueling, from New York to the Pribilof Islands. There Roberta is sequestered under the care of two Aleut women, encounters Fred Arnold, a stranded pilot who is slowly repairing his cracked-up airplane, and discovers that her captors are part of a seal-poaching ring.

The companion volume opens with Roberta still on the island but making plans for an escape. She befriends several of the poachers, flying one to a distant hospital when he is taken ill, and enlists their help in her escape. She steals an airplane from the group's Big Boss and gets away cleanly, only to be forced down in the tundra by a group of fighter planes. These prove to be part of a joint United States-Great Britain-Russia-Japan effort to smash the poaching ring. Mrs. Pollzoff and the ring's Big Boss are captured. Roberta is reunited with Fred Arnold and her parents, and learns to her delight that her dismissal from Lurtiss was merely window-dressing, part of Inspector Howe's scheme to give her credibility as an undercover agent. Her job restored, she returns home to great acclaim and satisfaction.

Roberta's engagement with aviation is a process of discovery. She joins the Lurtiss firm solely because it offers her a job. Not until she begins to settle into her work at the factory does she develop a desire to fly. The series of lectures that she transcribes piques her interest; she tastes some of the excitement of flight after clambering into the cockpit of a hangared craft and, after being given a joy-ride by one of the executives, yearns to learn to fly. From that point on, she is absorbed by the excitement of flight: during her joy-ride, "she glanced down at the world below, and laughed aloud with pure delight. It was even more splendid than her wildest dream had imagined." Various of the executives begin to give her lessons, and she solos within weeks.[42]

The four volumes of the "Airplane Girl" books make clear the technical knowledge that a pilot's license requires. Roberta's ground training includes "a stiff, concentrated drilling, and [she] had studied aerodynamics and meteorology; besides spending a third of her waking hours in the air since she had started to learn to be a sky-pilot." She has, in addition, "more than an average understanding of [radio] construction and operation; also, she had learned more during her period of training at Lurtiss Field for Mr. Wallace [the company instructor] considered that a pilot who did not understand sending and receiving, as well as rig-up, was only half trained."[43] Roberta masters these and other lessons with ease, absorbing them into her very being as would any pilot. When a superior praises her courage, Roberta replies that "When you are drilled in piloting as I was, you just go through things mechanically. If you were faced with a problem in the air, knew that it was up to you to keep your head, you'd get through it as well as I have."[44] Craine makes no claim for the uniqueness of Roberta's skills. They are those that any accomplished pilot, male or female, might reasonably be expected to have, and Roberta assimilates them in a wholly matter-of-fact way. This, she says, is what a pilot must learn if he or she is to fly; the pilot's sex is irrelevant.

In addition, the "Airplane Girl" books take note of the growing presence and acceptance of women in American general aviation. Roberta's employers initially see her simply as another member of the company secretarial pool, albeit an unusually conscientious one —a worker in a thoroughly conventional "woman's job." As they come to know her better, they recognize that her abilities benefit women in general as well as the Lurtiss Company in particular. "We have a reputation for having turned out, not only good planes, but some of the best flyers in the country," says the company's director of research and development. "Having an A-One girl sky-pilot in our service will promote the interest of women. We did not think of that when you started to learn, but we can see that it is a big advantage." By book's end the Lurtiss engineers are considering an airplane design with particular appeal for the woman pilot, recognizing women's new presence in the aviation marketplace. Roberta takes the new craft on its initial flight. After she pronounces it a "pilot's airplane" in its maneuverability and ease of handling, she is ecstatic when the company presents the first of the line to her. She has, by her skills, made a case for women in the cockpit, and has persuaded an important company that there is potential profit in the women's market. It is no small achievement.[45]

Taken together, *The Sky Girl*, Wirt's six volumes, and the "Airplane Girl" books offer a provocative introduction to aviation for their young readers. Susan Thompson learns piloting skills without difficulty, glimpses in her father's plant a hint of the aviation of the future, and comes away from her flying experiences feeling "sorry for the girls who lived in the years before flying was possible."[46] For her part, Ruth Darrow could easily continue her existence as a member of Brighton's privileged class, playing golf and giving parties in the accepted manner. Her father's status reflects upon her, and she is an established part of the social establishment who may well marry Sandy Marland. Yet she seeks more. Having mastered the basic skills of the sport flier, she focuses those skills to help her test other worlds and other experiences. Like Roberta Langwell, she challenges conventional thought; she seeks to establish herself in her world through her own efforts.

Jane Grant, while enjoying all the perks of affluence and status, is at home at the mechanic's bench, "never more happy than when she came home at night, smudged with oil and tired enough to drop," and capably flies the Reilly Cup race despite her father's "bromidical arguments." Cleo Bowman, determined to learn to fly, uses the family's straitened finances to justify her ambition. Her ability proven, she completes the requirements for a commercial license, takes her place alongside Jim Sherman and her father as one of the barnstorming troupe's pilots, and prepares the way for the restoration of her father's wealth and prominence. Both young women are capable, both are determined, and both break away, albeit quietly, from the accustomed and expected roles of their sex and class.[47]

In Roberta's case, the books affirm one of Amelia Earhart's contentions—that piloting skills are not the only avenue to an aviation career. All that is needed is an open, inquiring mind and the willingness to take on new responsibilities. Roberta readily accepts her role as stenographer, yet discovers that a "woman's job" conscientiously tended to can be the entry to a new, challenging, and progressive career. As a test pilot, Roberta enjoys equal status with the Lurtiss factory's other staff pilots, matching them skill for skill, and goes on to make a name for herself in her own right as a female flier. She has transcended the limitations of conventional work and proven her abilities in a new arena. Thus, all of these young women constitute a formidable group, and send a strong message to their readers. Women *are* capable of many unexpected accomplishments, if only given the chance.

Notes

1. A detailed account of the cult of the ace appears in Robert Wohl, *A Passion for Wings: Aviation and the Western Imagination, 1908-1918* (New Haven: Yale University Press, 1994), 239-250.

2. "National Movement to Popularize Aeronautics to be Launched by the Aero Club of America," *Aerial Age Weekly* 11 (10 April 1920): 170.

3. For typical prices and types of available aircraft, see "Navy Sale of Seaplanes," *Aerial Age Weekly* 11 (19 April 1920): 175, and "Classified Advertising," *Aerial Age Weekly* 13 (22 August 1921): 377.

4. See William M. Leary, *Aerial Pioneers: The U.S. Air Mail Service, 1918-1927* (Washington, DC: Smithsonian Institution Press, 1985), and Barry Rosenberg and Catherine Macaulay, *Mavericks of the Air: The First Daring Pilots of the U.S. Air Mail* (New York: William Morrow, 2006). Bogart Rogers, "Flying the Mail," *Cosmopolitan* 92 (March/April/May/June 1932): 24-27, 156-160; 80-83, 190, 192; 62-63, 159-162; 74-77, 148-149, is a nostalgic account capturing the air mail's romantic nature. F. Robert van der Linden, *Airlines & Air Mail: The Post Office and the Birth of the Commercial Aviation Industry* (Lexington: University Press of Kentucky, 2002), traces the development of modern airline companies from the early days of the air mail.

5. Colonel Charles A. Lindbergh, "Lindbergh Says His Mind is Ablaze with Noise and an Ocean of Faces," *New York Times*, 14 June 1927, 3; Colonel Charles A. Lindbergh, "Lindbergh Calls for Airways to Link Capitals of Continent," *New York Times*, 16 December 1927, 2.

6. Colonel Charles A. Lindbergh, "Lindbergh Writes of Aviation's Advance," *New York Times*, 26 August 1928, 1; Colonel Chas. A Lindbergh, "Differing Types of Planes Now Built to Serve Special Uses," *New York Times*, 18 November 1928, XX12; Colonel Charles A. Lindbergh, "Aircraft for Private Owners and How to

Choose One," *New York Times*, 25 November 1928, XX10. The literature discussing the Lindbergh phenomenon is vast, but a good starting point is John William Ward, "The Meaning of Lindbergh's Flight," *American Quarterly* 10 (1958): 3-16. An extensive bibliography of Lindberghiana, exhaustive up to its date of publication, is Perry D. Luckett, *Charles A. Lindbergh: A Bio-Bibliography* (Westport, CT: Greenwood Press, 1986). See also A. Scott Berg, *Lindbergh* (New York: G.P. Putnam, 1998).

7. George F. McLaughlin, "United States' Airplanes and Engines," *Aero Digest* 10 (May 1927): 402-403; Alexander Klemin, "Planes for Private Flying," *Scientific American* 140 (March 1929): 206-215; Alexander Klemin, "The Evolution of the Private Plane," *Sportsman Pilot* 14 (13 July 1935): 11, 80, 82.

8. Amelia Earhart, quoted in Capt. Hilton H. Railey, "Miss Earhart Held Victim of 'Career,'" *New York Times*, 11 September 1938, 49.

9. Nancy Woloch, *Women and the American Experience: A Concise History*, 2nd ed. (New York: McGraw-Hill, 2002), 256-257, 277-278; Susan Ware, *Still Missing: Amelia Earhart and the Search for Modern Feminism* (New York: W.W. Norton, 1993), 194-195.

10. Woloch, *Women and the American Experience*, 264-265, 306-307.

11. Ibid., 318-321; Ware, *Still Missing*, 192-195.

12. Betty D. Thornley, "Madame, the Aeroplane Waits," *Vogue* 55 (15 June 1920): 108; Howard Mingos, "The Ladies Take the Air," *Ladies Home Journal*, 44 (May 1928): 3-4, 159-160.

13. Alicia Patterson, "I Want to Be a Transport Pilot," *Liberty*, 7 September 1929, 19; Hugh Ammick, "The *Fimmale*" Wing," *U.S. Air Services* 19 (November 1929): 37; Ruth R. Nichols, "Aviation for You and for Me," *Ladies Home Journal* 46 (May 1929): 9, 159, 161; G. K. Spencer, "Pioneer Women of Aviation," *Sportsman Pilot* 3 (May 1930): 49.

14. Margery Brown, "Flying is Changing Women," *Pictorial Review* 31 (June 1930): 30, 108; T. J. C. Martyn, "Women Fliers of the Uncharted Skies," *New York Times*, 10 August 1930, 22; Ware, *Still Missing*, 263, n. 33.

15. The fullest account of the Derby is Gene Nora Jessen, *The Powder Puff Derby of 1929* (Naperville, IL: Sourcebooks, 2002). See also "The Women's Air Derby," *Literary Digest* 102 (7 September 1929): 9, and Kathleen Brooks-Pazmany, *United States Women in Aviation 1919-1929* (Washington, DC: Smithsonian Institution Press, 1991): 34-51.

16. General details of Earhart's life and activities are based upon Doris L. Rich, *Amelia Earhart: A Biography* (Washington, DC: Smithsonian Institution Press, 1989).

17. "Sick and Tired of Ocean Flights," *Literary Digest* 114 (13 August 1932): 30; "Would Bar Sea Hop by Amelia Earhart," *New York Times*, 30 December 1934, 15.

18. "Student, Worker as Well as a Flier," *New York Times*, 4 June 1928, 2; "City Greets Miss Earhart; Girl Flier, Shy and Smiling, Shares Praise with Mates," *New York Times*, 7 July 1928, 1; "A Woman Hops the Atlantic," *Literary Digest* 97 (30 June 1928): 9.

19. O. O. McIntyre, "I Want You to Meet a Real American Girl," *Cosmopolitan* 85 (November 1928): 21; Amelia Earhart, "Try Flying Yourself," *Cosmopolitan* 85 (November 1928): 34-35.

20. "Hoover Voices Nation's Pride; King Likely to Honor Flier," *New York Times*, 22 May 1932, 1; "Two Women Fliers Hail Achievement," *New York Times*, 22 May 1932, 36.

21. "Amelia Scores Again. . . ," *National Aeronautic Magazine* 10 (June 1932): 57; "The Society's Special Medal Awarded to Amelia Earhart," *National Geographic Magazine* 62 (September 1932): 363; Elizabeth MacRae Boykin, "Amelia Earhart at Home," *Better Homes & Gardens* 15 (February 1937): 46.

22. "Girl Flier thrilled by Motorcycle Ride," *New York Times*, 8 July 1928, 16; Earhart, "Try Flying Yourself," 32-33; Amelia Earhart, *The Fun of It: Random Records of My Own Flying and of Women in Aviation.* (1932; repr., Chicago: Academy Chicago Publishers, 1977), 99.

23. Earhart, "Try Flying Yourself," 35; Amelia Earhart, "Shall You Let Your Daughter Fly?" *Cosmopolitan* 86 (March 1929): 88; Earhart, *The Fun of It*, 172.

24. Amelia Earhart, "Fly America First," *Cosmopolitan* 87 (October 1929): 80, 134, 136; Amelia Earhart, "Is It Safe For You to Fly?" *Cosmopolitan* 86 (February 1929): 148; "Hourly Air Service to Capital Planned," *New York Times*, 3 June 1930, 3; Amelia Earhart, "The Most Traveled Road," *National Aeronautic Magazine* 8 (November 1930): 47-48; "Amelia Earhart New Vice-President," *National Aeronautic Magazine* 9 (May 1931): 34; Amelia Earhart, "Amelia Earhart's Own Story of Her Flight Over Pacific," *New York Times*, 13 June 1935, 1.

25. Amelia Earhart, "What Miss Earhart Thinks When She's Flying," *Cosmopolitan* 85 (December 1928): 196; Earhart, "Fly America First," 136; Amelia Earhart, "Flying is Fun!" *Cosmopolitan* 93 (August 1932): 39 (ellipsis in the original); Amelia Earhart, "Flying the Atlantic," *American Magazine* 114 (August 1932): 15, 72.

26. Ruth Nichols, *Wings for Life* (New York: J.P. Lippincott, 1957), 94. For the Ninety-Nines, see "The Ninety-Nines," http://www.centennialof flight.gov/essay/ Explorers_Record_Setters_and_Daredevils/99s/ (accessed 27 August 2008). The organization takes its name from the ninety-nine women pilots (out of 117 nationally) who responded to the original invitation to join. See Ware, *Still Missing*, 117-124, for Earhart's cooperation with other women's organizations.

27. "Women Are Held Back, Miss Earhart Finds," *New York Times*, 30 July 1929; Amelia Earhart, "Flying the Atlantic," 17; Amelia Earhart, *Last Flight*, arr. George Palmer Putnam (New York: Harcourt, Brace, 1937), 39.

28. Amelia Earhart, "Why Are Women Afraid to Fly?" *Cosmopolitan* 87 (July 1929): 71, 138; Amelia Earhart, *20 Hrs., 40 Min.: Our Flight in the Friendship* (1928; repr., Washington, DC: National Geographic Adventure Classics, 2003), 142; Earhart, *The Fun of It*, 143-144; Amelia Earhart, "Women and Courage," *Cosmopolitan* 93 (September 1932), 148.

29. Earhart, "Why Are Women Afraid to Fly?" 138.

30. Earhart, *20 Hrs., 40 Min.*, 115, 138; "President Hears Plea for Women's Rights; Amelia Earhart Cites Equality in the Air," *New York Times*, 23 September 1932, 1; Earhart, *Last Flight*, 12.

31. A convenient introduction to *St. Nicholas* is Susan R. Gannon, Suzanne Rahn, and Ruth Anne Thompson, eds., *St. Nicholas and Mary Mapes Dodge: The Legacy of a Children's Magazine Editor, 1873-1905* (Jefferson, NC: McFarland & Co., 2004).

32. Dorothy Verrill, *The Sky Girl* (New York: Century, 1930), 60, 142. Chums in later books may drift away for social or intellectual reasons, but the heroines will stay faithful to the True Belief of flight.

33. Ibid., 106-107, 161, 147, 193.

34. Ibid., 12-13, 25, 49, 198.

35. Melanie Rehak, *Girl Sleuth: Nancy Drew and the Women Who Created Her* (Orlando, FL: Harcourt Inc., 2005), 107-117. The Library of Congress received the deposit copy of *Ruth Darrow in the Air Derby* on 19 March 1930.

36. Terry Gwynne-Jones, *Farther and Faster: Aviation's Adventuring Years, 1909-1939* (Washington, DC: Smithsonian Institution Press, 1991), 161-178.

37. Mildred A. Wirt, *Ruth Darrow in the Air Derby or, Recovering the Silver Trophy* (New York: Barse & Co., 1930), 5-6, 43; Mildred A. Wirt, *Ruth Darrow in the Coast Guard* (New York: Grosset & Dunlap, 1931), 132-134, 14-15.

38. Mildred A. Wirt, *Courageous Wings* (Philadelphia: Penn Publishing, 1937), 19-21.

39. Wirt, *Ruth Darrow in the Air Derby*, 23, 31; Wirt, *Ruth Darrow in the Coast Guard*, 61; Mildred A. Wirt, *Ruth Darrow in the Fire Patrol or, Capturing the Redwood Thieves* (New York: Grosset & Dunlap, 1930), 44; Mildred A. Wirt, *The Sky Racers* (Philadelphia: Penn Publishing, 1935), 33.

40. Wirt, *Ruth Darrow in the Air Derby*, 43, 63; Wirt, *Sky Racers*, 27, 216-217.

41. Wirt, *Ruth Darrow in the Fire Patrol*, 52-53; Mildred A. Wirt, *Ruth Darrow in Yucatan* (New York: Grosset & Dunlap, 1931), 7; Mildred A. Wirt, *Courageous Wings* (Philadelphia: Penn Publishing, 1937), 97.

42. Harrison Bardwell [Edith J. Craine], *Roberta's Flying Courage* (1930; repr., West Lafayette, IN: Purdue University Press, 2003), 59, 61.

43. Bardwell, *Roberta's Flying Courage,* 127; Harrison Bardwell [Edith J. Craine], *The Airplane Girl and the Mystery of Seal Islands* (1931; repr., West Lafayette, IN: Purdue University Press, 2003), 179-180.

44. Harrison Bardwell [Edith J. Craine], *The Lurtiss Field Mystery* (1931; repr., West Lafayette, IN: Purdue University Press, 2003), 134.

45. Louise Thaden, *High, Wide, and Frightened* (1938; repr., Fayetteville: University of Arkansas Press, 2004), 9-24; Bardwell, *Roberta's Flying Courage,* 80-81, 246-247.

46. Verrill, *The Sky Girl,* 210.

47. Wirt, *Sky Racers,* 11, 7; Wirt, *Courageous Wings,* 144-146.

CHAPTER 4

Amelia's Daughters Face Reality:

1930-1940

The growing public air-mindedness and the appeal of
personal aircraft from 1920 onward fueled a dream of
the 1930s. This was the dream of an airplane so reliable
and so economical that it could be bought and operated as cheaply
as an automobile. An air-minded society could ask for no less, and
aviation notables encouraged their desire. Both Charles Lindbergh
and Amelia Earhart, as noted in Chapter 3, spoke of a time when
suburban garages would house a family airplane alongside the family auto. Men and women would "do [their] commuting by air," and
the rising generation of young persons would think no more of an
outing in an airplane than they did of an outing in an automobile.
Alexander Klemin, a respected engineering and aviation historian,
doubted the idealistic hope that "within the space of a few years our
skies will be darkened with airplanes." Nonetheless, he affirmed that
"a new generation is growing up which will be eager and determined to fly," and manufacturers, cities, and the populace in general must be prepared to accommodate it.[1]

The dream gained an added boost from Eugene L. Vidal,
Director of the Bureau of Air Commerce within the federal
Department of Commerce. A pilot himself and a partner with
Amelia Earhart in the operations of the Ludington Line, Vidal
sought to popularize general aviation. One way, he believed, would
be to develop aircraft that would be within the reach of the average
American consumer. Informally labeling these aircraft "poor man's

planes," he called for the development of an all-metal, two-seated light airplane that would sell for approximately $700. Operating such a craft, he argued, would cost "less than . . . an average-priced automobile," and "would not require 'superman' qualifications to fly it." Vidal's call produced several viable contenders: the Hammond Model Y, the highway-compatible Waterman Arrowplane, and Fred A. Weick's spin-proof Ercoupe. Of these, only the Ercoupe went into production, but all fed the public desire for personal aircraft.[2]

The growing possibility that aircraft might soon be within reach of an average person adds to the excitement of Edith Lavell's "Linda Carlton" stories (1931-1933; five titles). This series is the high point of aviation stories for America girls. Its books speak to Earhart's views on education, they show a young woman preparing herself for a varied career in aviation, they show a youth culture readily embracing air-mindedness, and they offer a heroine who, in her ambitions, is Earhartian through and through. Linda, the daughter of a land investor and rancher living in Spring City, Ohio, is affluent and socially prominent, possessing blue eyes, curly blond hair, and a circle of loyal friends.

Among these friends, two stand out: her best chum Louise Haydock, like Linda a member of the Spring City elite, and her steadfast beau Ralph Clavering, son of the wealthiest family in town. Linda is independent and mobile, she and her blue roadster familiar sights in the haunts of the well-to-do, yet her desire for self-determination is quickly evident. Whereas her classmates at Miss Graham's School are aiming at prestigious marriages and lives as the aristocrats of the community, Linda seeks a life on her own terms. Despite the pressures on her to blend into the rituals and routines of Spring City's social elite, Linda is determined to make her way in a realm traditionally dominated by males—that of aviation.

The five volumes of Linda's adventures are classic series-story fare, combining adventure, peril, a mystery element, and a modicum of romance to keep their readers engaged. The first volume, *Linda Carlton, Air Pilot* (1931), introduces eighteen-year-old Linda and her friends, on the brink of graduation from their elite, all-girl private school. Despite a class prophecy that she and Louise Haydock will be Spring City's next social leaders, Linda has other plans. She takes flying lessons from instructor Ted Mackay and receives an Arrow Sport airplane from her father as a gift. With Louise in tow, she makes increasingly lengthy flights, at last flying from Ohio to Colorado. In addition, she flies a famed surgeon to her ailing father's bedside and rehabilitates Ted Mackay's tarnished reputation when he is accused of stealing a $50,000 pearl necklace. As the book comes to an end, she is honored for her aviation skills and looks forward to a developing career as a flier.

Linda Carlton's Ocean Flight (1931) picks up three months after the events of the first volume, as Linda and Louise enter a St. Louis ground school where Linda plans to study for her mechanic's certification. She makes another mercy flight, carrying a strangling infant to a Philadelphia surgeon, and declines to join a flying club that the Claverings are sponsoring. Learning of a $25,000 prize for the first woman pilot flying the Atlantic, she begins planning for the trip. Louise, meanwhile, whose taste for partying exceeds her interest in flying, drops out of ground school and announces her engagement to Ted Mackay. When Mr. Carlton's import business is threatened by an unscrupulous competitor, Linda undertakes to help him, flying to New York, then to Canada on the trail of the wrong-doer. She thwarts the scheme to force her father out of business, but must parachute to safety when her crippled sports plane bursts into flames. His fortunes restored, Mr. Carlton buys Linda a Bellanca J-300 and she uses it to become the first woman to fly solo across the Atlantic, preceding Earhart by a year.

Volume three, *Linda Carlton's Island Adventure* (1931), finds Linda newly graduated from ground school with commercial and transport pilots' licenses (the highest ratings) plus full aero mechanic's certification. Using her prize money from the Atlantic

Linda Carlton shows off her Bellanca J-300 prior to her record-setting Atlantic flight. (Author's collection).

flight, she buys an autogiro and sets out for Georgia, planning to join a crop-dusting operation. En route, Linda is forced down and kidnaped by a gang of bank robbers. She escapes her captors with the help of Jackson Carter, son of an aristocratic southern family, whose hoity-toity mother promptly snubs Linda for her apparent forwardness and independent ways. Undeterred by the snub, she recovers the bank loot, uses the autogiro to help the police round up the gang, and is welcomed as an equal by the repentant Mrs. Carter.

Linda Carlton's Perilous Summer (1932), fourth in the series, opens with Linda summering with her aunt and assorted chums at the elite Green Falls Resort on the shores of Lake Michigan, where "her aunt knew practically everyone there." While on a flight in her autogiro, she rescues an amnesiac girl, Helen Tower, from an attacker and takes her under her wing. At the resort she meets Britisher Lord Dudley, tolerates his attentions, and gently refuses his proposal of marriage. She takes part in a flying treasure hunt with her friends, as they fly from spot to spot in their personal aircraft in accordance with cryptic clues given them. Linda handily wins the prize, a thousand-dollar check, and shares her windfall with Helen. When she discovers that "Lord Dudley" is actually Ed Tower, a scoundrel seeking to swindle Helen out of a substantial legacy, Linda pursues him in the autogiro, and after landing on the deck of the ocean liner in which he's fleeing, brings him to justice. She retrieves the papers that guarantee Helen her inheritance, turns Tower over to the authorities, and returns to Green Falls, nonchalantly flying her autogiro from Virginia back to Michigan.[3]

The final volume, *Linda Carlton's Hollywood Flight* (1933), takes Linda, now a nationally-known aviatrix, and new chum Dot Crowley on a cross-country flight to Hollywood, where an imposter is posing as Linda in a film under production. They are caught up in a web of confused identities and are unable to prove Linda's identity to the satisfaction of the California authorities, until they meet Secret Service agent Bertram Chase, who is trailing a counterfeiter. Chase helps to confirm Linda's identity, whereupon the imposter and her husband accomplice flee to Hawaii. Linda and Dot follow in a borrowed airplane, flying the Pacific without incident and serendipitously winning a $10,000 prize for the feat. Chase reveals the imposter's husband as the fugitive counterfeiter, and, at a festive dinner celebrating Linda's flight, proposes marriage and urges her to join the Secret Service. The series ends with Linda considering both offers.

Two major concerns dominate the series. One is Linda's commitment to aviation, as she embraces its possibilities and its future. The other is her challenge to blithely accepted social mores. Both make her a spokesperson for modernity and an exceptional role model for her young readers. Aviation appears as an enterprise open to female fliers and as a vehicle of progress, and the books quietly alert readers to women pilots' achievements. The opening pages of *Linda Carlton, Air Pilot* link Linda to Amelia Earhart and Elinor Smith (who set her first records as a teenaged pilot), and her skill at looping-the-loop causes Ralph Clavering to compare her to Laura Ingalls, who at the time held the world record of 980 consecutive loops. When a woman donor in 1931 establishes a prize for the first woman to fly the Atlantic alone, Earhart is mentioned as a possible competitor, but those in the know consider her "too good a sport to take honors from a younger, less-experienced flyer. . . . She has already won her place." While considering her own ocean flight, Linda goes on to laud Ruth Nichols and Mrs. Keith Miller (*sic*) as being among those "women [who] are working so hard to establish our place in aviation." Finally, in *Linda Carlton's Perilous Summer,* Linda proclaims Britisher Amy Johnson "The most courageous woman flyer in the whole world to-day!" in recognition of Johnson's twenty-day solo flight from England to Australia. The women pilots of the day and their achievements are Linda's inspiration (Johnson, like Linda, held both pilot's and mechanic's licenses), confirming her desire to earn her living in the exciting world of aviation.[4]

The technical advances that make aviation so progressive a realm are reflected in the three airplanes most closely associated with Linda's exploits. Unlike Susan Thompson, Ruth Darrow, and Roberta Langwell, Linda has no familial or vocational ties to aviation. She is simply a person who wants to fly, and, once qualified, buys her aircraft on the open market. Whereas earlier series either employ fictional aircraft or make only passing mention of real ones, the "Linda Carlton" books deal in detail with real aircraft, and Linda is the consumer for whom personal aircraft are intended. Linda's first ship, an Arrow Sport "Pursuit," is a graduation gift from her father, stimulating her to sign up for flying lessons.

The Arrow Sport was built by the Arrow Aircraft and Motors Corporation of Havelock, Nebraska. A "side by side, two place, bi-plane" priced at just under $3,000, it was certified by the Civil Aeronautics Authority in February 1929, and quickly gained popularity as a sport and training airplane. The "Pursuit" model shared the dual controls and side-by-seating of the other models, but was driven by a more powerful radial engine. Linda makes a number of notable flights in her Arrow, and, when it is sabotaged and crashes in flames, "Tears came into the young aviatrix's eyes, and she hugged her chum tightly in her grief. It was as if she had lost a very dear friend."[5] Her identification with the Arrow is profound, and she responds in ways befitting a member of the "flying generation."

Despite her dismay at losing the Arrow, Linda does not long remain airplaneless. For her Atlantic flight, she selects a Bellanca J-300. "It has everything to make it perfect!" she gushes to her father. "A capacity for carrying one hundred and five additional gallons of gasoline, besides the regular supply in the tanks of one hundred and eighty gallons! And a Wright three-hundred-horsepower engine, and a tachometer, and a magnetic compass—.... You can be sure it will have every modern invention, every safety device there is today." She chooses wisely in selecting this craft, for the Bellanca firm had a well-deserved reputation for producing sturdy, reliable aircraft suitable for long-distance flights. Charles Lindbergh attempted to buy a Bellanca WB-2 before turning to the Ryan works; a Bellanca J flew non-stop from Maine to Spain in July 1929; and a J-300 equipped much like Linda's flew non-stop from Brooklyn to Istanbul in July 1931.[6] As with the Arrow Sport, the books provide readers with the latest developments in modern aircraft.

No other aircraft, though, is more emblematic of 1930s modernity and progress than the machine associated with Linda's last three adventures—the Pitcairn-Cierva PCA-2 autogiro. Between 1928 and 1935, the autogiro was widely touted in the technical and the popular press as a safe, simple aircraft highly likely to replace the automobile. It was an ungainly appearing craft, with vestigial wings, a forward-mounted radial engine, and an enormous over-head rotor that served in lieu of a conventional wing. From that design, though, came its principal virtues, stability at slow speed and the ability to land and take off in a small space. Its inventor, Juan de la Cierva, called it "A New Way to Fly" in a 1929 *Saturday Evening Post* article, and later spoke of it as a "family flying machine" that "offers the immediate prospect of a real renaissance for aviation." Amelia Earhart, in one of her last articles for *Cosmopolitan*, anticipated the day when "autogiros will be rubbing shoulders with automobiles in our garage-hangars of tomorrow." Frank Ovington, a respected aviation journalist, called the craft "the 'missing link' that aviation is waiting for," and aviation advocate Brigadier-General William Mitchell, writing in *Woman's Home Companion*, lauded it as "The Automobile of the Air."[7]

Linda first encounters the autogiro in *Linda Carlton's Ocean Flight*, when one lands at the ground school where she is studying. She is enthralled by its possibilities, agreeing with her instructor when he says, "I believe it is the plane for the city dweller," where-upon one of her classmates proclaims, "Everyone can keep an auto-giro in his back yard." She buys her autogiro directly from the Pitcairn plant, having decided that it is the best ship for her pur-poses: "I want to take a job, and I think an autogiro will be the most convenient plane I can have." She considers her ship, named *Ladybug*, to be "the plane of the future, or of the present," and it proves to be everything she hopes. Its maneuvering capabilities fig-ure in all of her remaining adventures. She takes off from an island in *Linda Carlton's Island Adventure*, lands on a ship at sea to nab Ed Tower in *Linda Carlton's Perilous Summer*, and even lands on, and takes off from, the top of an office building in *Linda Carlton's*

Amelia Earhart and the Pitcairn PCA-2 autogiro. National Air and Space Museum, Smithsonian Institution (SI 85-3357).

Hollywood Flight.[8] In her knowledge of advanced aircraft technology, Linda is, indeed, an up-to-date, modern young woman.

Even more indicative of her modernity, however, is her determination not to be confined by conventional social norms. In her day-to-day life as a flier, she encounters false accusations, business conspiracies, and overt criminal behavior. These are evil, without question, and must be scotched as quickly as they appear. But what of the more conventional attributes of society? Might it not be possible for these, too, to be worthy of questioning? For Linda, the answer is an emphatic "Yes," culminating in her mid-series outburst, "I can't be bothered with social codes at a time like this." She has no quarrel with society and its mores as such. She readily takes part in the dances and parties offered by her friends, and is as comfortable in "a flowered chiffon" as she is in flying togs. Nonetheless, she is not one to accept society's dictates without question. Instead, she considers which actions are appropriate and which are inappropriate *for her.* From this self-evaluation comes the series' second major concern, Linda's response to the pressures of conventionality.[9]

Speaking for the societal side is Linda's Aunt Emily, Mr. Carlton's spinster sister, who, though she lives with the Carltons as chaperone and family doyenne, is herself financially secure and a person of stature in the community. For her, there is no other path for her niece to follow. Once graduated from Miss Graham's prestigious private school, Linda is to be formally introduced into Spring City society, have a year of parties, marry into a good family, and take her rightful place among the city's monied elite. Thus, to Aunt Emily, image matters, and she urges Linda to adopt more conventional feminine dress for her flight to the Green Falls Resort. "First impressions are always so important," she cautions Linda, "and there is sure to be a crowd [at Green Falls] there to meet you." Moreover, she has Linda's future well in mind: "She had been so happy about the friendship between Ralph [Clavering] and Linda—it was so eminently right! When her niece did decide to get married . . . . She couldn't imagine any young man who would suit her so well as Ralph Clavering. Such family! Such social position! And plenty of money!" Her goal firmly in hand, Aunt Emily bends every effort to make certain that Linda is seen in all the right places and by all the right people.[10]

Somewhat more broad-minded is Linda's father, the widower Thomas Carlton. Largely occupied with business matters, he has urged Linda to develop her independent side as well as her social side. In the opening volume of the series, readers learn that he has encouraged Linda "to shoot a gun, ride a horse, and drive a car"— all activities fostering independence and responsibility. He is perturbed, though, that she wants to be "one of those independent girls who insist upon earning their own living," and later reflects that, while Linda has indeed made a name for herself as an independent flier, "he didn't want her to miss the happiness that marriage would bring her." Though he has faith in his daughter's common sense and determination, even he cannot resist measuring her by the conventional standards of the era.[11] Facing outright opposition from her aunt and tepid support from her father, Linda must prove to them both the rightness of her determination.

In establishing herself as an independent person, Linda speaks for the modern American woman. She is always conscious of the importance of women's proving themselves to be competent, responsible citizens. When she hears that a woman has apparently preceded her across the Atlantic, she speaks of the feat as "history —great as the moment when the suffrage movement had been won!" Later, when she learns the news was a hoax, she criticizes the male pilot's female accomplice for having "brought dishonor on all our sex . . . , just when we women are working so hard to establish our place in aviation by honest methods." Though she relishes the acclaim that flying the Atlantic brings her, she can say, in all serious-ness, "I sincerely hope that more and more girls and women will be doing things in aviation, so that my little stunt will seem trivial. That is progress, you know."[12] Though she retains her femininity and social ease, Linda thinks of herself as an independent person, competent and capable in her chosen field of endeavor, and expects to be treated as such.

Two incidents attest to her success. The first is Aunt Emily's sur-render. Her aunt has never wavered in the belief that Linda should settle into the roles that society expects of her, yet she is sensible enough to accept the reality of Linda's achievements. Turning to her brother at series' end, Aunt Emily confesses the foolishness of her desires:

> 'I've learned my lesson, Tom,' she said, 'in this year and a half since Linda's been out of school. I had expected her to have a year of parties—to "come out," you know—and then marry some nice young man. But Linda has plans of her own, and I realize now that I might as well save my time as to try to arrange anything for her. . . . And, as for wealth and social position—well, they simply mean nothing in her

life. Besides, she doesn't need them; I can see that. Linda could go anywhere, be accepted at Court, if she wanted to, because of what she has accomplished herself."[13]

Spokesperson for the status quo though she may be, Aunt Emily is able to recognize that Linda's competence, responsibility, and serious-minded approach to aviation have won her as much prominence and social acceptance as her own more conventional means could have done.

The other is Linda's enigmatic response to Bert Chase's proposal, for she faces several choices. She might marry Bert, continue flying, and join the Secret Service. She might join the Service, stay single, and continue flying. She might marry and give up both flying and the Secret Service. Or she might stay single, spurn the Secret Service, and continue her life in flying. Which choice she makes is less important than her being able to decide. She is in total control of her career and future life. She, not the social milieu, will dictate the road she takes, and she emerges as the very model of a modern, independent young woman. The world has indeed changed, and the able, independent woman is to take her place in American society.

The girls' aviation series began to fade after the publication of the "Linda Carlton" tales. Only two new series appeared after 1931, both distinctly minor; taken together, they suggest a degree of discouragement on the part of authors and readers regarding women in aviation as well as a growing sense that flying was rapidly becoming more a corporate venture than an individual one. The Earharts of the world could make a living setting records and flying "stunts" for publicity—a realization confirmed a few years later, when *Independent Woman* referred to them as "the stars, the top-notches whose dazzling careers in relation to everyday jobs in aviation are on a par with Metropolitan Opera singers, to whom the hopeful aspirants of the chorus look for inspiration."[14] For the majority of women pilots, however, no such avenue to fame was practicable. The business of aviation was becoming a still more male-dominated enterprise, leaving women principally with the workaday jobs related to flying: operating a fixed-base enterprise, for example, giving flight instruction, joining a manufacturer's sales staff, or working in a clerical or (perhaps) managerial position with an airline. Although flying in and of itself retained its romantic appeal, the prospects for adventuresome careers dwindled rapidly. The reality of the world was catching up with the world of fiction.

The two clusters of books that follow Linda Carlton document the diminishing appeal of the "traditional" flying story. Bess Moyer's "Girl Flyer" series (1932; two titles) appeared while the "Linda Carlton" books were winding down. Published by the Goldsmith Company of New York, the books were billed as the tale of "two high spirited and adventurous girls . . . who go in for all outdoor sports; especially flying." Their adventures and their experiences in the "everyday occurrences of a modern flying field," the advertisement continues, "will be extremely interesting to any real girl." Another advertisement goes even further, remarking that the "Girl Flyer" books, along with several other Goldsmith-published series, will prove "a real boon" to "mothers who are deeply concerned for their children's inner life."[15] Clearly evident in both is the tacit assumption that stories of flying adventure, presented realistically, will be acceptable to parents and of interest *and* of benefit to the girl reader.

The series opens with *Gypsies of the Air,* which introduces sixteen-year-old twin sisters Terry and Prim Mapes, daughters of Dick Mapes, a retired air mail pilot. Dick now operates his own flying field, giving lessons and servicing air charters. After he is crippled in an air crash and confined to a wheelchair, the twins and their mother, with the help of Dick's former students Allan Graham and Syd Ames, keep the hand-to-mouth operation going. Allan, son of a well-to-do businessman who has been helping to fund Dick's enterprise, decides to fly the Atlantic to publicize the field. He and Syd disappear during the attempt, and Terry and Prim blithely set out to trace them. The girls easily find the boys' plane, which has been

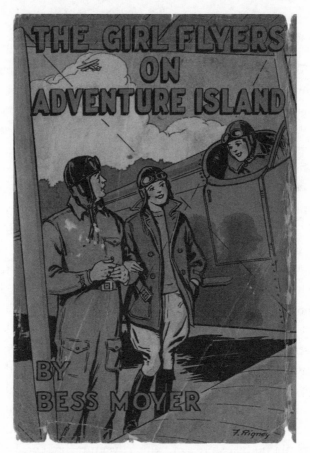

Terry and Prim Mapes share flying lore with a fellow aviator.
(Author's collection).

forced down on the Gulf of Saint Lawrence. They then discover that Allan and Syd have been kidnaped by Joe Arnold, a long-time rival of Dick's, and Bud Hyslop, Dick's ne'er-do-well mechanic. They free the boys, recover the aircraft, and return home safely, even though they must fend off an aerial machine-gun attack from Arnold and Hyslop en route.

The Girl Flyers on Adventure Island picks up immediately after the events of the first volume. When Arnold and Hyslop, who want to put Dick out of business and use the field as a base for their smuggling enterprises, learn that Dick is only leasing the land, they plan a trip to Peru to buy the field from Dick's absentee landlord.

When Terry and Prim hear of the plan, they themselves set out by air for Peru, carrying money and documents to take up Dick's option on the field. Pursued by Arnold and Hyslop, who have learned of their plan, the girls are forced down on a Caribbean island when an unexpected storm blows up. There the two fall into Arnold's and Hyslop's hands, but friendly islanders help them to escape, and they set off once again for Peru. Although the two male-factors arrive first and make their offer for the airfield, Terry para-chutes down to the owner's home to present Dick's case. Her brav-ery persuades the landlord to sell to her rather than the two scoundrels and she and Prim return home with the signed deed in hand. The book's final paragraph hints at a third volume telling of the search for a sacred emerald in "the Land of the Incas," but the work never appeared.

Throughout the books, Terry and Prim are presented as comple-mentary opposites. Terry is slender, active, and sharp-tongued; Prim is plump, easy-going, and diplomatic. Both are capable fliers, but Prim, like the traditionally more feminine sidekick, has had to strug-gle to learn piloting skills. For Terry, they come naturally: "Terry took to flying as a duck takes to the water," Moyer observes, "but with Prim it was always hard work. . . . She did not love flying as Terry did." Terry possesses the true "air sense" of the natural pilot, and the simple act of flying becomes a central part of her life. Her absorption with flight contrasts with the views of her mother. Mrs. Mapes, although supporting Dick in his flying, has never learned to fly, and considers herself "an old fashioned housewife." Because of her attitude, Moyer pointedly remarks, "the fearlessness of her mod-ern daughters frightened her."[16] Terry's skills in the cockpit and her feelings of happiness and security while in the air make a powerful message for the series' readers. Although conventional women may fear the idea of flying, progressive ones will find flying an activity in which women can participate with safety and satisfaction.

Moyer enlarges upon her message to her readers in several episodes. Early in the girls' childhood, in an encounter reinforcing

Amelia Earhart's comments on the training given young girls and hinting at Prim's struggling response to flight, Dick gives each of the toddlers a toy airplane and a doll. Prim, in the best feminine fashion, coos over the doll, but Terry spurns the doll and brandishes the airplane with delight. When Dick sees her reaction, he determines to make a pilot of her, because "There's a great future for women flyers. I'm sure of it." From childhood on, Terry's absorption with all things aeronautic is intense, ultimately leading her to the study of air frame construction and engine workings. With these skills mastered, she becomes "a good mechanic. . . . In the venture of the flying field, Dick called her his 'right hand man' and declared that she could do more work and understod [sic] more about planes than Bud Hyslop, his helper." Moreover, when Dick's accident takes him from active flying, "Terry took matters into her own hands and advertised for women flying students. Dick from his wheel chair directed the lessons and Terry demonstrated and took them up for flying instruction."[17] Having become a capable woman flier in her own right, Terry sets out to make aviation available to all women.

Accentuating Terry's efforts and reflecting some of the difficulties that a progressive woman must face is Bud Hyslop. A mechanic of only moderate ability, he recoils at any thought of a woman's attempting to match, much less surpass, his own limited skills. "'Women haven't any business around an airplane,' Bud had told Terry the first day he had come on the field. 'The kitchen is where they belong, and they should be made to stay there. . . . That's what I say, and I'll stick to it.'"[18] Moyer has him voice a prejudice held by many men, giving her an opportunity to use Terry and, to a lesser extent, Prim to give him the lie.

For all Dick's idealism and the opportunities he foresees for women fliers, the overall outcome of the books suggests the genre's loss of energy and focus. The "everyday occurrences" of a grass-strip operation are an uncomfortable fit for many female readers. After Linda Carlton's triumphs, air-minded readers doubtless would be disappointed to find the Mapes girls flying fictional air-craft. Aviation history and changes in the enterprise itself make clear that "stunts" such as ocean flights are not undertaken lightly, but require lengthy, careful, and expensive planning. The Andean expedition might have added substance to the series (as Ruth Darrow's trek to Yucatan did), but Moyer never had a chance to develop it. "Girl Flyers" Terry and Prim may be, but their opportunities to demonstrate their skills are fading fast.

The second series, the "Dorothy Dixon" books (1933; four titles) by "Dorothy Wayne," appears contemporaneously with the last of the "Linda Carlton" volumes, and shows an author grafting aviation onto an otherwise conventional adventure story to give it a more "modern" atmosphere. The result is a cluster of stories in which flying quickly becomes subordinate to melodrama—and the melodrama itself teeters on the edge of implausibility. The "Dixon" books were written by Noel E. Sainsbury, Jr., who adopted his wife's name for the purposes of the series. Sainsbury had been a naval aviator in the years immediately following World War I, and continued an active association with the naval reserves. He served in the United States Navy during the Second World War, retiring with the rank of lieutenant commander. Although trained as an engineer, he turned to fiction-writing in 1930, with his principal works being the "Great Ace" series (1928-1934; five titles) and the "Bill Bolton, Navy Aviator" series (1933; four titles), both written for boys. In each instance, the young protagonist has a naval background and flies realistically described seaplanes and amphibians of the sort used at the time.[19]

Even had Sainsbury not acknowledged his authorship of the Dorothy Dixon books, internal evidence would easily establish it. The four books, all appearing in 1933, are contemporaneous with the "Bolton" stories, and Bill Bolton is a major supporting character in each. The "Dixon" books also make several arch references to Sainsbury, his wife, and their daughter: "Where would I be without him?" asks Bill. "Look at the books he's written about me. . . . We're awfully fond of him and his wife and little girl." Dorothy thereupon chimes in, "I'm named for her [Sainsbury's wife], you know." The last book of the Dixon series, *Dorothy Dixon and the Double Cousin,* makes explicit reference to the final Bolton book, *Bill Bolton and the Winged Cartwheels* (1933), even including a footnoted reference to it.

Finally, and most persuasively, several of the highly detailed flying instruction sequences in the Dixon stories repeat word for word comparable sequences in the Bolton books. Both groups of episodes prove to be plagiarized from the same source, Lieutenant Barrett Studley's *Practical Flight Training* (1928). This was a manual for the beginning pilot based upon the flight manual Studley had written as an instructor at the Naval Air Station in Pensacola, Florida, and was no doubt a carry-over from Sainsbury's own cadet days. Although Sainsbury's brief use of actual aircraft and his liftings from his training manual attest to his initial determination to make Dorothy's flying experiences authentic, authenticity quickly gives way to melodrama.[20]

The Dixon books are unquestionably the most frenetic of the girls' series. The first, *Dorothy Dixon Wins Her Wings,* introduces sixteen-year-old Dorothy, the daughter of a widowed local bank president and living in New Canaan, Connecticut. Affluent, privileged, and very much a part of the New Canaan social scene, she is rescued from her capsized sailboat by Bill Bolton, who flies her to safety in his Loening amphibian. Dorothy learns to fly under Bill's tutelage and, when her father's bank is robbed, teams with Bill to trace the bandits, put an end to the Martinelli Gang, and give an assist to Scotland Yard. The second volume, *Dorothy Dixon and the Mystery Plane,* opens with Dorothy, herself now the owner of a Loening amphibian, becoming intrigued by the regular appearance of an unidentified airplane over the town harbor. She stumbles onto a plot to smuggle diamonds into the United States, and, despite various setbacks (including being chloroformed), enlists Bill's help to retrieve one shipment of diamonds, and brings the smugglers to justice.

Bill Bolton and his Loening to the rescue as Dorothy Dixon's sailboat goes under. (Author's collection).

Volume three, *Dorothy Dixon Solves the Conway Case,* opens with Dorothy and chum Betty Mayo being forced down in the Loening near a run-down mansion. The two help the mansion's young owner, George "Stoker" Conway, to escape from the ne'er-do-wells who are torturing him, summon Bill Bolton and one of his college friends for backup, and discover that the thieves are seeking

The Loening Cabin Amphibian, much esteemed by Bill Bolton and
Dorothy Dixon. National Air and Space Museum,
Smithsonian Institution (SI 80-5420).

the plans for a high-efficiency aerial engine designed by George's late father. Although Dorothy and Bill are hounded by the thieves, they escape with the help of the mumbling "darky" (*sic*) Uncle Abe "Ol' Man" River and retrieve the plans. All ends well when Dorothy and Bill complete an endurance flight of one hundred and one hours using the new engine. Events become even more action-packed in the final volume, *Dorothy Dixon and the Double Cousin*, when Dorothy, who is an exact double for her cousin, Janet Jordan, substitutes for Janet to infiltrate a nest of international spies and recover the formula for a new and deadly high explosive. Uncle Abe reappears at book's end as the Dixons' butler, Janet Jordan weds her intended, and the party by general agreement destroys the formula. The flying content is negligible, and the story is almost wholly an account of Dorothy's doings as she plays her double role and winkles out the spies.

For all their melodramatic excess, the Dorothy Dixon books do give at least a sketchy picture of the aviation world as Sainsbury knew it in 1933. The Loening amphibian favored by both Bill and Dorothy was familiar to Sainsbury from his time in the navy. A single-engine, open-cockpit biplane, it had a small cabin connecting the fuselage and its single float, and was considered "one of the most popular amphibians of the day." Bill himself at other times flies a Ryan M-1, a pleasure aircraft built by the same company that built Lindbergh's *Spirit of St. Louis*. The flying techniques discussed, from the forty-hour course of flight training Bill lays out for Dorothy to the neatly executed sideslip and short-field landing that she employs in the third volume, are up-to-date and accurate. To this extent, the books accurately represent the hardware and skills of flight in the early 1930s, and make the case that they can readily be mastered by any capable young woman.[21]

On the other hand, Dorothy herself is almost a caricature of the independent woman of the late Jazz Age. Taught by her father to shoot and to box, she is also a master of jiu jitsu and easily fells opponents twice her weight. By series' end she is traveling with "Flash," a throwing knife with "six inches of razor-keen, leaf-shaped blade . . . and three inches of carved ivory hilt, beautifully balanced" strapped to her thigh. She wields the weapon with pinpoint accuracy, demonstrating her skill by nailing a tossed macaroon to a hotel door, and has no qualms about using it (or any other convenient weapon) to protect herself. As she herself says, "If the gun is out of orders, Flash will have to go [with me]. Of course my jiu jitsu may help at a pinch, but Flash is more potent and ever so much quicker."[22]

Sainsbury attempts to establish Dorothy's modernity by having her speak throughout in late twenties' slang, and at one point she even simperingly lapses into the argot of a motion-picture gun-moll: "Them kind woids is a great comfort to a poor workin' goil. Do I pack a gat wid me, Mister?" She thinks of herself as "not the sort of girl who permits herself to be quietly wiped off the picture by an order from a boy friend!" She does not hesitate to spend an unchaperoned night with Bill Bolton when circumstances force them to rough it, and later shares the intimate confines of an airplane cockpit with him for their one-hundred-and-one-hour endurance flight. Her liberated modernity, as Anne Scott MacLeod points out, is so extreme as to overstrain "reader credulity," and "well beyond anything [readers'] own society was prepared to tolerate in girls."[23]

Her excesses notwithstanding, Dorothy possesses at heart the poise, skill, and self-assurance of the modern young woman, and she reveals throughout "a certain assurance . . . , a steely quality that came sometimes into her grey eyes, an indefinable air of strength and quiet courage." Bill quickly recognizes her natural ability as a pilot, and points out to Mr. Dixon that, in aviation, "sex has nothing to do with it [piloting skill]," letting her ability peek through the melodramatic context and convention-bound public attitudes.[24] In their adventures, Dorothy and Bill Bolton work as equals. The books suggest no hint of romance between them, and each respects the skills and expertise of the other. She is under no pressure to marry, and seems ready to continue her independent life as the series ends, a person in charge of her own future. Dorothy's flying exploits are secondary to her crime-solving adventures yet they confirm the accessibility of aviation to women, and her relations with Bill confirm her independence. The series' message to its readers, although almost lost in the fusillade of gunshots that punctuates the volumes, remains a progressive one.

The twenty-two "pure" aviation books published for girls during the 1930s document a pivotal time in American society and American women's history. Even as they express the optimism, liberalism, and idealism of Amelia Earhart and kindred feminist thinkers, they increasingly suggest the difficulties that the majority of contemporary American women, whether fliers or not, continued to encounter. Men, certainly, play a role in posing these difficulties. Male attitudes toward women's physical weakness, presumed lesser intellectual capacity, and overall "flightiness" were in great part unchanged despite the evidence presented by women.[25]

This stereotypical opposition, though, appears only occasionally in the books, and the outspoken defender of male superiority almost always turns out to be morally unsound or inferior in ability. The men in the foreground are intelligent, open-minded, and willing to accept the evidence of their eyes. The books, therefore, do not attack male attitudes as such. Instead, they offer a picture of a society in which work and societal obstacles to women will disappear in the face of women's demonstrated competence. Unfortunately, it is also a society in which economics, technology, and societal elements coalesce in ways that hinder, even block, the progressive dreams of American women pilots.

The American society of the girls' books is an open one. Women and men may well continue to be rivals within an enterprise, but their contests will take place according to objective rules and only individual capability will decide the "winner." Women will be unfettered in their movement into the so-called "man's world," and they will find acceptance in proportion to their skills. This is the society for which Amelia Earhart spoke, pointing to the traditional ways in which women—unthinkingly, perhaps, but no less definitely—had been held back:

> Because this world has been arranged heretofore so that women could not be active as individuals, it has been assumed that they neither wanted to nor ever could be. However, so many "impossibilities" have been proved baseless in the last quarter century that there is no telling now where limitations to feminine activities—if any—will be henceforth. I am not one to set any bounds upon the work of men or women nor restrict them except by the natural laws of individual aptitude.[26]

Her views were echoed in *Equal Rights,* the journal of the National Woman's Party, as she was preparing for her final flight. Calling Earhart an "Ardent Feminist," the magazine went on to editorialize that "All women will not fly oceans. Neither will all men. Freedom, not restriction, makes for progress." Given the liberty to do so, women will prove their worth in aviation and in all other parts of contemporary life.[27]

Earhart's vision of society is one that Susan Thompson, Roberta Langwell, Ruth Darrow, Jane Grant, Cleo Bowman, the Mapes girls, Dorothy Dixon, and Linda Carlton share. Capable fliers all, they meet men's (and society's) challenges head-on, proving their right to equality. Susan looks ahead to a life-time of sport flying, whatever else the future might bring. Roberta moves from the secretarial pool to the flight line, working alongside equally competent (and male) test pilots, and giving no sign of forfeiting her job for domesticity. Ruth lands her airplane on the deck of an aircraft carrier and proves her mettle in the rigors of the Central American jungle. She may in time marry Sandy Marland, but she is unlikely to give up either her privileged life-style or her flying activities. Linda earns her way in the classroom, winning transport and commercial licenses along with full mechanic's certification, *and* in the air, crossing the Atlantic to France, the Pacific to Hawaii, embracing the latest in aircraft technology, and proving to all comers her liberation from constricting convention.

Linda, of all the books' heroines, is the most Earhartian. As George Palmer Putnam remarks of Earhart,

> She saw the modern world as a sphere in which . . . one had to tune oneself to the almost lightning changes produced by science and invention. She never feared the erosion of human beings by science and invention, but felt that as women more than any other group had been affected by them, they had also become the greatest beneficiaries of them.[28]

Women must—and can—accommodate themselves to the technological world as well as men. Although each of her fictional contem-
poraries contributes something to the series' portrayal of the modern woman, Linda most fully personifies independence and liberation for her host of young readers.

The woman pilot was a readily identifiable female heroine,
appealing to the young readers of the series books. As a series character, she served as "an excellent symbol of women's emancipation
in the post-suffrage era," personifying the independence and the
modernity of aviation. There was just one problem. For all their
prominence, women fliers like Earhart appeared to some segments
of the American public as only themselves, not representatives of
womankind. Despite Earhart's insistence that "it takes from forty to
a hundred men on the ground to keep one plane in the air. That is
from forty to a hundred jobs per plane—and I don't think all those
jobs need forever be held by men," their exploits created no jobs of
equal stature. While "every business had special service jobs intended
for women," the star turns such as Earhart's career were open only
to a privileged few and access to the specialized non-piloting tasks
was difficult if not impossible to attain.[29] The majority of women
were caught up in the confluence of economics, technology, and
changing societal trends in ways that inexorably held them back.

For the 1930s, the economic situation stood front and center.
The United States was in the midst of the Great Depression. Jobs
were scarce, wages were low, and single women were increasingly
seeking work in the general job market. The necessities of
Depression-era existence had to take priority over the uncertainties
of an emerging occupation. Adding to the economic pressure was
the cost of airplanes. Whereas the craft were once within the reach
of an at least average middle-class consumer, they now were available only to the well-off. Only the Mapes twins, living upon the proceeds of their father's small-scale operation, must watch their pen-
nies, and even they have personal aircraft. Ruth Darrow, Linda
Carlton, and even Dorothy Dixon, whatever their other merits, are

comfortably fixed. Ruth's father is a high-ranking military officer with a steady income; Linda's is a diversified businessman able to resist Depression-era fluctuations; Dorothy's is a bank president whose well-capitalized firm is in no danger of failing. All have money to spare.

And money was necessary. Vidal's dream of a practical $700 airplane was never realized, and a steady increase in the price of private aircraft reflected their growing technological sophistication. Linda's Arrow Sport listed for $3,000 in pre-Depression cash and a Bellanca WB-2, less sophisticated than the J-300 Linda acquires, still cost $15,000 in 1927. Topping the list was Earhart's Lockheed 10-E Electra, the craft in which she planned to fly around the world. Its estimated cost in 1937 was $80,000 (the equivalent of $1.5 million in present-day funds), and repairs following the crack-up during her first attempt required another $50,000. Only with the help of the Purdue Research Fund was she able to obtain the airplane, and few persons, male or female, had access to such an organization.[30] Modern aircraft were out of reach of the ordinary flier, however hopeful her dreams.

Technology played its part, as well. Aircraft were becoming more complex as such innovations as radio receivers for the nationwide navigational beam, variable-pitch propellers, and the Handley-Page "slot" for better low-speed control were assimilated into modern aircraft. These required new flying skills that many considered beyond women's reach. Airplanes were also becoming bigger, especially among the commercial aircraft, where airline flying seemed to hold out at least a chance for women to make a career. The Ford 5-AT Trimotor, boasting sixteen seats, had entered service as early as 1926; it was followed by the Boeing 80-A, a twenty-seat, tri-motored biplane, in 1928, and the Boeing 247-D, a speedy twin-engined, all-metal monoplane seating ten, in 1933.[31] These were for the times large, heavy aircraft lacking any form of hydraulic or mechanical "boost" for the control systems, and offered an ideal opportunity for commercial pilots to attack women's physical prowess.

The test came in 1934, when Central Airlines, flying Ford Trimotors on a mail route between Washington, DC, and Detroit, hired Helen Richey as a co-pilot. Richey was undeniably qualified for the job. She was a graduate of Carnegie Technical Institute, an experienced pilot with all federally required licenses, and holder of a women's endurance record. As the nation's first woman airline pilot, she won public notice when she flew a Central craft along the entire route with professional ease. Other articles trumpeted her elevation and her ability. W. B. Courtney described her hiring as "perhaps the most consequential phenomenon of the year in commercial aviation" and praised her common sense and rich experience. Seven months later, the *Literary Digest* dubbed her "Queen Helen" and "a symbol of emancipation to the nation's women in aviation," pointing to her breaking of "the industry's last barrier to women job-seekers."[32]

Ability notwithstanding, Richey faced increasing opposition from Central's male pilots. The pilots' union denied her membership, and Central forbade her to fly in rough weather, claiming that she would not be strong enough to handle the controls in an emergency. Richey thereupon resigned her post in late 1935, after barely a year of service. This situation generated considerable discussion among men *and* women pilots. Two women fliers, Ruth Haviland and Ruth Nichols, supported the company, agreeing that women were physically too weak to handle the larger commercial craft. Amelia Earhart supported Richey's cause, unsuccessfully taking her case to the Department of Commerce seeking her reinstatement. Although the Bureau of Air Commerce subsequently hired Richey to work with Louise Thaden and Phoebe Omlie in developing a nation-wide series of navigational markers, no American woman would again formally take the controls of a commercial airliner until 1973.[33]

Perhaps the greatest challenge to the woman flier came from society itself. Public interest in aviation and flying "stunts" was dwindling as fewer and fewer "firsts" remained to be claimed. The decline was reflected in press coverage. A typical case is that of the *New York Times*. Between 1928 and 1936, it published 1,268 articles concerning women fliers; of these, three hundred and twenty-nine (or 26 percent) concerned Earhart. After her disappearance in 1937, coverage for the 1938-1942 period, bringing matters to the start of the Second World War, dropped to one hundred and ninety articles, of which thirty-four (or 18 percent) dealt with Earhart.[34] Casual distance flights and increasingly arcane records no longer commanded the attention they once held, and the accomplishments of women fliers, which once featured largely in the daily publications, began to fade from sight.

Complicating matters was a nation-wide shift in cultural values as the 1930s led into the 1940s. Although Franklin D. Roosevelt's "New Deal" and the activism of First Lady Eleanor Roosevelt brought new involvement of women in political and governmental matters, general societal trends began to emphasize more conventional roles for women. The result was greater attention to family and home, and what historian Nancy Woloch describes as "a conservative division of gender roles, an apparent retreat from public affairs, and a pronounced antifeminist mood." There was little or no place for the female flier in this new milieu, and the vanishing of the girls' books reflects it. Terri and Prim Mapes never got to have their Andean adventure, and the energy of Dorothy Dixon's antics did not carry her affairs beyond 1933. External reality had caught up with the idealistic fantasies of fiction, and fiction could not compete.[35]

As the times changed, women in aviation began to be seen in a new light, one that served "to exclude women from piloting altogether." The self-reliant women of the girls' books who once were presented as pilots increasingly appear as passive passengers consuming aviation rather than advancing it. The changing perception of women in aviation was summed up poignantly in *Aviation*'s farewell to Amelia Earhart in 1937. The leading technical journal of the times, it first remarked in its editorial that she personified "the spirit of the era of single-handed achievement in aviation *which we have just passed.*" Then, its tone openly elegiac, it concluded: "The real tragedy of Amelia Earhart is that hers was the psychology of the Age of the Vikings applied at a time when aviation had already passed over into the Age of the Clipper."[36] Individual derring-do was being supplanted by corporate blandness, and the women of aviation were experiencing the consequences. The corporate world gave no thought to their skills. If they were to fly for a living, women had to find other opportunities.

Notes

1. Colonel Charles A. Lindbergh, "Lindbergh Calls for Airways to Link Capitals of Continent," *New York Times*, 16 December 1927, 2; Amelia Earhart, "Try Flying Yourself," *Cosmopolitan* 85 (November 1928): 35; Amelia Earhart, "Your Next Garage may house an Autogiro," *Cosmopolitan* 91 (August 1931): 58; Alexander Klemin, "An Airplane in Every Garage?", *Scribner's Magazine* 98 (September 1935): 182. See also Joseph J. Corn, *The Winged Gospel: America's Romance with Aviation, 1900-1950* (New York: Oxford University Press, 1983), 91-111.

2. "200 Plane Experts to Hold a Parley," *New York Times*, 23 May 1934, 10; "10,000 'Baby Planes' At $700 Proposed," *New York Times*, 9 November 1933, 23; Reginald M. Cleveland, "Interest in Tiny Planes," *New York Times*, 8 December 1935, XX9. For the Ercoupe, see "Erco 415-C Ercoupe," http://www.nasm.si.edu/research/aero/aircraft/erco415.htm (accessed 13 November 2007).

3. Edith Lavell, *Linda Carlton's Perilous Summer* (New York: A.L. Burt, 1932), 54.

4. Edith Lavell, *Linda Carlton, Air Pilot* (Akron, OH: Saalfield, 1931), 8, 86; Edith Lavell, *Linda Carlton's Ocean Flight* (Akron, OH: Saalfield, 1931), 208-259; Edith Lavell, *Linda Carlton's Perilous Summer*, 28. See also Bruce Gould, "Girls Have Wings, Too! How Elinor Smith, 17, Set an Endurance Record," *St. Nicholas* 56 (June 1929): 631, 674; Helena Huntington Smith, "New Woman" [Elinor Smith], *New Yorker* 6 (10 May 1930): 28-31; "This Month's Cover" [Laura Ingalls], *U.S. Air*

132   *From Birdwomen to Skygirls*

Services 19 (June 1934): 32-33; Clair Price, "Amy Johnson Wings Her Way to Fame," *New York Times Magazine*, 1 June 1930, 4, 19.

5. Arrow Aircraft & Motors Corporation. Common Stock Notification. *New York Times*, 15 April 1929, 43; "Arrow Sport A2-60," http://www.nasm.si.edu/research/aero/aircraft/arrowsport.htm (accessed 13 November 2007); Lavell, *Linda Carlton's Ocean Flight*, 138.

6. Lavell, *Linda Carlton's Ocean Flight*, 201-202; Alan Abel and Drina Welch Abel, *Bellanca's Golden Age*, Golden Age of Aviation Series 4 (Brawley, CA: Wind Canyon Books, 2004), 28-32, 42, 55-56.

7. Juan de la Cierva, "A New Way to Fly," *Saturday Evening Post* 202 (2 November 1929): 20-21; "Autogiro is Hailed as Family Machine," *New York Times*, 6 June 1931, 14; Earhart, "Your Next Garage May House an Autogiro," 58; Earle Ovington, "The Airplane and Autogiro Compared," *Popular Aviation* 9 (November 1931): 36; Brigadier-General William Mitchell, "The Automobile of the Air," *Woman's Home Companion* 59 (May 1932): 18-19, 126. See also Peter W. Brooks, *Cierva Autogiros: The Development of Rotary-Wing Flight* (Washington, DC: Smithsonian Institution Press, 1988).

8. Lavell, *Linda Carlton's Ocean Flight*, 214; Edith Lavell, *Linda Carlton's Island Adventure* (Akron, OH: Saalfield, 1931), 19, 25; Edith Lavell, *Linda Carlton's Hollywood Flight* (New York: A.L. Burt, 1933), 31-34.

9. Lavell, *Linda Carlton's Island Adventure*, 121; Lavell, *Linda Carlton's Perilous Summer*, 73.

10. Lavell, *Linda Carlton, Air Pilot*, 83, 144.

11. Ibid., 22, 58; Edith Lavell, *Linda Carlton's Hollywood Flight*, 37, 249.

12. Lavell, *Linda Carlton's Ocean Flight*, 249, 259; Lavell, *Linda Carlton's Island Adventure*, 13-14.

13. Lavell, *Linda Carlton's Hollywood Flight*, 220. Ellipsis in the original.

14. Corn, *Winged Gospel*, 111; Julietta A. Arthur, "Airways to Earning," *Independent Woman* 19 (February 1940), 34-35.

15. "Books for Girls" [back dust jacket advertisement], Bess Moyer, *The Girl Flyers on Adventure Island* (New York: Goldsmith Publishing, 1932), unpaged; [untitled back dust jacket advertisement], Bess Moyer, *Gypsies of the Air* (New York: Goldsmith Publishing, 1932), unpaged.

16. Moyer, *Gypsies of the Air*, 12, 19, 23; Moyer, *Girl Flyers on Adventure Island*, 12.

17. Moyer, *Gypsies of the Air*, 22-23, 30.

18. Ibid., 29.

19. "Sainsbury, Noel Everingham, Jr.," *Who Was Who in America*, vol. 7, 1977-1981 (Chicago: Marquis Who's Who, 1981): 498.

20. Dorothy Wayne [Noel E. Sainsbury, Jr.], *Dorothy Dixon Wins Her Wings* (Chicago: Goldsmith Publishing, 1933), 143-144; Lieutenant Barrett Studley, *Practical Flight Training* (New York: Macmillan, 1928), vii.

21. Klemin, "Planes for Private Flying," 212-213; W. L. LePage, "The Development of the Amphibian Airplane," *Aviation* 22 (25 April 1927): 828-831; "Loening Cabin Amphibian," *Aviation* 24 (9 April 1928): 888, 902-906; "The Ryan M-1 Monoplane," *Aero Digest* 8 (May 1926): 276; Wayne, *Dorothy Dixon Wins Her Wings,* 111-113; Dorothy Wayne [Noel E. Sainsbury, Jr.], *Dorothy Dixon Solves the Conway Case* (Chicago: Goldsmith, 1933), 16-18.

22. Dorothy Wayne [Noel E. Sainsbury, Jr.], *Dorothy Dixon and the Double Cousin* (Chicago: Goldsmith, 1933), 63, 61.

23. Ibid., 60; Wayne, *Dorothy Dixon Solves the Conway Case,* 183, 245-246; Anne Scott MacLeod, In "Nancy Drew and Her Rivals: No Contest," *American Childhood: Essays on Children's Literature of the Nineteenth and Twentieth Centuries* (Athens, GA: University of Georgia Press, 1994), 38.

24. Wayne, *Dorothy Dixon and the Double Cousin,* 56; Wayne, *Dorothy Dixon Solves the Conway Case,* 182-185.

25. Captain Charles W. Purcell, "What I Think about Women! A Rip-snorting Opinion of Women's Place in Aviation," *Popular Aviation* 8 (April 1931): 15-16, 54, is an extreme yet typical example.

26. Amelia Earhart, quoted in George Palmer Putnam, *Soaring Wings: A Biography of Amelia Earhart* (New York: Harcourt, Brace, 1939), 89-90.

27. "Amelia Earhart, Ardent Feminist," *Equal Rights,* 15 June 1937, 82; see also Ware, *Still Missing,* 24-25.

28. Putnam, *Soaring Wings,* 139.

29. Ware, *Still Missing,* 63; Woloch, *Women and the American Experience,* 264; Amelia Earhart, quoted in Putnam, *Soaring Wings,* 245.

30. Abel and Abel, *Bellanca's Golden Age,* 24; Rich, *Amelia Earhart,* 220-227, 248-249.

31. R. E. G. Davies, *Airlines of the United States since 1914* (Washington, DC: Smithsonian Institution Press, 1998), 655, 652, 658.

32. W. B. Courtney, "Ladybird," *Collier's* 95 (30 March 1935): 16, 43; "'Queen Helen' of Air," *Literary Digest* 120 (26 October 1935): 34.

33. "First Woman Airline Co-Pilot Flies Plane from Capital to Detroit With 7 Passengers," *New York Times,* 1 January 1935, 22; "Says Man's Strength Is Needed," *New York Times,* 8 November 1935, 25; "Electric Rudder Is Urged," *New York Times,* 7 November 1935, 25; "Miss Earhart Backs Flier," *New York Times,* 8 November 1935, 25; "Feminists Stirred Over Woman Flier," *New York Times,* 8 November 1935, 25; "Helen Richey Gets Post," *New York Times,* 14 December 1935, 13;

Deborah G. Douglas, *American Women and Flight since 1940* (Lexington: University Press of Kentucky, 2004), 176.

34. Dean Jaros, *Heroes Without Legacy: American Airwomen, 1912-1944* (Niwot: University Press of Colorado, 1993), 80.

35. Woloch, *Women and the American Experience,* 300, 314-315.

36. Jaros, *Heroes Without Legacy,* 97-98; "A. E.," *Aviation* 36 (August 1937): 22 [emphasis added].

CHAPTER 5

The Stewardess Enters the Scene:

1930-1945

When Ruthe S. Wheeler published *Jane, Stewardess of the Air Lines* in 1934, she had little idea she was creating a genre. Her only concern was to produce a salable career story touched with information, laced with adventure, and interwoven with a hint of romance. She intended to capitalize upon what was then considered as one of the latest, most modern occupations for women, pair it with the rapidly developing world of American commercial aviation, and present an informative, exciting story for her young readers. In this, she succeeded—and also created the genre of the "stewardess story," the literary formula that puts its young heroines into the cabin of an airliner and records their adventures as they encounter pilots, passengers, and miscellaneous folk. The authors who followed her lead, all of them women, took Wheeler's model and extended it from the era of tri-motored biplanes to that of the high-flying jet liner. Their books constitute a cluster of works reaching from 1934 until the late 1950s, glamorizing the stewardess's life while reflecting the sweeping changes in both American commercial aviation and American attitudes toward women in aviation, the workplace, and the home.

The story of American commercial aviation leads directly to that of the airline stewardess. Commercial aviation in the United States dates from the mid-1920s, as the several elements needed for a national air transport system slowly fell into place. The govern-

ment air mail service had been operating since 1918. Its needs stimulated the completion in 1925 of a transcontinental system of lighted beacons that made night flying practicable, and twenty-four hour flying of the mail became a commonplace. At the same time, the federal Air Mail Act of 1925, the "Kelly Act," established eight regional air routes and opened them to bids from independent contractors. This shifted the carriage of air mail from a government agency to private enterprise, and from the winners came the first commercial American air carriers. The following year, the Air Commerce Act of 1926 gave the federal government the authority to establish standards for the licensing of pilots and in general reg-

Opposite: *Interior (looking forward) of a United Air Lines 5-AT trimotor, 1932. National Air and Space Museum, Smithsonian Institution (SI 75-7267).*
Top: *The "City of Columbus," a Ford 5-AT trimotor in Transcontinental Air Transport Livery—competitor to the Boeing 80-A. National Air and Space Museum, Smithsonian Institution (SI 75-15206).*
Above: *Eastern Air Transport stewardesses alongside a Curtiss Condor. Their uniforms bear a striking resemblance to a registered nurse's cap and whites. National Air and Space Museum, Smithsonian Institution (88-18944).*

ulate aviation development, leading to the formation of the Civil Aviation Authority (CAA) and a systematizing of government oversight of general and commercial aviation.[1]

The carriers stimulated by the Kelly Act quickly began a series of mergers and takeovers that absorbed numerous minor companies and created a network of truly national airlines. Most of the companies, large or small, flew passengers on occasion (sometimes at freight rates). Transcontinental Air Transport (TAT), however, organized in 1929 with the assistance of Charles Lindbergh and dubbed "The Lindbergh Line," became the first line deliberately planned as a passenger carrier. Flying Ford 5-AT tri-motors for daytime segments and connecting with the Pennsylvania and Santa Fe Railroads for night-time travel, it reduced coast-to-coast travel time to forty-eight hours. It never proved profitable and in 1930 merged with Western Air Express to create Transcontinental and Western Air (TWA). Other mergers were taking place as well, involving a network of routes linking New York and Miami, a second network spanning the southern and middle United States, and a third in the Northwest comprising Boeing Air Transport and its associated routes. These produced the so-called "Big Four" carriers: TWA, plus Eastern Air Transport (1930), American Airways (1930), and United Air Lines (1931), respectively. Barely four years after Lindbergh's trans-Atlantic flight of 1927, a national air-commerce system was in place.[2]

The carriers realized that they must win over their passengers, persuading the public to fly when normally individuals would travel by railroad or bus. Airline advertising began to present air travel as safe, luxurious, and sophisticated. Meanwhile, descriptive articles and first-person accounts began to appear in national publications, all stressing the modernity of the craft, the safety of the operations, and the comfort of the flight. One regional trade journal, *Southern Aviation*, for example, praised airport cleanliness, calling on-site conditions "exact counterparts of those noted at railway depots—*sans* soot, smoke, grime, and the customary motley assemblage of uncouth human derelicts who are usually wont to loiter about a railroad station." Amelia Earhart, who had joined TAT middle management, wrote in 1930 of "Women's Influence on Air Transport Luxury" for *Aeronautic Review,* noting that "the utmost in luxury can be obtained on the better air lines in this country."[3]

The *Literary Digest* in 1932 called attention to efforts directed toward "Putting Luxury in the Air," stressing the creature comforts offered by the aircraft. The same year, Francis Vivian Drake, writing in the *Atlantic Monthly,* stressed the speed, economy, and pleasure of transcontinental flight, observing that his flight from Chicago to the Pacific, which took twenty-two days in wagon-train times, now required only twenty hours. In late 1933, Reginald M. Cleveland, in *Scientific American,* stated flatly that the modern airliner was "The acme of modern design, both in relation to aerodynamic efficiency and in relation to what might be termed the comfort features for the passengers." In 1937, United Airlines began "Skylounge" service between New York and Chicago. An extra-fare, luxury service, it offered passengers swivel chairs with special upholstery, china and silver tableware, bridge tables, and individual toilet kits. By 1938, J. C. Furnas, writing in *Scribner's,* openly reviewed the airlines' intentions and approvingly discussed their "campaign to make America air-minded . . . [and] the publicity designed to overcome fear."[4]

Women in the aviation workplace, meanwhile, faced a dilemma. Commercial aviation in the 1930s had no place for women in the cockpit. The one experiment in hiring a woman pilot ended in a blaze of notoriety. As noted in Chapter 4, Central Airlines, a regional carrier, hired Helen Richey as a co-pilot, but refused to allow her to fly in bad weather or at night. Richey's resignation created substantial public controversy, but Central held to its position and prospects for women pilots faded. Work in clerical or, occasionally, lower management positions was available, but women who wished to fly professionally had to look elsewhere. There was no lack of attention to non-flying work. As early as 1930, *U.S. Air Services* listed two dozen women who were working in aviation-

related but non-flying jobs, from aircraft sales to airport management. *Time* magazine in 1937 wrote of several women who were
working as women's liaisons for three of the major airlines, while
Julietta K. Arthur devoted four pages of *Independent Woman* in
1940 to identifying "Airways to Earning."[5] Job opportunities there
were, but they did not involve flying.

Three plans to involve women in active flying emerged prior to
World War II: the Betsy Ross Corps, the Women's Air Reserve, and
the Women Flyers of America. The first of these was a quasi-mili-
tary group established in 1931 "to weld flying womanhood into a
group capable of and willing to serve its country if need be." The
Corps was created by Opal Kunz, an accomplished air-racer and a
veteran of the Powder Puff Derby, who saw it as a way of providing
"a woman's flying corps which will perform service behind the lines
in time of stress or trouble, and in peacetime as well." It attracted a
number of notable women pilots, including Marjorie Stinson,
Phoebe Omlie, and Ruth Elder, but never managed to achieve its
announced goal.[6]

The Women's Air Reserve, also created in 1931, was an offshoot
of the Betsy Ross Corps. Florence ("Pancho") Barnes, a flamboyant
air-racer and stunt pilot, grew bored with what she saw as the
Corps' inactivity, and proceeded to found her own group, the
Women's Air Reserve, with its headquarters on the West Coast. It,
too, attracted well-known women fliers, including Louise Thaden,
Evelyn ("Bobbi") Trout, and Blanche Noyes among its numbers.
Like the Corps, it was structured along military lines, with Barnes
as Commanding General, and was intended to "aid in disasters
where it was impossible to reach people except by plane," and to
help women fliers in "proving their self-sufficiency, proving their
competence to the men who would deny them an equal place in
aviation and in the military." The group gave over one weekend a
month to various flying exercises, and, in 1934, did achieve a two-
month-long flying outing to New York and Washington, DC, to

lobby for governmental support for women in aviation. It lapsed soon afterward.[7]

Far more successful than either the Betsy Ross Corps or the Women's Air Reserve was the Women Flyers of America (WFA), created in 1940. Unlike the other two groups, which were primarily for women already holding pilot's licenses, the WFA saw itself as a means of providing inexpensive flying lessons to encourage women who wanted to learn to fly. This, the organizers believed, would create a pool of licensed, competent pilots who could be called into domestic service in a national emergency. Opal Kunz, again a founding member, pointed out that "We do know that every girl who can fly can release a man for active duty at the front." By August of 1940, the WFA had enrolled more than a thousand members, and, in October of that year, was the focus of "Now You Can Learn to Fly," an article in *Independent Woman*. It also attracted more notice than had either of its forebears. An unnamed Washington official remarked that "It is quite possible that in the event of war a very definite place can be found for women in aeronautical services, perhaps in conjunction with the training of pilots or in some related civilian capacity," and, the next year, Colonel Robert Olds of the Air Corps Ferry Command circularized the WFA membership to determine whether any would be able to aid "in the delivery of planes to the airfields for which they are destined."[8] Although their piloting skills were ignored by the airlines, determined women were managing to keep current with aviation, develop their competence as pilots, and look ahead to a turbulent future. Those who wished to fly professionally, however, had to turn to the stewardess corps.

Before the coming of the stewardesses, in-flight services for passengers, when provided, were carried out by the co-pilot. He would distribute box lunches, deal with the air-sick, and answer questions when not otherwise occupied in the cockpit. The creation of a stewardess corps was initially proposed by Ellen Church, a trained nurse who was herself a pilot. Her proposal caught the attention of Stephen Stimpson, a district manager for Boeing Air Transport, who pushed for its adoption. The presence of attractive young women in the cabin, he wrote the Boeing central authorities, would offer "a great psychological punch," with a "tremendous effect . . . on the traveling public." The women, moreover, would be of additional value to the line "not only in the neater and nicer method of serving food but looking out for the passengers' welfare." Boeing reluctantly agreed to a three-month trial run in the spring of 1930, and Church selected a cadre of seven other women, all of them white and all of them registered nurses, to make up the "Original Eight." Nurses' training, she reasoned, would equip the women to work under discipline and to deal calmly with emergencies. Knowing that a nurse was on board, moreover, would reassure queasy passengers; in the very earliest days of the stewardess's work on other lines, some wore their RN uniforms in lieu of airline livery. Recognizing the limitations on lift and space in the aircraft then flying, Church set stringent limitations on the women's weight and stature, and went on to outfit them with businesslike green uniforms that gave a professional appearance and provided warmth in the drafty cabins of the day.[9]

The experiment proved a success. By 1932, W. B. Courtney, writing in *Collier's,* praised the presence of the stewardesses, calling their work "a profession of many facets" involving the ability to be "a saleswoman, an information bureau, a diplomat, an entertainment committee, [and] a dietitian." Francis Vivian Drake, again writing in *Atlantic Monthly,* spoke of the stewardess's work as "the newest career in the world. And, equally, the strangest," and went on to note an airline official's stress upon the importance of "character" among the women. *Airwoman,* the official publication of the Ninety-Nines, the women pilots' organization, noted the nearly three hundred women working as stewardesses in 1935, and commented upon "how far the air stewardess profession has traveled." The next year, *Literary Digest* reported on the intellectual and emo-

*Boeing Air Transport's (United Air Lines) "Original Eight" stewardesses,
alongside a Boeing 80-A, May 1930. Ellen Church stands by the door at left rear.
National Air and Space Museum, Smithsonian Institution (SI 78-14836).*

tional requirements of the work, concluding that "transport pilots
and passenger air-plane hostesses to-day form the most carefully
picked professional group in the world," while Frederick Graham,
writing in the *New York Times Magazine* in early 1940, observed
that "the average passenger has come to consider the airline hostess
quite as essential . . . as the pilot and the plane."[10] All of the accounts,
though, assumed—correctly—that the stewardess would be white,
single, and a registered nurse. This pattern of selection spread, and
before the end of the decade, the airline stewardess had become a
familiar figure embodying competence and dependability for the
air-traveling public.

As stewardesses became more and more a part of the operations of commercial aviation, their duties expanded. In addition to

reassuring the passengers and distributing meals, the women soon became responsible for the entire internal economy of the aircraft. Before take-off, they were responsible for checking and confirming the inventory of in-flight supplies and the operation of cabin accessories—lights, air vents, reclining seats, and other amenities, as well as the meals and beverages scheduled for service. At embarkation, they checked tickets against the manifest (a task made unnecessary by the modern computer), assigned seats, and saw to pre-take-off safety arrangements. The senior stewardess aboard any flight had to sign off on the satisfactory status of interior facilities, taking over the airplane from the commissary department as formally as the pilot took over responsibility of the ship from the maintenance crew.[11] The work may have been clerical in its nature, but the airplane could not take off without clearance from both the cockpit and the cabin.

The airlines were aided in their quest for customers by a steady advance in aircraft technology. The initial airplanes placed in commercial service were primarily the Ford 5-AT tri-motor, an all-metal, high-winged monoplane that seated fourteen and cruised at 125 miles per hour, and the Boeing 80-A, a three-engined biplane seating eighteen and also cruising at 125 mph. Both gave adequate service and, for all their shortcomings, marked a genuine advance in airline comfort and safety. They quickly were supplanted, though, by two strikingly advanced airplanes. The first was the Boeing 247, an all-metal, twin-engined monoplane seating ten. Its streamlining boosted its cruising speed to 170 mph, while its soundproofing and ventilation systems gave passengers a quiet, comfortable flight that was a far cry from the noisy and drafty Fords. It entered service with United Air Lines in 1933, promptly setting a trans-continental speed record and justifiably winning the label of "the first modern airliner." Its success with United prompted other airlines to seek the 247 for their fleets, but Boeing, the parent company of United, withheld external sales until United's needs were satisfied.[12]

Boeing's refusal to supply competitors with the 247 gave rise to

Top: *The first modern airliner: the Boeing 247 in United Air Lines livery. National Air and Space Museum, Smithsonian Institution (SI 82-5412).*
Above: *The airplane that changed the world: a Douglas DC-3 in American Airlines livery. National Air and Space Museum, Smithsonian Institution (SI 75-15208).*

the second airplane and revolutionized commercial aviation. Jack Frye, president of TWA, frustrated in his efforts to buy 247s for TWA, circulated a proposal to other manufacturers soliciting a competitive design. Only Douglas Aircraft Company responded, and from their submission came the first of the famed "DC" series of commercial airplanes. From the prototype DC-1 came the DC-2, a twin-engined, low-winged monoplane seating fourteen passengers and cruising at 200 mph; when it went into service in 1934, it set speed records between New York and Chicago four times in a single week. Other airlines, recognizing the DC-2's superiority, placed their own orders and the craft became a familiar sight on airfields domestic and international. Then, in 1935, American Airlines asked Douglas to develop a stretched version of the craft that would accommodate berths for "sleeper service." This craft, the Douglas Sleeper Transport (DST), took to the air in 1935, providing seating for twenty-one passengers or berths for sixteen. Douglas undertook further modifications of the DST on its own, and from them came the DC-3—an aircraft called "the greatest airliner ever built." It was the first airplane that could make money through passenger service alone, and its reliability, speed, and economy of operation made it a legendary ship in the history of aviation.[13]

The rapid development of domestic air travel came to a virtual standstill with the start of the Second World War. Faced with an urgent need for aircraft, the army requisitioned ships from the commercial lines, taking at times as many as half or two-thirds of companies' entire fleets. Douglas Aircraft, which had been in the late stages of developing the DC-4, a four-engined transport equipped with tricycle landing gear, had its entire production of the craft diverted to military purposes. The nine Boeing Model 307 Stratoliners, the only four-engined, pressurized liner then flying, were all pressed into service, leaving Pan American and TWA without long-range, high-altitude equipment. Crew members were also absorbed by the military, at times flying the aircraft wearing their airline uniforms instead of military garb. The army began construction of military bases across North America, and the first transAtlantic flights began in February 1943. From these early stages came the Air Transport Command (ATC), which ferried aircraft, personnel, and supplies throughout the world.[14]

Despite the reduction of their fleets, the commercial airlines, in

United Air Lines stewardesses of 1940 get their wings alongside a DC-3.
National Air and Space Museum, Smithsonian Institution (SI 89-21546).

collaboration with the government and the military, struggled to maintain at least a semblance of domestic service. Bookings were placed on a priority basis, allowing persons with a high priority (military, governmental personnel) to "bump" lower-ranked passengers at any stage of a flight; ships were daily flown 20 to 30 percent more hours than in peacetime; and flamboyant advertising of the de luxe service available en route went by the board. The stewardess corps itself changed dramatically as many of its members entered the military as nurses, requiring the airlines to relax admissions requirements to recruit replacement cabin staff. For all the difficulties, though, the airlines kept up a domestic presence, and the lessons taught by flying for the military helped prepare them for post-war changes.[15]

The growing acceptance of stewardesses by the airlines and their passengers is evident from two sources. One is sheer numbers. The "Original Eight" began their work with United Air Lines in May 1930. By mid-1935, their numbers had grown to 150; in addition, Western Air Express employed ten stewardesses, American Airlines sixty, and Transcontinental & Western Air (TWA) was in the process of hiring sixty. The carriers were recognizing the effectiveness of the stewardesses in winning and keeping passengers. The other is the visibility of the young women in the general realm of popular culture. By 1933, admiring articles were appearing in middle- and upper-middle-class periodicals, ranging from *Collier's* to *Atlantic Monthly,* and Columbia Pictures was in the process of shooting *Air Hostess,* a film starring Evalyn Knapp and featuring the aircraft and crews of United Air Lines.[16] These, however, constituted information directed toward the adults who were potential passengers for the airlines. Even more telling is the appearance of the "stewardess story," a formulaic career story intended for pre-teen and teenaged girl readers. Beginning in 1934, these books detailed the training and life of the stewardess in ways that made the work seem irresistible. Their emphases change with the evolving nature of commercial flight, however, making them a capsule record of the changing nature of the stewardess's image.

Two freestanding volumes, Ruthe S. Wheeler's *Jane, Stewardess of the Air Lines* (1934) and Betty Baxter Anderson's *Peggy Wayne, Sky Girl* (1941), establish the formula for the larger genre, although a later cluster of works, Patricia O'Malley's "Carol Rogers" books (1941-1946; three titles) and "Caddie Palmer" series (1944-1946; two titles) offers some modifications. The formula features a heroine, normally a "classic" American girl from the heartland—i.e., the Midwest. A registered nurse in her late teens or early twenties, she enters the stewardess training offered by an airline and moves through its schooling to become a full-fledged stewardess. In the company of one of the line's pilots, she may take flying lessons and earn a license, all the while finding prestige, glamor, sophistication, and (often) romance in her work. The books always reflect to some degree the evolving nature of aircraft technology and the airline industry, and add to it a solid if rose-colored (not to say overly dramatic) picture of the responsibilities of an in-flight stewardess. Thus, Wheeler's and Anderson's books become pioneering works bridging earlier views of women's possibilities in the aviation marketplace and with those extant in the contemporary airline industry. In their way, they look as much backward to the flying stories of the 1930s, when women still had general access to the cockpit, as they do to their present, with their forward-looking presentation of the most modern of occupations for women.

Ruthe S. Wheeler's *Jane, Stewardess of the Air Lines* was the second of a cluster of four career-related books that Wheeler published with the Goldsmith Publishing Company between 1932 and 1935. The first of these, *Helen in the Editor's Chair* (1932), offered a relatively conventional view of the work opportunities available in publishing for the modern woman, while the last two, *Janet Hardy in Hollywood* and *Janet Hardy in Radio City* (both 1935), moved into the world of the more up-to-date media. In *Jane,* Wheeler takes up the newest of women's occupations, envisioning the work as seamlessly melding the flying world of the 1930s' independent aviatrix with that of the newly anointed adjunct to the world of commercial flight.

Jane Cameron and her best friend Sue Hawley, new graduates of the nursing program at Good Samaritan Hospital in University City, Iowa, are urged by their supervisor to apply for stewardess posts with Federated Airways. They fly to Chicago for their interview, en route aiding a passenger stricken with appendicitis, and are accepted into the program. Experiencing an early crash tests their mettle, but they persevere and Jane graduates at the top of the class. She is assigned to the Federated headquarters in Cheyenne, Wyoming, flying in Boeing Model 80 trimotored biplanes. There she garners publicity for herself and Federated by accompanying a wealthy matron, Mrs. Van Verity Vaness, on a special chartered

Jane Cameron's flying workplace: the Boeing 80A-1 airliner.
National Air and Space Museum, Smithsonian Institution (SI 83-16414).

flight across the country. Jane becomes a regular on the Cheyenne-Chicago route, takes flying lessons from her friend Charlie Fisher, and earns a pilot's license. She enjoys Charlie's company during off times, but there is no hint of any serious romance, and whether the company dismisses a stewardess when she marries is not mentioned.

Incident follows upon incident. When a jealous classmate attempts to discredit Jane by contaminating on-board food supplies for her flight, Jane is investigated, but exonerated. She later takes part in an urgent, mid-winter flight to carry medical personnel and medicine to an isolated Wyoming town stricken by a diphtheria epidemic, and foils gangsters' efforts to hijack a Federated liner and kidnap child film star Jackie Condon. Her skills as a private pilot win her an after-hours flying job doing stunts for Mammoth Films as the company shoots a story based upon the operations of Federated Airways, and she parachutes to safety when a Mammoth special effect malfunctions and sets her airplane ablaze. Federated then retires its Model 80 trimotors for the new, twin-engined Boeing 247, and when the resulting increase in business compels the company to take on more stewardess trainees, Jane is offered the job of assistant chief stewardess. She ends her first year with Federated in a position of still greater responsibility, looking forward to her career and new experiences to come.

Several things are notable about Jane's situation. Her employer, Federated Airways, is clearly a surrogate for United Air Lines. Its headquarters, like United's, are in Cheyenne, it flies the same routes used by United, and it is equipped with the same aircraft as United. The Boeing Model 80 entered service with United in 1928, giving reliable and relatively comfortable service until it was replaced by the Boeing Model 247, which entered service with the line in 1933. The Model 80 is described early in the story as "a great tri-motor biplane," impressing Jane with its "double row of comfortable reclining seats" and its enclosed pantry and lavatory at the rear of the cabin.[17]

When the 247 comes onto the scene, it represents cutting-edge technology, as the book makes plain. Charlie Fisher, returning from a training session at the company's plant in Tacoma, Washington, has only praise for it. "'They're the greatest ships ever built,' he told Jane and Sue. . . . 'Why, we'll be able to outrun the lightning. They carry ten passengers, two pilots and a stewardess.'" And, when the first aircraft appears on the flight line, Jane sees it as "a thing of beauty, all metal, with one low wing. . . . The interior . . . was not as roomy as the bulking tri-motors, but the seats were more comfortable and the pantry which the stewardess used was complete to the latest detail."[18] It is an aircraft as well-suited to the stewardess's duties as it is to the pilot's.

Also paralleling United's practices are the uniforms worn by the stewardess staff, described so as to catch a female reader's eye. United's were a "dark green jersey double-breasted jacket and shirt, with a green tam shaped like a shower cap, and a flowing green jer-

Interior (looking aft) of a United Air Lines Boeing 247.
National Air and Space Museum, Smithsonian Institution (SI 82-8663).

sey cape with gray collar and silver buttons." Those of Federated, as donned by Jane, are "smoke-green," with a smartly cut coat and "fashionable box pleats in the skirt. The beret, set at a jaunty angle, had only one ornament, a pair of silver wings." In it, Jane indeed cuts "an attractive figure." She is an asset to the airline and a person radiating competence to her passengers.[19] From this uniform, with only modest variations, principally in the uniform color and the shape of the cap, came the uniforms of all the airlines' stewardess corps, giving way to more extreme forms of dress only in the 1960s.

A third notable element of the book is its dealing with the airlines' announced purpose for creating a stewardess corps. United, as has been noted, was prompted to initiate the service by a memo from a district manager, stressing "the psychology of having young women as regular members of the crew." Federated, for its part, states in its recruiting letter that it "has been considering a plan to improve its service to passengers and to provide even further for their welfare and comfort while they are guests aboard our transport planes. We have come to the conclusion that the addition of a stewardess *to our flying crews* is essential."[20] For both organizations, the stewardess's role originates as a marketing device, but Federated injects the element of flight.

Neither proposal, real or fictional, equivocates about management's view of the stewardess's work. The recommendation to United held from the outset that the job was intended to encourage passengers to become more regular patrons of air transport. Federated's letter echoes this assumption, but makes one small change. Rather than stressing the economic as well as the psychological benefits of the stewardess's presence, it speaks of the women as *members of the flying crew.* Federated's (and Wheeler's) distinction is important, for it implies that the stewardess is as much a part of the proper functioning of the aircraft as are the pilot and co-pilot. She is a member of the team, not just a mere servant—a view that Jane embraces wholeheartedly. Seeing herself as being "one of the pioneers in this new profession for girls," she turns down a lucrative offer to leave the airline and work as nurse-companion for Mrs. Van Verity Vaness. She cannot accept the offer, she says, for "there seems to be a real future for girls in aviation and I want to make the most of my opportunity."[21] The work, its responsibilities, and its possibilities are genuine, and she wants to be a part of expanding this new opportunity for women. As a minor airline executive she has some authority, and she intends to exercise it in contributing to aviation.

Seven years after the appearance of Jane's adventures, Betty Baxter Anderson published *Peggy Wayne, Sky Girl* (1941), the first of a seven-book series subtitled "Career Stories for Older Girls." Following Peggy Wayne came *Connie Benton, Reporter* (1941), *Ann Porter, Nurse* (1942), *Nancy Blake, Copywriter* (1942), *Julia Brent of* the WAAC (1943), *Four Girls and a Radio* (1944), and *Holly Saunders, Designer* (1947), all published by Cupples & Leon, a well-established series-book publisher. All save Julia Brent's activities in the Women's Auxiliary Army Corps and Ann Porter's work as nurse dealt with occupations not exclusively "women's jobs," and suggested how an aspiring young woman might make her way in the contemporary mercantile world. Peggy Wayne's adventures, inaugurating the series, may well reflect the uproar over Helen Richey's brief sojourn with Central Airlines, for they make evident Anderson's desire to show women's aviation work in all its forms, up to and including active professional duty in the cockpit of a commercial aircraft.

Following their graduation from Iowa Wesleyan University's school of nursing, Peggy Wayne and her best chum Jane Fuller enroll as "hostess" candidates with Skylines, Inc. They, along with their sultry classmate Inez Hunt, pass easily through the training course and begin their work. Peggy strikes up a friendship with First Officer Tex Martin and with his encouragement takes flying lessons in her spare time, ultimately earning a private pilot's license. Once licensed, she passes a test of high-altitude endurance in a pressure chamber and polishes her flying skills with occasional lessons in Skylines' Link Trainer, an early flight simulator used to train pilots in instrument flying. Her work, meanwhile, proves anything but uneventful. Her nursing skills enable her to save the life of fading film star Norma Blaine when the latter is stricken with in-flight appendicitis. She accompanies a special flight of celebrated child radio stars, the Junior Mental Giants, to San Francisco, teaching the youngsters something of aeronautics, and she joins a mercy flight of medical personnel and supplies to Barkley, Kansas, which is experiencing a diphtheria epidemic while cut off from the outside world by a raging sleet storm.

Peggy's finest hour, however, comes when she is selected to work the inaugural flight of Skylines' new forty-passenger, four-engined, pressurized Stratoliner. The ship, carrying a revolutionary new direction-finding device, is hijacked by three criminals, one of whom proves to be Inez Hunt's off-duty beau. When the hijackers incapacitate the pilot and co-pilot, Peggy, recalling her high tolerance for anoxia, smashes a galley window at stratosphere altitude and depressurizes the aircraft. Lack of oxygen knocks out the criminals, enabling her to get to the cockpit and its supplementary oxygen. She then calls upon her piloting skills to take the craft to a breathable altitude, picks up the navigational "beam," and safely lands ship, crew, and criminals in Dallas, Texas. Inez Hunt, meanwhile, confesses her complicity in the plot and is summarily fired; Peggy wins the acclaim of the Skylines executives and the public, and accepts Tex Martin's offer of marriage, even though she knows it means leaving the hostess corps.

Like that of Jane Cameron, Peggy's career has several links to the real world. Skylines bears a notable resemblance to Transcontinental and Western Airways (TWA), particularly in the routes it flies and its calling the cabin attendants "hostesses," a label distinctive to TWA. The book spells out in concrete terms the duties of a working hostess, from passenger care to maintaining cabin inventory and keeping flight records. Peggy also extends her understanding of aeronautics on her own time. During her flying lessons, her instructor gives her a detailed description of the federal regulations governing student pilots and quizzes her knowledge of the mechanics of flight and the operation of the various systems of an airplane, and Peggy informs herself about the principal women fliers of the day, notably Jacqueline Cochran, Anne Morrow Lindbergh, and Amelia Earhart.[22]

Although the book makes no bones about the hostess's role in encouraging passengers to fly, it also presents the hostess corps as an advanced professional sisterhood, a distinctive group of young women with a responsible role to fill in advancing commercial aviation. Tex Martin tells Peggy that "Part of a hostess' job is to sell the airline to the passengers," while an advertising executive reminds her that "The vast general public is still pretty much in the dark about commercial aviation. . . . It's our job to sell that lethargic group of tourists . . . that aviation has a number of advantages." Yet, though the hostess is unquestionably a part of a commercial enterprise, she is an individual set apart by her nature and her work. She has, first of all, undergone an exhaustive selection process, intended to weed out the insincere, the "chorus girls" and the "thrill-seekers." (The screening echoes Stephen Stimpson's explicit ruling out of "the flapper type of girl.") She and her associates, as in *Jane, Stewardess of the Air Lines,* have been trained "to become regular members of flight crews." For her employer and the public, she is "a new symbol of charm and dignity," one of "a noble band of women."[23] A hostess is a special person who lends substance to the airline experience.

The evolution of airline technology also shares in Peggy's world. The chief hostess's description of the flight line in Chicago at the book's outset captures a pivotal moment in airline hardware: "Most of the lines use Douglas DC-3s for twenty-one passengers, just like the Skyliner you came in on. But over there's a Midcontinent Boeing 237-D [*sic*] with the shield-and-silver streak. Those three in front of Hangar Three are Overland's sleepers, also DC-3s." The juxtaposition of the 247-D, the DC-3, and the sleeper transport illustrates the changing nature of commercial flight as the DC-3 comes to dominate American air transport and longer flights and overnight flights become a reality. Later in the story, Peggy encounters a four-engined Boeing Model 314, with two internal decks and seats for seventy-four passengers, the last of the great trans-oceanic flying boats. And, by story's end, Skylines is preparing to introduce the Skyliner, an aircraft identical in all its specifications to the original version of the Douglas DC-4. The first pressurized ship in the Skylines fleet, it has a tricycle landing gear, four Pratt & Whitney engines, and, with its cabin pressurization, a service ceiling of 23,000 feet. In the space of a year, Peggy has seen commercial aviation go from the earliest modern airliner to the most advanced. The girls who read of her adventures see the progress as well.[24]

*Breakfast in bed aboard a United Air Lines Douglas Sleeper Transport,
precursor of the DC-3. National Air and Space Museum,
Smithsonian Institution (SI 2005-22907).*

For all its similarities to *Jane, Stewardess of the Air Lines, Peggy
Wayne, Sky Girl* stands apart in one remarkable way. Even as it
approvingly details the airline hostess's work and life, it goes on to
make an overt call for the active engagement of women in aviation.
As Peggy progresses in her flying lessons, she develops a "great
dream": "Why shouldn't women, one day, pilot the big transport
planes? Why should the highest goal in commercial aviation be limited to two thousand men?" She is aware of the military's siphoning
off experienced pilots from the airlines for its defense reserve, and
she is conscious of the government's Civilian Pilot Training
Program, which provided low-cost flying lessons to the public but
included only a small number of women candidates. "So," the nar-
rator concludes, "Peggy dared to dream. Perhaps, in the immediate

future, women would have a chance to prove their right to an equal place in airliner cockpits."[25]

Peggy understands that the likelihood of women's attaining the cockpit is almost nonexistent, but this does not stop her from arguing her cause. While flying with Tex Martin and the Skylines personnel director in the latter's private plane, she asks bluntly: "Mr. Hallett, why doesn't Skylines hire women pilots?" He answers: "We need pilots badly, but we're not in such desperate circumstances that we have to do that." Whereupon Peggy presses the issue: "You wouldn't be afraid to hire Jacqueline Cochran, would you? Or Anne Lindbergh?" The executive, cornered, hedges: "Well, now, Miss Cochran is more of a speed merchant. That's an entirely different sort of flying. And I don't think Mrs. Lindbergh really needs the job." Realizing that she has made her point, Peggy drops the matter and the three amicably continue their flight. Her dream, however, remains alive.[26]

In the final pages of the book, after Peggy has successfully piloted the immense Stratoliner to safety, she good-naturedly twits the personnel director once more: "This seems the best possible moment for me to ask if you've changed your mind about women transport pilots?" To her surprise, Mr. Hallett bends:

> 'We're seriously considering putting on some "flying freighters." We might add some women transport pilots to our rosters as first officers on those. . . . Miss Wayne, this remarkable piece of flying that you carried out today will contribute a great deal toward breaking down the prejudices against women transport pilots, I am convinced. Skylines, I know, will be on your side.'

At this point, Tex Martin chimes in, taking the debate one step further: "If you do hire women pilots, Mr. Hallett, [I hope] you won't make any silly rules about their having to quit when they get married." On this, too, Hallett yields, and the book ends with his telling the chief hostess, "You may have lost a trio of hostesses today, Miss Huston, but I believe Skylines gained a great new pilot."[27]

Peggy's victory is a qualified one, but is a victory nonetheless. Skylines may not be ready to put female pilots in front of passengers, limiting them to first-officer status on all-freight flights, but Hallett is at least open to both the employment of women in flight status and the freeing them of the no-marriage requirement that so often proved the bane of the hostess's life. Moreover, he commits Skylines to supporting efforts to win over the public's opposition to women commercial pilots, and, in the last line of the book, he speaks of Peggy not as a first officer but as "a great new pilot." At least one of the major air line companies, fictionally if not literally, has opened the door, however slightly, to a major step forward for women in aviation. It is a notable moment in both the history of the stewardess story and the history of women fliers and it is, alas, fictional.

Wheeler's and Anderson's books evoke the world of commercial aviation as it was taking shape as a national enterprise, and both look ahead to a period of steady progress in the expansion of the companies and the nature of the stewardess's duties. In the public mind, as Drew Whitelegg points out, the stewardess's job by the end of the 1930s "had achieved a certain gravitas." Its relatively high pay was an asset in the Depression years, and its combination of glamour and sophisticated travel made it attractive to scores of young women.[28] The Second World War changed all that. Following the Japanese attack upon Pearl Harbor in 1941, commercial aviation shifted to a war footing. The government commandeered significant numbers of the airlines' craft. Airline pilots and aircraft were impressed into duty ferrying aircraft and supplies. General aviation came to a standstill, as private pilots entered the Army Air Corps and gasoline shortages effectively grounded their airplanes. Air travel itself shrank to essential flights. Commercial aviation was being forced into a period of dramatic adaptation and evolution even before it had found its real identity as a mature industry.

These adaptations appear in Patricia O'Malley's "Carol Rogers" books, which take a somewhat different approach to women's place in aviation. O'Malley's own career supplies much of the background, for her work in the field was principally administrative. She joined the Civil Aeronautics Authority in 1938, working as the agency's director of publicity, then became manager of the publicity department of TWA, working out of Washington, DC. Her career gained her a degree of notice in feminist circles, and she went on to become a general advocate for the engagement of women in all aspects of aviation.[29] The "Carol Rogers" books show a range of ways in which women can find responsible work in the larger field of airline operations. A spin-off series, the "Caddie Palmer" books (1944-1946; two titles), shows its young heroine making her way not as a stewardess but in airline middle management.

O'Malley's *Wings for Carol* (1941), the series' initial volume, opens with the European-educated, convent-raised Carol Rogers, the orphaned daughter of a diplomat, enrolling as a stewardess candidate with Universal Airlines. She is accompanied by her best chum Foster Allen, like Carol a registered nurse, and the two progress steadily through their training. In the process, they meet pilots Grant Lowrie and Jack Prior, developing attachments to both. Carol's success in training stirs the jealousy of classmate Iris Wakefield, but leads her to other successes reflecting the glamor of a stewardess's job. She works as Universal's liaison with Hollywood, accompanying the mother of film star Lisa Tablay to a well-publicized reunion. By happy chance, Tablay's mother is a friend dating back to Carol's childhood in France, and the coincidence provides ample publicity fodder for Universal and Tablay's studio. She takes part in a national fashion tour when Morris and Harold Wapeer, New York clothing manufacturers, arrange to use Universal's new Stratoliner to publicize Wapeer's latest clothing lines. She makes her peace with Iris Wakefield when the two fly an emergency run with medical supplies for a flood-isolated city, and looks ahead to her coming career with Universal.

*Carol Rogers leaves a DC-3 with her male colleagues
the background. (Author's collection)*

That career takes a new turn in *Wider Wings* (1942) when the chief stewardess, noticing Carol's chafing under the Universal routine, suggests she look into an administrative job opening with Texas-based Benton Airways. A small, family-owned airline, Benton in many respects resembles Braniff Airways. Like its contemporary Braniff at the time, it is replacing its original fleet of aircraft with larger DC-2s and wants to start a stewardess service. Carol joins the company as Chief Stewardess, asks the Wapeers to design Southwestern-themed uniforms for the stewardesses, and shepherds the first class of candidates through its training. When she meets the wife of a Guatemalan diplomat, an old friend of her mother, she is invited to visit the family's home in Guatemala City. Carol accepts, using vacation time for the junket. She revels briefly in the exoticism of Guatemalan life, then flies on to Panama City to take part in Foster Allen's wedding to Jack Prior. The book ends with the news of the Japanese attack on Pearl Harbor, Grant Lowrie's announcement that he is going on active duty with the Army Air Corps, and Carol's agreement to a *de facto* engagement with him.[30]

War Wings for Carol (1943) finds Carol the assistant to the vice-president of New England Air Lines (NEA), which is flying supplies and ferrying aircraft for the fledgling Air Transport Command. She has resigned her job with Benton Airways, thinking that she and Grant would marry immediately; however, he is sent abroad on a hush-hush assignment, and Carol has had to find new work. She negotiates New England Air's purchase of an idle tourist camp to serve as housing for the growing NEA staff. She organizes a stewardess corps when NEA starts a small passenger service, again turning to the Wapeers for uniforms, and helps the army capture an on-site spy. She renews an acquaintance with Whitey McIntyre, a Benton mechanic who is now a co-pilot, and hires a local girl, Caddy Palmer, to help in the office. Given leave time, Carol flies to New York to visit with Foster and arrives just as Grant Lowrie's flight unexpectedly comes in from Asia. The two promptly set out to find a marriage license. They are facing the future together, but their ultimate status and the direction of their careers is left for the reader to reflect upon.

O'Malley shifts her attention from Carol to Caddy Palmer at this point, in *Airline Girl* (1944) relating how Caddy has joined TWA's publicity division in Washington, DC. There she reunites with Whitey McIntyre, and arranges the fanfare for the record-setting flight of a new airplane that is joining the line, the four-engined Lockheed Constellation. The other volume of Caddy's adventures, *Winging Her Way* (1946), finds Caddy taking over the publicity division when her supervisor is transferred to Paris. She briefs a reporter on the several stages of stewardess training, makes a national trip with a beauty consultant to publicize TWA's "Charm Classes" for its stewardesses, and flies with a plane-load of reporters as they observe the revolutionary technique of ground-controlled approach. When Whitey is discharged from the army, he takes an airline management job in South America; Caddy isn't yet ready to marry, but looks ahead to a future marriage/career with Whitey in Latin America.

O'Malley throughout both series makes a strong case for the breadth of stewardesses' knowledge and their pivotal role in the operations of an airline. Universal insists that its stewardesses have at least a passing familiarity with aircraft technology and operating procedures, a practice echoed by Carol when she sets up the training program for the Benton stewardess candidates. What's more, she insists upon candidates "who've read a lot and can think for themselves. Knowing what's going on in the world is half the battle with passengers." As trained nurses, the stewardesses constitute a disciplined corps that can accept new conditions on short notice. Dwelling upon this realization, Carol ruminates that commercial flying is an enterprise in which "miracles were accepted casually by men who seemed to realize no other existence than that above the earth.... Nurses were not surprised at miracles. They were used to them.... A nurse could keep her head in a time of emergency and could handle people well from her long experience with temperamental patients." Knowledge and skills, working together, make the women a valuable adjunct to the airline's operations.[31]

Throughout their work, the trainees are instilled with a sense of their responsibilities to themselves and to their employer. The stewardess's job, as a Universal official spells out early in the series, "is not easy and ... requires the peculiar combination of qualities that make a good diplomat." When those qualities are effectively employed, the outcome benefits both airline and passengers, and the stewardess is a necessary, even critical, part of the process: "The hostess represents the airline to the public.... A thousand people

*The original (pre-war) version of the Douglas DC-4, as featured in
Betty Baxter Anderson's* Peggy Wayne, Sky Girl *(1941) and Patricia O'Malley's*
Wings for Carol *(1941). National Air and Space Museum,
Smithsonian Institution (SI 89-70).*

worked hard in the treasury, engineering, operations, sales and
public relations departments so that the twenty-one people on each
airplane would be pleased. Actually in many cases it is the hostess
who either sells or unsells the individual company to the passengers." They, like their colleagues, work to carry out the airline's mission of service, and it becomes "the responsibility of every stewardess, *as a member of the crew of the airplane,* to keep this constant-
ly in mind."[32] As the airline's contact person with the traveling public, the stewardess is as essential to the operations of the enterprise
as the flight crew and engineering staff.

Perhaps because of O'Malley's own familiarity with commercial aviation, both the "Carol Rogers" books and the "Caddy
Palmer" books quietly reflect the changing nature of aircraft technology as the stories move from the pre-World-War II era to postwar times. Taken as a unit, the stories illustrate the evolution of
airplanes from the small ships of an earlier time to the four-
engined, high-flying craft of the late 1940s and after. Although the

DC-3 is never mentioned by name, it is unquestionably the air-plane in which Carol first learns her trade; she works in a twin-engined, tail-wheel landing gear craft that seats twenty-one pas-sengers. She gets a glimpse of United Air Lines' "flying laboratory," a refitted Boeing 247, "a bullet-nosed ship, standing closer to the ground than those the girls were used to seeing, [that] was painted a heavy battleship gray," when Grant Lowrie begins a stint of research flying. She is present when Universal introduces its "Stratoliner," an airplane, like Peggy Wayne's "Stratoliner," indis-tinguishable from the forty-seat Douglas DC-4 and representative of the latest stages in aeronautical progress.[33] Crashes, moreover, so prevalent in the early books, are rarely if ever mentioned, tacitly establishing the growing safety of modern aircraft. Carol is watch-ing technological history unfold as she carries out her duties.

Carol—and Caddy after her—also learn that a great part of that unfolding history is driven by a combination of technology and economics. Even before she leaves Universal, Carol and a technician friend agree that larger aircraft are going to be needed, and they marvel that the Stratoliner can carry up to sixty passengers. When she joins Benton Airways, she learns that the First Officer has been distributing box lunches to the passengers of its ten-passenger Lockheed Electras. The larger Douglas DC-2s about to join the line, with their more complex cockpits and fourteen-seat cabins, will require a dedicated cabin attendant. Finally, her time with New England Air Lines acquaints her with DC-3s refitted as C-47s and DC-4s altered to C-54s, both stripped of their airline luxury for the new mission of war support. Caddy Palmer then picks up the thread as her work with TWA introduces her to the Lockheed Constellation, a four-engined, sixty-seat, high-speed liner that would ultimately make non-stop transcontinental and trans-Atlantic flights practicable. She is present when it makes its initial flight for TWA in April, 1944 witnessing its arrival following a seven-hour flight from California with Howard Hughes and TWA president Jack Frye at the controls.[34] As she and Carol both come to understand, when the demand for airline seats grows, the technology must grow with it and new super-ships like the Constellation are the result.

The issue of what properly constitutes "woman's work" within the airlines also figures in O'Malley's series. Although O'Malley tacitly omits mention of pilot's status, the doors of aviation are otherwise open for women at all levels. Carol's boss at New England Air Lines, Mr. Ingram, talks with her about the company's overall procedures and goals, then goes on to muse:

> 'It's a big job for a girl and I thought a long time before I made up my mind to take you. But women must shoulder men's work, and I suppose we'll see more of it before this thing ends.'
>
> After a few minutes of reflection, during which Carol sat quietly, he added, 'And they always do it as well. . . or better. It's a sad commentary on the stronger sex, Miss Rogers, but it's true.'

Carol takes Ingram's concession to heart, easily shouldering the diverse duties and responsibilities of her new position, and going on to defend the ability of women against Whitey Palmer's condescension toward female air-traffic controllers. "Carol refused to let him dismiss her sex so lightly. 'It is not simple,' she said with spirit, challenging his masculine vanity. 'And you needn't be so patronizing. It takes brains and a pretty high I.Q. to hold down one of these jobs.'"[35] Carol's defense is not unexpected, but Ingram's acknowledgment that women can out-do men is. He is a seasoned executive in a traditionally male-dominated occupation, yet because of the pressures of war has come to realize that his previous assumptions were far from valid.

Caddy's work also provides O'Malley with an opportunity to comment upon the range of possibilities for women. She has already spoken of middle-level management and air controller's duties; when Caddy sets out to write a release detailing women at work around the TWA base, she is awed by her findings. A male crew chief tells her that his best mechanic, seen working on a brake assembly, is a woman. Interviewing her, Caddy is nonplused to discover that the mechanic "could fly, as well as repair planes, and that before the war had been a saleswoman for an advertising agency." As her search widens, she finds women carrying out diverse jobs throughout the shops. Some are doing laboratory work, others are overhauling engines, still others are shifting cargo, and yet more are skillfully welding and painting equipment. All of them, O'Malley observes, are "making good in most of the fields which had hitherto been one hundred per cent masculine." These occupations closely approximate real-life ones. Pan American employed 814 women mechanics in 1942, and one all-woman maintenance crew was recognized as the most accomplished of 1943.[36] From flight line to executive suite, there is a place for women in O'Malley's world. One precedent, however, still holds true: there was no place in that era for women in the cockpit.

Commercial aviation within the books is nonetheless open to women. Apart from actual control of an aircraft, it offers them many of the same career possibilities that it offers men. Like Peggy Wayne's boss before him, Caddy Palmer's boss, Mr. Baron, grows to understand that women's competence extends far beyond the home, and he spells out his understanding to Caddy:

> 'When the war broke out, the airline business was a man's world, but that's all changed. It's a woman's business as well now and we feel that it will continue to be so. And we want our girls to think of their jobs as careers, not just makeshifts until they marry, or get something else to do. We want them to take pride in working for us.'[37]

His vision is singularly far-reaching. He understands that women have made their place in the airline industry; that they will continue to fill that place and others in the future; that what the industry offers them is a lifetime career opportunity comparable to those found in other businesses. The stewardess is, and will continue to be, a necessary part of commercial aviation, but work in other capacities and at other levels is also opening to women, and Baron is ready, even eager, to accept them.

Other women commentators on the times seem to concur with O'Malley. The journalist Dickey Meyer, writing in *Girls at Work in Aviation* (1943), lists sixteen areas in which women were contributing to the defense effort; these, she suggests, can well carry over into peacetime. The women working in the realm of aviation "give us a glimpse beyond the present," looking toward a future when "everyone will fly in the postwar world." That future will come about in great part because it has been placed squarely in [the women's] own hands, and they are grasping it firmly." They can grasp that opportunity because they have learned "that there are no remaining doors closed to them simply because they are women."[38] Slowly but steadily, women are making their way in all ranks of the industry, and their access to the cockpit may yet come about.

Notes

1. See F. Robert van der Linden, *Airlines & Air Mail: The Post Office and the Birth of the Commercial Aviation Industry* (Lexington: University Press of Kentucky, 2002). An account of the development of lighted airways is Robert Dane, "Midnight Suns of the Air Mail," *Aero Digest* 7 (July 1925): 12-18.

2. James P. Wines, "The 48 Hr. Coast to Coast Air-Rail Service of Transcontinental Air Transport," *Aviation* 27 (6 July 1929): 26-29; "All Aboard the Lindbergh Limited!" *Literary Digest* 100 (2 March 1929): 54, 56-58; R. E. G. Davies, *Airlines of the United States Since 1914* (Washington, DC: Smithsonian Institution Press, 1998), 56-108.

3. Sherman J. Kline, "Development and Operation of the Safeway System," *Southern Aviation* 2 (15 October 1930): 16; Amelia Earhart, "Women's Influence on Air Transport Luxury," *Aeronautic Review* 8 (March 1930): 32.

4. "Putting Luxury in the Air," *Literary Digest* 112 (9 January 1932): 34; Francis Vivian Drake, "Pegasus Express," *Atlantic Monthly* 149 (June 1932): 670; Reginald M. Cleveland, "Air Transport Becomes luxurious," *Scientific American* 149 (December 1933): 265; "Skylounge Luxury," *National Aeronautics* 15 (February 1937): 22-23; J. C. Furnas, "Mr. Milquetoast in the Sky," *Scribner's* 104 (September 1938): 7.

5. "Women Take to the Air," *U.S. Air Services* 15 (May 1930): 44-45; "Airwomen," *Time* 29 (8 March 1937): 48-49; Julietta K. Arthur, "Airways to Earning," *Independent Woman* 19 (February 1940): 34-35, 55-56.

6. Horace S. Mazet, "Pro Patria et Gloria," *Sportsman Pilot* 6 (August 1931): 30.

7. "Thaden, Louise McPhetridge," Document File CT-141000-01, National Air and Space Museum Library, Smithsonian Institution: Washington, DC; Lauren Kessler, *The Happy Bottom Riding Club: The Life and Times of Pancho Barnes* (New York: Random House, 2000), 100-105.

8. Frederick Graham, "Air Currents," *New York Times*, 23 June 1940, XX9; "Women for War Flying," *New York Times*, 11 August 1940, 114; Julietta K. Arthur, "Now You Can Learn to Fly," *Independent Woman* 19 (October 1940): 336; "Army May Use Women to Ferry New Airplanes," *New York Times*, 3 July 1941, 12. The Women Flyers of America disbanded in 1954.

9. Steve A. Stimpson, quoted in Frank J. Taylor, *High Horizons: Daredevil Flying Postmen to Modern Magic Carpet—the United Air Lines Story*, new Rev. ed. (New York: McGraw-Hill, 1964), 70-71. For the RN uniform, see W. B. Courtney, "High-Flying Ladies," *Collier's* 90 (28 August 1932): 30, and Taylor, *High Horizons*, 68.

10. Courtney, "High-Flying Ladies," 30; Francis Vivian Drake, "Air Stewardess," *Atlantic Monthly* 151 (February 1933): 186; "The Service is Excellent as the Stewardess Profession Grows Up," *Airwoman* 2 (August 1935): 11; "Flying Supermen and Superwomen," *Literary Digest* 122 (14 November 1936): 22; Frederick Graham, "Winged Hostess," *New York Times Magazine*, 7 January 1940, 117.

11. "AM 23-3: NK to GX," *Fortune* 19 (February 1939): 112, 114. In Patricia O'Malley's *Wings for Carol* (New York: Dodd, Mead, 1941), a senior stewardess, completing her checklist, says to Carol, "From now on we are responsible for the ship" (89-90).

12. "All Aboard the Lindbergh Limited!" 54, 56; "The Tri-Motored Ford Air Transport," *Aero Digest* 10 (June 1927): 582; Peter M. Bowers, *Boeing Aircraft Since 1916* (New York: Funk & Wagnalls, 1968), 122-126; F. Robert van der Linden, *The Boeing 247: The First Modern Airliner* (Seattle: University of Washington Press,

1991), 75-76, 88-89; "Boeing's new Model 247 transport," *Aviation* 32 (April 1933): 124-125.

13. Douglas J. Ingells, *The Plane that Changed the World: a Biography of the DC-3* (Fallbrook, CA: Aero Publishers, 1966), 28-46, 72, 85-89; Max Karant, "Air-Sleepers On American Line," *Popular Aviation* 18 (January 1936): 25-26, 72; "Sleepers: New Douglas Ships Have More Lift, Space, Comfort," *Newsweek* 8 (4 July 1936): 25.

14. Davies, *Airlines of the United States since 1914,* 267-287; Bowers, *Boeing Aircraft Since 1916,* 201-206; Roger E. Bilstein, *Flight in America: From the Wrights to the Astronauts,* rev. ed. (Baltimore: Johns Hopkins University Press, 1994), 161-63; "DC-4," *Time* 31 (23 May 1938): 33-34, 36-38. Ernest K. Gann, *Fate is the Hunter* (New York: Simon & Schuster, 1961) is an impressionistic but vivid memoir of flying in the early days of the ATC.

15. Davies, *Airlines of the United States since 1914,* 287-292; "Air Stewardesses Mark Anniversary," *Western Flying* 25 (May 1945): 62, 84. See also Dickey Meyer, *Girls at Work in Aviation* (Garden City: Doubleday, Doran & Co., 1943): 198-199, and Alfred Toombs, "Flight Nurse," *Woman's Home Companion* 70 (December 1944): 36, 117-118.

16. "The Service is Excellent as the Stewardess Profession Grows Up," 11; Courtney, "High-Flying Ladies," 29-30; Drake, "Air Stewardess," 185-193; Leo Freedman, "The Duties of an Air Hostess," *Popular Aviation* 12 (February 1933): 81-82, 124-125.

17. Ruthe S. Wheeler, *Jane, Stewardess of the Air Lines* (Chicago: Goldsmith Publishing Co., 1934), 31-33; R. E. G. Davies, *Airlines of the United States since 1914* (Washington, DC: Smithsonian Institution Press, 1982), 653, 658. See also Peter M. Bowers, *Boeing Aircraft Since 1916* (New York: Funk & Wagnalls, 1968), 122-126, 182-187.

18. For the Model 247, see F. Robert van der Linden, *The Boeing 247: The First Modern Airliner* (Seattle: University of Washington Press, 1991); Wheeler, *Jane, Stewardess of the Air Lines,* 210, 212.

19. Frank J. Taylor, *High Horizons,* rev. ed. (New York: McGraw-Hill Book Co., 1964), 71; Wheeler, *Jane, Stewardess of the Air Lines,* 102-103.

20. Taylor, *High Horizons,* 71; Wheeler, *Jane, Stewardess of the Air Lines,* 18. Emphasis added.

21. Wheeler, *Jane, Stewardess of the Air Lines,* 24,134.

22. Margaret Case Harriman, "Ring Bell for Hostess," *Woman's Home Companion* 64 (December 1937): 12; Betty Baxter Anderson, *Peggy Wayne, Sky Girl* (New York: Cupples & Leon, 1941), 3, 13, 60-61, 99-110; Taylor, *High Horizons,* 71. Jacqueline Cochran, holder of numerous speed records and the first woman to fly faster than sound, is discussed more fully in Chapter 6.

23. Anderson, *Peggy Wayne, Sky Girl*, 85, 91, 11-12; Taylor, *High Horizons*, 71. For selectivity, see "5,000 Seek 20 Jobs as Air Stewardesses," *New York Times*, 17 October 1939, 27.

24. Anderson, *Peggy Wayne, Sky Girl*, 292-30, 141-142, 187. For the Boeing 314 and the DC-4, see "Giants of 1938," *Aviation* 37 (July 1938): 20-21, 30-33.

25. Anderson, *Peggy Wayne, Sky Girl*, 110-111. For the Civilian Pilot Training Program, see Dominick A. Pisano, *To Fill the Skies With Pilots: The Civilian Pilot Training Program* (Washington, DC: Smithsonian Institution Press, 1993).

26. Anderson, *Peggy Wayne, Sky Girl*, 173-175.

27 Ibid., 244-246.

28. Drew Whitelegg, *Working the Skies: The Fast-Paced, Disorienting World of the Flight Attendant* (New York: New York University Press, 2007), 38.

29. Back cover matter, O'Malley, *Wings for Carol* (New York: Dodd, Mead, 1941); Julietta K. Arthur, "Airways to Earning," *Independent Woman* 19 (February 1940): 35; Patricia O'Malley, "Women With Wings," *Senior Scholastic* 42 (19-24 April 1943): 23-24.

30. For the Braniff parallels, see "Braniff Welds the Southwest," *National Aeronautics* 15 (July 1937): 10-11.

31. O'Malley, *Wings for Carol*, 46, 57; Patricia O'Malley, *Wider Wings* (New York: Junior Literary Guild and Greystone Press, 1942), 53, 55, 70.

32. O'Malley, *Wings for Carol*, 23,32 (italics added); O'Malley, *Wider Wings*, 139-140.

33. O'Malley, *Wings for Carol*, 88-93, 66, 212. For the "flying laboratory," see William Garvey and David Fisher, *The Age of Flight: A History of America's Pioneering Airline* (Greensboro, NC: Pace Communications, 2002), 85-86.

34. O'Malley, *Wings for Carol*, 206; O'Malley, *Wider Wings*, 24, 29-30, 34; Patricia O'Malley, *War Wings for Carol* (New York: Dodd, Mead, 1943), 58-59; Patricia O'Malley, *Airline Girl* (New York: Dodd, Mead, 1944), 193. For the Constellation, see Davies, *Airlines of the United States Since 1914*, 326-329. Although given the designation C-69, the Constellation did not enter military service until after war's end.

35. O'Malley, *War Wings for Carol*, 19, 152. Ellipsis in the original.

36. O'Malley, *Airline Girl*, 51-52; Deborah G. Douglas, *American Women and Flight since 1940* (Lexington: University Press of Kentucky, 2004), 36.

37. Patricia O'Malley, *Winging Her Way* (New York: Dodd, Mead, 1946), 145. "Baron's" name, with its evocation of the autocratic lord of a medieval fiefdom, may be an inadvertent pun, for his heart is otherwise in all respects in the right place.

38. Meyer, *Girls at Work in Aviation*, 205, 208-209.

*Norman Rockwell's "Rosie the Riveter," a popular personification
of the woman war-worker. Norman Rockwell Museum, Stockbridge, Massachusetts.
Printed by permission of the Norman Rockwell Family Agency.
Copyright © 1943 Norman Rockwell Family Entities.*

CHAPTER 6

World War II,

Working Women, and Aviation:

1940-1960

After the United States entered World War II in December 1941, customs, conventions, and attitudes seemed to change for both men and women. Men were needed to man the weapons and fly the aircraft of the modern military; women, the workplace recognized, were needed to fill the home front jobs once held by men. These jobs came in many forms and at many levels, blue collar to white collar, clerical to executive. For many Americans, however, the iconic image of Rosie the Riveter personified women's role in the war effort. Whether embodied in the ubiquitous poster featuring a dungaree-clad woman, her hair wrapped in a turban, brandishing a fist and proclaiming "We Can Do It!" or in Norman Rockwell's memorable *Saturday Evening Post* cover of 29 May 1943, showing a muscular Rosie at ease, eating her lunchtime sandwich while resting her feet on a copy of *Mein Kampf,* the woman engaged in heavy industry became the symbol of the wartime working woman.

Nature and art merged to make the image a central one in American life. Recognizing the patterns imposed upon women's vision of themselves prior to the coming of war, government agencies embarked on a concentrated publicity campaign "to convince women that they had the stamina and skill to do jobs formerly held by men." In magazine stories and advertisements, on billboards or in cinema newsreels, the American public saw image after image of women ably dealing with jobs traditionally considered "men's." Whether shown as welders, machinists, riveters, or builders and operators of heavy machinery, these women workers were presented in ways that "not only publicized their increased presence but also helped validate their new roles."[1] Almost overnight, women were being told that they could—and *should*—take their place alongside men throughout the industrial workplace. The effect of this campaign was extraordinary.

Women were obviously needed throughout the workplace as the nation shifted to wartime status. Many were absorbed into office and clerical work, reflecting the needs of burgeoning local and national agencies and the work traditionally assigned to women. Others, though, in increasingly significant numbers, turned to industry. The transition was not entirely smooth. Some heavy industries, such as ship-building and steel-making, initially resisted adding women, as did their unions. When United States Steel began employing women, however, the female workers readily adapted to assignments as welders, crane operators, furnace operators, foundry helpers, and comparable jobs, establishing "that in time of crisis no job is too tough for American women." Other defense plants preparing explosives, ammunition, aircraft, and other necessary supplies quickly moved to put women workers on the assembly line. Ammunition plants had over 100,000 women workers by 1943, while better than 250,000 women were employed making electrical equipment. Before the war, women constituted roughly 1 percent of the aviation industry workforce; by late 1943, they were some 65 percent of that workforce.[2]

These employment trends continued until more than 25 percent of the 16 million working women in the United States were engaged in defense industry work. That work had its benefits and its shortcomings. The eventual acceptance of women workers by the industrial unions offered them a chance to move up within the workplace. Although the wages paid women were often lower than those paid men, they were still high for the times (sometimes as much as 40 percent higher than comparable peacetime wages), giving women workers an unaccustomed source of income and a new degree of financial independence. The jobs were often physically demanding, and until the women performing them built up their muscles and their skill, they frequently fell short of the quotas assigned men. Yet, once adapted to the work, the women almost always proved the equal of their male counterparts, and sometimes their superiors. In the workplace and in the public mind, they were cementing the lasting image of "Rosie the Riveter."[3]

Women also found a place in the military. The first of the armed forces to accept women was the army, inaugurating the Women's Army Auxiliary Corps (WAAC) in June 1942. This organization had been proposed in Congress prior to the United States' entering the war, but was not authorized until after Pearl Harbor. Initial limits on the number of women to be accepted were quickly raised to 150,000 and, in 1943, the WAAC was formally integrated into the army as the Women's Army Corps (WAC). Other services quickly followed suit as congressional approval was given. The navy, which had proposed a women's auxiliary as early as 1938, added the Women Accepted for Volunteer Emergency Service (WAVES) in July 1942. The WAVES were followed by the Coast Guard's SPARs, the name taken from the Guard motto, "*Semper Paratus*—Always Ready," in November, 1942, and the Marine Corps Women's Reserve (MCWR) in February 1943.[4]

Women's participation in the four service auxiliaries was substantial. By war's end, some 350,000 women overall were a part of the United States military. WAVES enlistment reached 86,000 by 1945; the SPARs achieved close to 11,000; and the MCWR numbered 8,500. The remainder constituted the WAC, the only one of the four auxiliaries to include African Americans. For all the enthusiasm reflected by the women recruits, however, enlistment provided them little change. Many WAAC volunteers, a contemporary report said, "wanted to fly bombers [and] shoot big guns." Instead, they were directed to duties as "typists, hygienists, chauffeurs, cooks, bakers, accountants, telegraphers [and] the aircraft warning service." All of these duties came under the rubric of traditional "women's work." These same duties characterized much of women's contributions to the other services, although the navy and the Marine Corps offered a somewhat greater variety through their aviation branches. There women found work as gunnery instructors, navigators, photographic interpreters, air traffic controllers, metal-workers, electronics technicians, parachute-riggers, and other special applications. The Army Air Corps, in contrast, restricted its women recruits largely to aircraft warning duties, and even these jobs were transferred to civilian operators by early 1943. Although all of the services operated aeronautical wings, none permitted women to pilot aircraft.[5]

As in peacetime, women who wanted to fly in the national service had to look elsewhere. A 1942 article surveying civilian work in the aeronautical industry offered the possibility of women's serving as flight controllers, meteorologists, and tower communicators, but called these positions "difficult and hard to come by" and glossed over the absence of flying work by noting that "the job of flying airplanes is one of the least that women can and are doing in war service." Some women found positions as civilian flight instructors teaching air cadet recruits to fly or as civilian test pilots for the aircraft manufacturers, carrying out "check-out" flights as airplanes came off the assembly line, but these appointments, too, were comparatively rare.[6] It remained for two determined women, both of them pilots and both prominent, to create a means of employing qualified women in flying duty.

The first of these was Nancy Harkness Love, a one-time employee of the Bureau of Air Commerce, an occasional air racer, and a pioneer in testing tricycle landing gear for aircraft, flying the Hammond Y craft submitted for Eugene Vidal's "poor man's plane" competition. She proposed a corps of women pilots with commercial licenses and cross-country flying experience who would fly training and other light aircraft from their factories to their assigned bases. The commander of the Army Air Transport Command accepted the proposal, and, on 10 September 1942, the army announced the creation of the Women's Auxiliary Ferrying Command (WAFs). Although authorized by the military and engaged in flying military aircraft, the WAFs remained civilians, employed only as civil service workers; their initial authorization was for a corps of fifty women, forty to fly and ten to deal with administrative work. Nancy Love was appointed commander, and the Service began its recruiting. By July 1943, when the group underwent a change in organization, its pilots were actively engaged in ferrying high-performance fighter craft, and Love herself had won authorization to fly the Boeing B-17 four-engined heavy bomber.[7]

Although the WAFs faced a degree of opposition from within the ranks of the Army Air Corps, a greater challenge came in the form of the second woman, Jacqueline Cochran, an aviation celebrity who had her own ideas about women's place in military flying. Cochran was an ambitious, often abrasive person whose life and career attested to her determination to achieve her goals whatever the cost. She was largely self-taught, lacking even a high-school education, and began her rise to prominence as a teenaged hairsetter in a Florida beauty shop. Using the skills she learned there, she worked her way to New York and found a job at the fashionable Antoine's beauty salon in the Saks Fifth Avenue department store. The contacts made at Antoine's enabled her to involve herself in New York society, where she met investor Floyd Odlum. After a four-year affair, the two married in 1936 and Cochran began her climb to aviation prominence.[8]

Cochran earned her initial flying license in 1932, followed by her commercial and transport ratings in 1933. She immediately began a series of publicity-seeking flights: she was the only American to enter the England-to-Australia MacRobertson Race of 1934, she took part in the cross-country Bendix Race of 1935, and

Top: *Nancy Harkness Love and Frank Hawks with a Gwinn Aircar Model 1.*
Permission to reprint from the Ianuzzi Family and H.A. Bruno LLC.
Above: *Vincent Bendix, Jacqueline Cochran, and Major Alexander de Seversky*
(l-r) following Cochran's 1938 Bendix Trophy Race victory in a Seversky Pursuit
(background). National Air and Space Museum,
Smithsonian Institution (SI 84-14781).

she set her first speed record (the women's world record for unlimited speed) in 1937. In the same period she established a cosmetics business, "Jacqueline Cochran's Wings to Beauty Cosmetics," undertook a national marketing campaign for her products, and opened beauty salons under her name in Chicago and Los Angeles. Meanwhile, she flew. By the end of 1937 she held six national and world speed records and had won first place in the Women's Division of the Bendix Race. *National Aeronautics* called her "one of the world's outstanding feminine pilots," placing her alongside such notables as Juan Terry Tripp, president of Pan American Airlines; Roscoe Turner, the only racing pilot to win the Thompson Trophy three times; and World War I ace Eddie Rickenbacker. *U.S. Air Services* featured her on its cover in January 1938, dubbing her "America's outstanding aviatrix."[9] She was gaining prominence within aviation circles.

Cochran soon began to attract notice outside those circles. In 1938, the *New York Times Magazine* featured an article dubbing her "First Lady of the Air Lanes." She was presented with a gold medal by First Lady Eleanor Roosevelt on the occasion of her winning the Harmon Trophy two years in succession. (The Clifford B. Harmon Trophy honored the outstanding woman flier of the year; Cochran would go on to win it a total of fourteen times.) She was widely publicized for piloting an Army Air Corps Lockheed Hudson bomber during a trans-Atlantic flight in 1941, and a second article in the *New York Times Magazine* in the same year spoke of her seventeen speed records and proclaimed her "the No. 1 woman flier of America." Her activity continued after the Second World War, when in 1953 she became the first woman to break the sound barrier, flying a Canadair F-86 Sabre jet, and, in 1964, flying a Lockheed F-104G Starfighter, the first woman to surpass Mach 2 with a record speed of almost 1,500 mph.[10]

Cochran had strong views about the place of women in wartime aviation, and used her celebrity to press her case. As early as 1939 she had written to Eleanor Roosevelt recommending the use of women pilots in the national service. In July 1941, she submitted a formal plan for creating a squadron of women pilots within the Army Air Corps to ferry aircraft. When Nancy Love received authorization to organize the WAFs, Cochran resubmitted her proposal and, on 14 September 1942 (barely four days after the announcement of Love's appointment), was named director of women's flying training. This was a program to train women pilots in cross-country flying, creating a pool of pilots to be used for non-combat flying "to release as many male pilots as possible." It was designated the Women's Flying Training Detachment (WFTD) and, like the WAFs, was a civilian enterprise. Cochran began recruiting immediately, and, by early 1943, was overseeing the WFTD at Avenger Field in Sweetwater, Texas.[11]

A degree of rivalry quickly developed between Love and Cochran, as each sought greater support for her training enterprise. The rivalry was peacefully resolved in mid-1943, when General Henry H. ("Hap") Arnold, Commanding General of the Army Air Corps, appointed Cochran Director of Women Pilots in the Air Forces and reassigned Love to administrative duties in the ferrying division of the Air Transport Command. The two programs were consolidated under Cochran's supervision and renamed the Women Airforce Service Pilots (WASP). From this consolidation came one of the most successful—and little-known—operations of the Second World War. Despite an initial ignoring of them by the press, the organization attracted a steady stream of volunteers from throughout the country, and graduated a total of 1,074 women pilots before its disbanding in 1944.[12]

During the eighteen months of the group's existence, it amassed an impressive record. WASP duties ranged from ferrying aircraft and working as check pilots to carrying out engineering tests and towing targets for anti-aircraft and aerial gunnery practice. In ferrying operations alone, the organization flew 9,224,000 miles and ferried seventy-seven types of aircraft, training planes, bombers, and high-performance fighters constituting every version of aircraft in active service. WASPs demonstrated the ease of flying the Martin B-26 medium bomber to reluctant airmen, who feared its high landing speeds. Several were checked out to fly the Boeing B-29, the most advanced bomber of the war. One, Ann Baumgartner, worked in flight testing at Wright Field, and became the first woman to fly the XP-59, the United States' first jet aircraft. The work was not without its hazards; thirty-eight of the women were killed in crashes during the life of the program. Yet, despite the gloomy predictions of male critics, the WASP's fatal accident rate of 0.060 percent per thousand hours flight time marginally bettered that of male pilots (0.062 percent) and their overall accident rate of 0.693 percent per thousand hours was notably better than the rate for male fliers (0.707 percent).[13]

As the WASP program flourished, it began to draw media attention. Some was favorable. Barbara Selby, writing in *Flying* in 1943, gave a laudatory overview of the program and noted the diverse backgrounds of many of the graduates, who ranged from a public relations counselor to the wife of an FBI agent. *Life* magazine, in a report also published in 1943, wrote of "Girl Pilots" and featured several pages (including its cover) of photographs showing the WASPs in training at Avenger Field, although putting somewhat more emphasis on the women's glamour than upon their flying skills. John Stuart talked approvingly of "The WASP" in *Flying* in early 1944, while Marjorie Kimler, in "They've Done It Again" in March 1944, described her WASP training for readers of the *Ladies' Home Journal*. Other accounts, however, were sharply critical, and increasingly preached the injustices being worked upon qualified male fliers. By mid-1944, *Time* magazine, in "Unnecessary and Undesirable?," reported on a Congressional committee's findings that the program was expensive and unnecessary.[14]

Driving the criticism was a growing protest from male pilots who, as civilian flight instructors, Army Air Force pilot-instructors, and army air cadets, had been exempt from duty in the "walking army" of front-line troops. By 1944, the war was clearly going in the

Allies' favor, and more forces were needed on the ground than in the air. The protest rose to a crescendo when the air force proposed militarizing the still-civilian WASP, making them an official branch of the army as were the WAC. The action would free still more men for ground combat; Jacqueline Cochran endorsed the measure and gave it her full support. However, critics claimed such a move would unfairly discriminate against male pilots, giving their work to women and putting them unnecessarily in harm's way. A strenuous lobbying campaign on behalf of the men won the day; Congress refused to militarize the WASP and the Army Air Force, given no other option, disbanded the program as of 20 December 1944.[15] Women pilots found themselves back where they started, and perhaps even worse off than before the war.

As war's end neared, public attitudes toward working women also underwent a profound change. Whereas Rosie the Riveter had been held up for admiration, women in the factories and the trades were now seen as threats to the returning veterans, holding jobs that the men badly needed. More and more, these women came to be seen as a hindrance to demobilization, and the national media, which "had exhorted women to work in the factory . . . , began to encourage women to return to the home and family." Mary Anderson, head of the Department of Labor's Women's Bureau, discussed the return of women to the workplace in the *New York Times Magazine* as early as 1943, arguing for the protection of their jobs. On the other hand, a 1944 editorial in *Life* magazine quoted statistics showing that "54% of the women now working want to quit when peace comes."[16] The public soon had an opportunity to see what war's end might bring.

Factories began the sudden and unexplained laying-off of women as early as August 1944, with dismissals out of proportion to the number of women actually working. Maureen Honey, an expert on the phenomenon of Rosie the Riveter, remarks that "Disruptions to family life caused it to become highly valued and . . . women were expected to subordinate personal ambition in order to bolster the family unit. These tendencies were accelerated, not initiated, by the demobilization period when social readjustment was occurring on a massive scale." And massive it was. In mid-1946, barely nine months after the war's end, the then director of the Women's Bureau called the readjustment "the most tremendous reshuffling of human resources . . . . that the country ever has known." Women no longer needed in the workplace were expected to give way to men; their place, even more so than it had been prior to the war, was in the home. For those women who hoped to fly, there were once again few options remaining beyond taking up the work of the airline stewardess.[17]

As the airlines returned to full-time commercial service, they also faced changes. Aviation technology had produced bigger aircraft capable of longer flights. Prior to the war, the only four-engined land plane flying in commercial service was the Boeing Model 307 Stratoliner, and it flew only from July 1940 through December 1941 before being called into military service. By war's end, four-engined craft were commonplace, their technology perfected by the Douglas C-54, the Boeing B-17, the Consolidated B-24, and the pressurized, high-altitude Boeing B-29. With greater size came greater range, so that the Douglas DC-4 (and its successor, the DC-6) and the Lockheed Constellation, all of them four-engined and now pressurized, were capable of transcontinental and transoceanic flights. Postwar developments included the Douglas DC-6B and DC-7, along with the Boeing Model 377 Stratocruiser, all of which did notable service in opening the Pacific area to commercial flight.[18]

The larger aircraft, for their part, required larger crews. The two-man cockpit of the Boeing 247 and the Douglas DC-3 became a thing of the past, as airlines added flight engineers, navigators, and radio operators to the crew. Larger aircraft also meant larger numbers of passengers per plane, and these required more stewardesses. Winning and keeping those passengers compelled the airlines to renew their efforts to "sell" commercial aviation. Airlines had earlier dropped their requirement of nursing certification for stewardesses, and some even conceded that while a college degree for a stewardess was an asset, it was not a necessity. This action opened the door to the employment of many young women who otherwise would have been ineligible for the work and gave the airlines a greater opportunity to shape their corporate images. Where once they had touted nursing-qualified stewardesses as the personification of professionalism and capability, the airlines now placed new emphasis on stewardesses' looks and personality. They sought passengers—not just *new* passengers, but those who might routinely be flying on a competing airline—and did so by creating advertisements portraying air travel as reliable, comfortable, *and* accompanied by attractive young women.

The airlines also had to deal with a dramatic shift in postwar attitudes toward women in general. Although the independent, tough-minded Rosie the Riveter had been an admired *persona* during the war, postwar American women were increasingly urged to return to the home. There they would shed their wartime shell of mechanical and technological expertise and become, once again, wives, mothers, and home-makers. This attitude extended even to what in the past had been seen as promising career paths. Now, rather than being a means to an end, women's careers became thought of as work to be pursued while waiting for marriage. In the public mind, the ultimate goal of a woman in the workplace was not to rise in her occupation, but rather to achieve the security of home, family, and domesticity. Nowhere was this more apparent than in the work of the airline stewardess. As Kathleen M. Barry points out, the surgically deft, professionally capable prewar stewardess now became "a young woman enjoying the chance to travel briefly while training for the ultimate female 'profession' of home-making."[19] Such an image brought its own set of problems for airline management and stewardess candidates alike, for it entailed the combining of an image of wholesome attractiveness with that of the coolly capable cabin stewardess, able to deal with all exigencies from in-flight emergencies to the skillful arranging of a meal-time dinner tray.

The shifting world of the airline stewardess appears early in the wartime and postwar series, and grows in prominence as the books proceed. Elisabeth Lansing's "Nancy Naylor" books (1939-1947; six titles), are the only stewardess stories to deal overtly with World War II, taking their young heroine through stewardess training and service and on into military service. Even the formula, however, yields to wartime circumstances, and Lansing's stewardess must deal with issues and situations unanticipated by Jane Cameron or Peggy Wayne. Stewardesses' lives and activities appear in a new and complex context, and the dream of women's achieving the cockpit, already fading, dims still further as the rosy image of a home and family grows in importance.

Lansing, a Rhode Island-born writer and editor, began her "Nancy Naylor" books in 1939. She had already published a tourist's guide to New York for young people, and went on to write nearly three dozen other books, including the "Ann Bartlett" series (1941-1946; five titles) about a navy nurse, and a scattering of other works of fiction and non-fiction. The "Nancy Naylor" stories appeared as airline stewardesses were beginning to emerge as distinctive, even respected figures, and they chronicle the transition of a young woman from graduate nurse to New England housewife. Lansing also to a degree makes readers aware of the secondary effects of war, for Nancy's life and attitudes, like those of her husband-to-be, are affected by their wartime experiences overseas.

Sky Service (1939), the first of the series, opens with twenty-one-year-old Nancy Naylor, a graduate nurse living with her parents in Granville, Illinois, enrolling as a stewardess trainee with Consolidated Airlines. The job's attraction for her, apart from its singularly high pay, is the inherent excitement of flying. Her attorney father and homemaker mother are initially taken aback, but reluctantly endorse her decision. At Consolidated's headquarters in Newark, New Jersey, Nancy befriends Elly Jackson, who is unabashedly seeking a husband; Jean Fowler, who becomes her best friend; and co-pilot Jim Taylor, who is immediately attracted to her. Her training complete, Nancy is momentarily caught up in the arrest of a spy for whom she has hidden a packet of secret papers, but establishes her innocence and is assigned to Consolidated's base in Kansas City.

Flights with Jean and Elly become largely routine, with two notable exceptions. In the first, Nancy's natural empathy impresses a fragile old woman. The woman proves to be the widow of a wealthy oil man, and, struck by Nancy's patent sincerity, leaves her a legacy of five thousand dollars. Nancy later uses this windfall for flying lessons. The other comes when Nancy's flight from Chicago to Kansas City with her young brother Tommy on board is forced down by bad weather. Jim, who has been promoted to captain and is flying the craft, ventures into the snow to seek help, leaving Nancy to deal with the injured co-pilot and the frightened passengers. This she manages with unruffled competence, splinting the former's broken arm and calming the latter with time-filling games. Jim returns with help, the passengers and crew are carried to safety, and Jim tells Nancy of his affection for her.

The second book, *Nancy Naylor: Air Pilot* (1941), finds Nancy working out of La Guardia Airport in New York. When Jim Taylor resigns his post to become an army flight instructor, Nancy joins the Women Flyers of America, takes flying lessons in her spare time, and earns her private pilot's license. She is accompanied in her lessons by timorous Grace Staples, and strikes up an acquaintance with Grace's dashing brother, Richard. Nancy continues her flying during off hours, and at one point helps the army rescue Jim following a training-flight crash. Her work with Consolidated, though, begins to suffer, and, after a series of in-flight misadventures, she is suspended from active duty. When Richard Staples learns that she is jobless, he engages Nancy to fly him in his private plane on business trips for his bank.

During these trips Nancy becomes suspicious of Staples's

actions. She sees him meeting with persons seemingly unrelated to a bank's business, and notes he is being followed by a dark, sinister, heavy-set man. Matters quickly come to a head: Staples is a spy, and uses Nancy to persuade Jim to slip him the plans for a secret new aviation device. Jim yields after Staples takes Nancy hostage and appears on the scene with the documents. As Staples takes the papers, the FBI, in the person of the sinister shadower, bursts in and captures him red-handed. Jim's leak of the device, as was Nancy's suspension, has been arranged by the FBI, and the book ends with Nancy eagerly hoping to be assigned to Consolidated's new route to South America.

She gets her wish in *Nancy Naylor Flies South* (1943), the third volume in the series. After special training for the Miami—Buenos Aires flight, Nancy moves to Miami. Her first flights on the route are tranquil, although she saves a small boy from a traffic accident during a layover in Cali, Colombia. The boy's parents, the Pendillo y Santara family, are duly grateful, and tell Nancy to feel free to call upon them at any time. Matters change, however, with Nancy's next flight. The aircraft is forced down at a deserted emergency field, and Nancy and her passengers are compelled to hike to safety through the jungle, fending off insects and threatening natives. Her next flight is still more eventful. The aircraft, with Nancy, the crew, and a famed diplomat traveling incognito, is hijacked, and Nancy discovers that Señor Pendillo is the leader of a Nazi spy ring. Nancy and the diplomat escape in a small plane with Nancy at the controls; the authorities capture the spies, and Nancy announces her intention of joining the Army Nurse Corps.

The fourth and fifth volumes, *Nancy Naylor: Flight Nurse* (1944) and *Nancy Naylor: Captain of Flight Nurses* (1946), take Nancy to war. In *Nancy Naylor: Flight Nurse* she resigns her stewardess job and enlists as a Flight Evacuation Nurse in the United States Army. During four weeks of basic military training and eight weeks of specialized flight nurse training she learns military protocol, new ways to deal with wounds, and the effects of poison gas.

Her training completed, she is assigned to Tunis in the North African Theater. There she flies in and out of combat zones, seeing a graphically described range of wounds and narrowly escaping injury herself. She and the wounded Jim cross paths and decide to marry at once, but Nancy is assigned to Italy and their plans must be postponed.

Nancy Naylor: Captain of Flight Nurses finds Nancy in England on the eve of D-Day (6 June 1944). With the invasion under way, she flies in and out of France tending the wounded and with Jim accompanies a unit of the French Resistance during the liberation of Paris. Her military superiors reprimand her for this show of irresponsibility, but she receives the *Croix de Guerre* for her aid to the French. Promoted to captain and put in charge of her own flight section, she is stranded behind German lines, but locates a group of escaping Allied soldiers and makes her way back to safety. Granted a month's leave, she returns to Illinois and happily renews her acquaintance with her family.

The final book of the series, *Nancy Naylor, Visiting Nurse* (1947), opens in September 1945; Nancy is twenty-four and has just been discharged from the nurse corps. Her father, to everyone's amazement, announces that he is closing his law practice and moving the entire family to the ancestral Naylor home in Lyons Center, Vermont. The family complies without protest, and he, Mrs. Naylor, and Tommy soon find their niches in Lyons Center. Nancy, however, troubled because of a series of coolly indifferent letters from Jim, cannot fit in. At last she agrees to help the town's sole physician, Doc Conway, who badly needs assistance in dealing with the larger health problems of the community. Nancy establishes herself as caring and competent, but is shattered when Jim abruptly breaks off their engagement.

Having no other recourse, she loses herself in her work, teaching a clueless young couple proper infant-care practices, encouraging immunizations among the townspeople, saving an injured boy from hypothermia in the snow, and setting up health examinations

Nancy Naylor remains unruffled as shells burst nearby.
A C-47 waits in the background. Copyright © 1944
Thomas Y. Crowell Co. (Author's collection).

at the one-room schoolhouse. Jim at this point reappears, confessing to Nancy that he has been confined in a neuropsychiatric ward. His wounds threatened to cost him an arm, and he slipped into a funk worrying that the loss of a limb would jeopardize Nancy's affection and their marriage. Nancy reassures him of her love whatever his physical condition, resigns her visiting nurse's appointment because Jim "won't hear of [her] keeping up [her] job," and looks forward to a future as neither stewardess nor nurse, but simply Mrs. James Taylor.[20]

A glowing Nancy Naylor prepares for life as a New
England matron. Copyright © 1947
Thomas Y. Crowell Co. (Author's collection).

Like their predecessors, the "Nancy Naylor" books present the
stewardess's work as desirable, absorbing, and responsible. Nancy
considers her being selected a piece of "the greatest luck," for flying
is "the most marvelous, exciting thing in the world!" She does not
hesitate to accept Consolidated's strictures on age, height, body
weight, and marital status, and even agrees to submitting a photograph because "they want you to be as nice looking as possible." As
their training proceeds, she and her classmates learn emergency
procedures, passenger service practices, and the operations of the
meteorological and radio services of the airline. These studies

admit them to a new and distinctive world, one that "would have been utterly bewildering to a layman."[21]

By book's end, Nancy is at home with the many facets of her work, from preparing meals in the DC-3's "compact little kitchenette" to improvising "bridge tournaments, cribbage, and any game her small supply of amusements afforded" to occupy her passengers. Eventually, she equates the nurse's profession with the stewardess's. As she embarks on her new venture as a visiting nurse, Nancy reflects that, "As an airline hostess and an Army nurse she had been actively engaged in nursing work." Now, as a visiting nurse, "she was once more doing something that she had a right to do; that all her training and skill had fitted her for."[22] The key words in this final passage are "once more." All along, she has been using her special knowledge and skills, making a stewardess's work as responsible and as professional as a nurse's. Both are acceptable (and admirable) occupations for a woman.

Adding to Nancy's belief in the responsibility of her job is her growing sense of being an accepted member of the aircrew. Her stewardess training and her work bring her to see Consolidated as a special family. Early on, as she visits Consolidated's crew room, she watches the pilots and the stewardesses exchange ready conversation and jokes; the room has, Nancy thinks, "an atmosphere of friendly goodwill . . . which made [her] long to be one of this exalted company and feel that she really belonged there." She soon blends in with the group, as her ripening relationship with Jim Taylor and her growing competence in her work give her confidence and recognition. This, in turn, leads to her identification with the corporation, the crew, and the airplane itself. Initially she loves "to feel that she was an essential part of [the] mighty plane and that her work was important to the functioning of its purpose." Her identification grows throughout the series, until readers are told that "Nancy was proud to be a *necessary* part of the smooth functioning of [the] huge monster."[23] The "exalted company" of flight crew and cabin crew work together in seamless cooperation, each contributing its essential part to the successful carrying-out of Consolidated's mission.

Paralleling these elements within the series is a third, quietly stated concern: that of women in the American workplace. Nancy's family do not oppose her *working;* she is, after all, a registered nurse and would normally be looking ahead to a career in medical services. Nor do they necessarily consider the stewardess's job a backward move; Mr. Naylor, in fact, sees it as "a glorious adventure, romantic and filled with promise." Yet Lansing looks beyond the middle class's easy acceptance of the stewardess's job to raise some issues concerning women in general. Nancy, for example, is far from being as vehement about the perceived superiority of men as is Peggy Wayne, yet she bristles at the rumor that Consolidated may use stewards rather than stewardesses on its Latin America flights: "'I suppose they think men are the only ones who are capable of flying on the South American run,' replied Nancy bitterly." Then her ingenuity and expertise in thwarting a hijacking lead even Señor Pendillo, steeped in the tradition of *machismo*, to give her grudging credit: "American women sometimes try to step into a man's world and learn their work. With women of your country it is well to take extra precautions."[24]

Still later, Nancy's wartime success in improvising a fiery tank trap wins awkward praise from a battle-hardened army sergeant, who was "obviously overcoming a tremendous reluctance to give credit for the idea to a mere girl." Even in the midst of a combat firefight, Nancy can feel a "sense of gratified pride" at the sergeant's yielding to acknowledge her contribution. And, although her female peers are not yet willing to see women in the cockpits of commercial aircraft, they can look ahead to a possible role for themselves in aviation. After Nancy enrolls in the Women Flyers of America, she embraces the group's sense of purpose: "Perhaps the day will come when [women] will even fly the commercial airplanes, though of course there is no definite plan for that. I imagine women would be used mostly to fly small relief planes to flood areas, or work of that sort which men do now. Oh, there are lots of things a woman flyer could do."[25]

Without turning her books into volumes of preaching, Lansing conveys to her young readers a sense that women are more than merely secondary personnel. They have necessary roles to fill and can, if given the opportunity, make their mark in occupations formerly thought to be the bailiwick of men. But, simultaneously, she feeds the growing image of the postwar domestic woman. Nancy, for all her experience and capabilities, dreams of marriage and a home possessing "an air of lived-in hospitality in its wide doorway and the many-paned Colonial windows which now glowed with the rosy light of the setting sun." Jim will commute to his managerial position with a regional airline and Nancy will tend the home— thinking, as she walks down the bridal aisle on her father's arm, "This is where I belong. . . . This is what I have been working and waiting for all my life."[26] She has made the transition from prewar professional to postwar wife.

The two stewardess series to emerge after World War II convey all of the preceding changes, and add some of their own. Their wholesome young protagonists are attractive, intelligent, and personable. Neither has a college degree nor any kind of professional certification, and both quickly attract a retinue of male admirers. Both easily make the transition from twenty-one passenger DC-3s to larger-capacity craft, and both revel in the exoticism of the romantic ports that longer-range flights make possible. While the authors of both series stress different facets of the airline industry and the stewardess's life, both nonetheless dwell upon the increasing domesticity of the stewardess's role, tacitly reflect the job's evolution from professional service to glamorous "domestic" service in the decades immediately following the war, and hint at still more changes to come as aircraft technology continues its progress.

First are the "Vicki Barr, Flight Stewardess" stories by Helen Wells and Julie Tatham (1947-1964; sixteen titles). The two writers had already shared the earlier "Cherry Ames" nursing series (1943-1968; twenty-six titles), so their second assignment was a natural one. Wells wrote twelve of the Barr books while three, *The Clue of the Broken Blossom* (1950), *Behind the White Veil* (1951), and *The Mystery at Hartwood House* (1952), were by Tatham. The last volume, *The Brass Idol Mystery* (1964), was published as by "Wells," but was actually written by pulp novelist Walter B. Gibson.[27] For all of their claim to be stewardess stories, Vicki Barr's adventures, starting in 1947, are just that: adventures. The daughter of an Illinois economics professor, Vicki yearns for excitement in her life and turns to Federal Airlines to find it. Though she has only two years of college and is underage (she is twenty while Federal has set twenty-one as a minimum), her looks and personality win her a spot in a stewardess training class and she sets out on her new life.

The first book, *Silver Wings for Vicki* (1947), briefly relates her training, introduces a cadre of close friends, notably Minnesotan Jean Cox, who has a pilot's license, and Charmion Wilson from New Hampshire, young widow of a famous test pilot. It also supplies the *de rigeur* male admirers—the Lindberghian copilot Dean Fletcher and the newspaper reporter Pete Carmody, who are joined later by flight instructor Bill Avery. In her first assignment, working a New York to Memphis route, Vicki encounters a range of notables who reflect the airlines' glorification of air travel: a Brazilian diplomat, a nuclear scientist, and a famed woman sculptor. Celebrities notwithstanding, Vicki grows suspicious of a succession of men carrying identical briefcases, initiates an inquiry, and uncovers a jewel-smuggling ring. Acclaim follows, and she is on her way as stewardess *and* as detective.

Succeeding volumes steadily emphasize Vicki's detective skills over those of the stewardess. Volume two announces that *Vicki Finds the Answer* (1947), and volume three, *The Hidden Valley Mystery* (1948), introduces "mystery" as a recurring element in the series titles. Subsequent titles feature such words as "secret" (1949), "clue" (1950), "peril" (1953), and "search" (1957), with "mystery" leading the way by its presence in six titles overall. By the final volume, *The Brass Idol Mystery* (1964), the series had become dominated by increasingly bizarre investigations in ever more remote locations. Indeed, of the sixteen volumes of the series, none alludes to the stewardess's work in its title, and only three make any reference to flying: *Silver Wings for Vicki, Peril Over the Airport* (1953), and *The Mystery of Flight 908* (1962).

Airline stewardess she may be, but Vicki's first love is mystery-solving. Flying is but a means of bringing her to the next thrilling adventure or exotic locale. Various of her later adventures take her to the Caribbean, France, and India, and the mysteries she encounters in each place dominate the story. Her essentially detectival nature becomes explicit in the sixth book, *Behind the White Veil* (1951). In the opening pages of the story she thinks of her passenger manifest as revealing "clues to the personalities" of her charges, and she later remarks proudly that "I've found that in my career I can combine business with my favorite hobby which is scenting out mysteries." Her work may be in the realm of commercial aviation, but her soul is that of Nancy Drew. She deals capably with puzzle after puzzle as the stories progress, and the details of her stewardess's work are less and less prominent as the mystery elements take center stage.[28]

Their mystery elements notwithstanding, the "Vicki Barr" stories give at least token acknowledgment of a few possibilities that aviation may hold for women. *Silver Wings for Vicki* makes reference to "the women pioneers in aviation" and mentions Phoebe Omlie by name, but the significance is lost on Vicki, who is "still comparatively ignorant of flying." Later, when Vicki announces to a group of her friends her plans to earn a pilot's license, pilot Jim Bolton gloats that "Airlines' pilot jobs aren't open to women." Jean Cox snaps back: "They will some day! You wait and see, smarty!" Jim concedes that he had only been needling Vicki, and goes on to list what he sees as appropriate aviation occupations for women: sport flying for personal pleasure, flying charter passengers, working as a test pilot or a dealer's demonstrator, ferrying aircraft for the government, or flying cargo. None, significantly, involves contact with traditional airline passengers, and none carries the visibility and prestige of an airline captain. Women can fly, he agrees, but he grudgingly gives them only second-tier status.[29]

The sex's potential is more readily recognized when Vicki joins the Women Fliers [*sic*] of America, described as an organization primarily intended to link women aviators for social and educational purposes. When she attends one of the group's dinners in New York, she is struck by the women's diversity: they are young and old, highly educated and secretarially trained, seasoned WASP or ATC pilots and low-time newcomers to flying, nationally famous and wholly unknown. None, however, is actively engaged in commercial flight, save for one who does "personnel work for a big airline" and "another beauty who was a stewardess on still another airline." Although they are all pilots, they too are denied front-rank standing.[30]

Its *pro forma* tip of the hat to women pilots out of the way, the series goes on to offer a new slant on the stewardess's work. Vicki lacks the two principal qualifications for the work, age and education, but makes up for them with her looks, personality, and physique. As the chief stewardess says to her at the close of their interview, "Real beauty isn't necessary, but you have to be nice to look at; well groomed, pleasant, and not too tall or heavy. After all, a plane must carry the biggest payload possible, and the heavier the crew the less paying weight we can carry." The work is, she continues, "primarily a personality job," and Vicki makes the grade. Matching these qualifications is Vicki's motivation for seeking the job. The first word of the first volume is "Adventure!," and a stewardess instructor, while acknowledging the hard work of the transport business, adds, "For fun and excitement I wouldn't trade flying for anything in the world!" The books traffic in excitement combined with a healthy domesticity; when Vicki's class is at last walked through an actual airplane, she is "thrilled" to think of "playing hostess to dozens of people on this beautifully appointed ship."[31]

In this latter reaction lies a hint of the stewardess's new world. The stewardesses who join Federal Airlines are chosen for glamour and personality. They serve to *attract* passengers through their visibility in publicity work ("You'll symbolize the girl in aviation," says an instructor.) and they work to *retain* passengers through their in-flight personality and service. "The stewardess," says the same instructor bluntly, "should make the trip so pleasant that the passengers will want to fly with Federal again. You are Federal's diplomat." To this end, Federal's training is focused upon the domestic side of the stewardess's duties. Wells and Tatham make virtually no reference to emergency procedures throughout Vicki's training. They omit the crashes and medical emergencies of the earlier books and dwell instead on the nature of the Federal stewardess: "A stewardess with passengers in her plane . . . is like a hostess entertaining guests in her own home. She sees that they are comfortable, chats with them, serves them meals. More than that, the stewardess looks out for her passengers, really takes care of them."[32] If mystery is the principal plot element in the series, the stewardess's role as domestic hostess is a strong second.

Vicki embraces the role enthusiastically. For her, even the endless cataloging and inventorying of in-flight supplies available for passengers' comfort is a joy; she blissfully checks blankets, chewing gum, toys for on-board children, newspapers and magazines, frozen breakfasts, urns of coffee and containers of fruit juice, all with the eye of a person eager to please:

> Vicki felt like a conscientious housekeeper expecting guests. "Well, I *am* playing hostess." She smiled to herself, thinking that after all her job was pretty much like Marie's [the operator of a small hotel] work at the pension. "Except that Marie doesn't have twenty-one guests practically every day, and isn't responsible for their well-being a mile or more above the earth."

She is so engaged in the role that her workspace becomes a *de facto* home: "Vicki always felt like a hostess when she was on duty. The comfortable, up-to-date ship was her air-borne apartment, and the little galley in the back, her kitchenette."[33] To herself as much as to the passengers, she is the open-handed hostess whose only aim is the pleasure of her guests.

If the "Vicki Barr" books relegate the stewardess's domesticity and attractiveness to the background in favor of their mystery plots, Margaret Hill's "Beth Dean" stories (1953-1958; three titles) place the qualities front and center. Hill was a Colorado-born writer and public school teacher working principally in Colorado and Wyoming. The "Beth Dean" books show Beth slowly coming to believe in the romance and glamour she has been told live in her duties. Her growing absorption in her work transcends an early love interest, and even a more serious romance developing at series' end may well prove subordinate to the romance of the work—at least for a while. She is the stewardess of the 1950s *par excellence,* and her career illustrates the overall consequences of the airlines' changed marketing.

Goal in the Sky (1953), the first of the series, opens with Beth a junior in college, uncertain as to what she wants to do with her future. She has the tentative possibility of marriage to hometown veterinarian Kirk Arnold, but is lukewarm toward the prospect. When she learns that her family's Montana dude ranch has money problems, she leaves school and applies for a stewardess's job with Sky Lanes Airline. She is accepted despite her lack of a college degree, and sent to San Antonio, Texas, for training. As her training proceeds, she takes part in a commercial film being made about stewardesses, undergoes an extensive and detailed cosmetic make-over, and wins a commendation for her attention to a child passenger who is stricken with in-flight appendicitis. She is assigned to a Sky Lanes base in Oregon for a three-month probationary trial, and sets out on her career, her relationship with Kirk as yet unresolved.

*Beth Dean awaits her first passenger as a DC-4 soars
overhead. Illustration copyright © 1953 by
Manning de V. Lee. (Author's collection).*

In *Hostess in the Sky* (1955), Beth and classmate Corrie
Womack take up residence in Bernard, Oregon, and begin their
work with Sky Lanes. Beth experiences a number of problems as
time passes, all intended to show the range of matters a stewardess
may have to deal with. A stowaway youngster on one of her earliest
flights tests her resourcefulness. Dealing with him introduces her to
the school counselor Peter Harcourt and the two become close
friends. Other problems involve utensils omitted from the food
service, a wolfish traveler with partying on his mind, an "experi-
mentally" educated small boy whose lack of discipline makes life
miserable for the other passengers, a drunk and his bottle, and a

forced landing at a small airport. The latter necessitates her finding housing and entertainment for the stranded passengers despite the limited resources of the adjacent town. She handles all with easy aplomb.

The ingenuity Beth displays in dealing with these encounters brings her to the attention of Sky Lanes' management, and the company begins to use her in its public relations efforts. When Sky Lanes introduces its new, long-range, ninety-passenger "Skyblazer" craft, Beth is tapped to help show it off. She then appears on a television program for teenagers to speak of career opportunities in commercial aviation. She covers an airshow for the company newsletter, and witnesses a crash when an unauthorized plane enters restricted air space. Her appearance on television prompts Peter Harcourt to renew their acquaintance, and Beth finds herself increasingly attracted to him, heightening her quandary over her mixed feelings concerning Kirk Arnold. The problem is unresolved when she is assigned to San Antonio for a refresher course, and she leaves Bernard with Peter's "Good night, Skygirl" echoing in her mind.

The final volume, *Senior Hostess* (1958), finds Beth in San Antonio, where her refresher training includes preparation for the new, jet-propelled "Sky Monarch." Accompanied by flutterbudget trainee Penny Jordan (a tacit acknowledgment of the airlines' lower admissions standards), she flies to Hawaii to help inaugurate Monarch service from the mainland, then is assigned to an Alaska-Washington State route with Penny as junior hostess. Penny's flippancy proves a constant irritant to Beth, who cannot understand why Penny is kept on while she and her other peers strive to toe the Federal line. Beth appears on another television show, this time making a strong statement about flight safety, and draws the attentions of Bill Norgren, a passenger on the inaugural Hawaii flight. Her interest in Bill is shaken when Peter Harcourt re-enters the story, and the series ends with Beth giving Peter a New Year's kiss and briefly rethinking the importance of her career.

Like the other series, the "Beth Dean" books show an airline industry in transition. Beth trains in both DC-3s and DC-4s, and defends the DC-3 for its contributions to commercial aviation, but quickly moves on to larger craft. The ninety-passenger Stratoblazer closely resembles the Boeing Model 377 Stratocruiser, which entered service on Pan American Airways' San Francisco-Honolulu route in 1949 and United Airlines' flights between the same two cities in 1950. A double-decked, four-engined, pressurized aircraft, the Stratocruiser could carry from fifty-five to one hundred passengers. When configured with berths for sleeper service, it featured twenty-eight upper and lower berths and five seats. Its most distinctive feature was a fourteen-seat lower deck, which usually was fitted out as a luxury lounge and bar area. The Stratoblazer mirrors the 377: it carries five hostesses, features reclining swivel seats in its main cabin and berths in the sleeper cabin, and boasts a lower-deck facility divided into a lounge and a library. Like United Airlines' Hawaii flights, the Sky Lanes Stratoblazers on the Hawaii run offer a "late buffet supper" of hors d'oeuvres, cold meats, fruit, and cheese. Finally, although the jet-propelled Sky Monarch is not described in detail, its swept-back wings and cruising speed of five hundred and fifty miles per hour match those of the all-jet Boeing 707, which entered service on Pan American's transatlantic route in 1958.[34]

Also in transition is the nature of the stewardess herself. From the outset, Beth is instilled with the belief that the stewardess is first and foremost a public figure. She exists to make her passengers comfortable, to deal with their questions, and to convince them of Sky Lanes' superiority over its competitors. In the opening days of Beth's training, Marjorie Petti, the Chief Hostess, spells out that "An air hostess comes in contact with a cross section of humanity. She must learn to appear at ease with any type of individual." Understanding of the public is more important than education, she continues: "We have found that girls with public contact experience —librarians, clerks, waitresses, schoolteachers, for instance—are

A Boeing 377 Stratocruiser in Pan American Airlines livery. The lobed, double-deck fuselage is readily apparent. National Air and Space Museum, Smithsonian Institution (SI 89-13139).

often more successful as airline hostesses than girls with more education but less business experience."[35] The examples Miss Petti singles out are all jobs traditionally associated with women, a linkage that becomes important as the series proceeds.

Beth's indoctrination begins even before she reaches her first interview. A Sky Lanes representative, visiting her college, casts the work as principally domestic when he specifies that "We prefer 'hostess' because that describes the role we want our girls to play on the plane. A hostess should be gracious and charming whether in her own home or in the cabin of an airliner," and she must "possess or acquire neatness, poise, tact, good grooming, warmth in her manner toward others." There is no mention of the emergency skills that the nurse-related stories make so much of. In fact, at no point do readers learn of Beth's receiving training in emergency procedures, and the only crash mentioned in detail occurs when a reck-

Interior (looking aft) of a Boeing 377 main cabin.
National Air and Space Museum, Smithsonian Institution
(SI 71-865).

less pilot flying an obsolete warplane plunges to earth during an airshow.[36]

As her training continues, Beth is led more deeply into her pub-lic-relations role. She is, and *must be,* a symbol of all that Sky Lanes represents, for how well she conducts her work is often how the line is judged. An instructor makes this explicit:

> You, the hostess, are the airline's link with the passen-gers—in many cases, the only personal contact between company and passenger. In that capacity you are at all times a sales person. It is up to you to give a sample of the service for which the airline likes to be known. Passengers often choose an airline on the basis of the courtesy and consideration shown by its employees.

Beth's realization of her publicity value becomes even more explicit following the air-show crash. She has worn her uniform to the show so "people would realize she knew something about flying," and her supervisor is ecstatic when a photograph of Beth at the scene is published, for it shows her "in her Sky Lanes uniform administering to a shock victim." The victim's condition is less important than the good publicity for Sky Lanes, and Beth's tardy return to base is readily forgiven.[37]

The passenger must always come first, being treated as a special individual and with personal warmth—but behind that warmth is the constant presence of Sky Lanes, for it must fill its seats. This is, of course, not an unusual motif throughout the stewardess series. What is notable about its presence in the "Beth Dean" series is the degree to which the author brings it to the foreground, spelling out the commercial implications of the hostess's role. The part she plays is not in complementing the operations of the aircraft itself, but in maintaining a loyal customer base for the line's operations. Even the label, "hostess," plays a subliminal part in that commercial role, implying that the individual's duties are less flight-related than they are socially determined. Beth's training does not take her to the overtly sexualized extremes utilized by the airlines of the 1960s and 1970s, with their revealing uniforms and double-entendre advertising, but it helps to prepare the way for such developments. She is the glamorous part of the airline, and she has company obligations she must live up to. Significantly, she does not give the nature of those obligations a second thought.[38]

Sky Lanes' shaping of the hostess corps to their corporate vision begins with the outer woman. Sky Lanes openly picks its hostess candidates for looks and personality, then imposes its own standards of beauty upon them. Beth's classmates are tall and short (within the specified limits), dark and blonde, out-going and reticent, yet each must conform to Sky Lanes specifications. The company will not hire, for example, a hostess "who has a visible scar," lest passengers think "she received the scar in a plane accident."

Later, Beth learns that Sky Lanes seeks candidates with "an appealing personality" and "reasonably even teeth, attractive smiles and clear complexions." Midway through their training, Beth and her class participate in the much-anticipated Glamour Day. Here they are explicitly trained in charm, personality, and the appropriate speaking voice. They have their hair restyled so as to accentuate their faces and undergo a cosmetic makeover intended to bring them to the generally accepted "standard of beauty." The outcome, as one of Beth's classmates remarks, will modify them all so that "any resemblance to the girls chosen for training will be purely coincidental."[39]

The external remaking of the hostess corps completed, that of the internal begins. There is a corporate model as well as a physical one. Sky Lanes requires absolute adherence to its rules and procedures: lecturing Beth on a minor misadventure, an instructor tells her, "We have discovered over the years that the girls who conform without rebellion to the few principles we have, run into less trouble when they get out on their own as full-fledged hostesses." The indoctrination continues throughout the training, and in a final evaluation before graduation, Beth is lectured on "the importance of irreproachable conduct, particularly while in uniform, [and] the importance of care in the selection of friends." The stewardess's behavior, whether personal or public, reflects on Sky Lanes' public image, and the company is determined to ensure that its hostesses are seen as corporate assets. Its emphasis on its own brand of "acceptable" looks and behavior anticipates Arlie Russell Hochschild's observation that, for the air lines, "a 'professional' flight attendant is one who has completely accepted the rules of standardization," one who has entirely surrendered herself to the company.[40]

For her part, Beth tranquilly accepts the remaking, emotionally and intellectually as well as physically. She is ready for it even before she begins her training, as Sky Lanes' "irresistible uniforms [and] the attractive salaries and promises of vacations with pay" give her the reassurance she lacked in her thinking about careers. She happily accepts Sky Lanes' imposed standards as she encounters them. Indeed, she extols them during her appearance on the teen-oriented television program "Young People's World," giving a nostalgic account of Glamour Day: "We got free facials and all kinds of advice about exercises, make-up tricks, safe dieting and hair styling. . . . We scarcely knew our own classmates when they got through with us."[41] The loss of an outward physical identity, much less her intellectual and emotional identity, means nothing to her. She is happy to live as a *tabula rasa* upon which the standards of Sky Lanes are written, and therein lies the tragedy of both Beth Dean and the airline stewardess.

Beth never realizes that she is a creation of Sky Lanes Airways. The twenty-first century reader, on the other hand, sees this from the outset. Beth's studies at college have prepared her for nothing: "What on earth could she do?" she thinks to herself. "This was what she got for spending two years on that vague something known as 'liberal arts' instead of learning how to do something specific." She openly admits her lack of preparation to her education-major roommate: "I can't *do* anything. I'm not trained for anything. I wish I had something special to work toward. Some sort of goal." Her counterparts in the earlier series brought with them a sense of professional identity and purpose created by their nursing training; they saw themselves as skilled individuals who were applying those skills to a new and promising career. Beth, on the other hand, in a seemingly careerist society, brings no sense of identity, no sense of skill, no sense of purpose to the work. She picks the stewardess's job almost at random, telling a group of teenagers in the second book that "I was interested in just any old career, but this one seemed the most attractive."[42] She is what Sky Lanes has made her—a young woman attracted to the work because of its pay and glamour, who has become a company clone in the name of commerce. Unprepared for any other life, she can look forward only to submerging herself in marriage and homemaking when her career has run its brief course.

What matters is that this message is one wholly credible to the teenaged girls of the 1950s. What the twenty-first century reader sees as powerful social coercion seems in its time to be an approving account of female behavior. Girls do not need a complete education, nor do they need a lifetime career. Work for them, however glamorous and exotic it may be, is only preparation for their lives as wives and mothers in the near future. Stewardesses' tenure during the 1930s and early 1940s was relatively brief, to be sure. The average stewardess of 1938 worked for barely two years before resigning to marry, and those women who stayed on were compelled to resign at age thirty-five.[43] Even so, the job was not seen as merely a pathway to marriage; it was presented as a career that would give individuals stature and dignity. Technology and circumstances brought about sweeping changes, however, and the profession of the 1930s became the time-filler of the 1950s.

Vicki Barr's mysteries and Beth Dean's corporate absorption effectively mark the end of the stewardess story. The 1960s and after brought new forms of story-telling to dominate the girls' books scene, ranging from the passionately romantic to the wildly fantastic, and a television-raised generation demanded more of its reading than low-key stories of successful job fulfillment. The series' ending in 1964 and 1959, respectively, is no accident; by those years, the nature of commercial aviation had changed forever, and the stewardess—now a "cabin attendant"—was no longer the stuff of career fiction. From nurse professional to in-flight nurturer, the stewardess's work was always one of service. How that service was marketed by the airlines and how it was carried out as the Dean and Barr series wind down add to the poignancy of the series' demise.

As late as 1941, stewardesses were still viewed as professional as well as attractive, and their varied skills made them an asset to the airlines. An April 1941 issue of *Life* focused on the work of

American Airlines stewardess Joan Waltermire, describing her as "hostess, nurse, sister, [and] entertainer" for the sixteen passengers aboard her DC-3 and reporting her work during the five-hour flight from New York to Chicago. The latter, the article observes, was a favorite route for Joan, for "a fairly long non-stop flight like AM-7 gives the stewardess plenty of time to do her work and get acquainted with her passengers." When the profession observed its fifteenth anniversary in 1945, a complimentary article in an aviation trade journal called stewardesses "an institution" whose members "have stimulated air travel, and have given gracious, dependable service through pioneering days, subsequent peace days, war days." It ended on a singularly prescient note: "More stewardesses will be needed for new routes, for additional schedules on established routes and for larger aircraft." The days of the DC-3 and leisurely flight times were numbered.[44]

The end of the superficial glamor of the stewardess's work began in the mid-1960s. The airlines, seeking more and more passengers to fill the increasing number of seats, turned to discount fares and "cost-efficient" flying. Fewer cabin attendants flying longer hours had to deal with more passengers, and the personalized nature of the stewardess's work began to fade. When the airlines were deregulated in the early 1980s, the loss of glamor was complete. Unlike the earlier days, when cabin attendants "were able to do what they were asked to do, what they often came to *want* to do," the attendants' work became more a matter of dealing with increasing numbers of passengers unaccustomed to flying and rushing to complete meal and drink service in crowded aircraft in reduced time. In Arlie Russell Hochschild's memorable description, "The cruise ship [had] become a Greyhound bus."[45]

Working conditions, moreover, were aggravated by the airlines' merchandising of the stewardess as an in-flight sex object. National Airlines introduced the arch "I'm Jane—Fly Me" advertising campaign in 1971; Continental Airlines countered with "We Really Move Our Tails For You;" and PSA, a California carrier, equipped its stewardesses with buttons translating the airline's logo as "Pure, Sober, and Available." The tailored uniforms of the past gave way to clinging shorts, miniskirts, and, in the case of TWA, an all-paper "British Wench" outfit. This garb, appearing in the early days of the women's liberation movement, unsurprisingly created a backlash as stewardesses and their union fought to counteract the sexy, "swinging stewardess" image. From this confrontation came the gender-neutral label "flight attendant," and the stewardess was no more. Changing circumstances, new attitudes toward women in the workplace, economic concerns, and technological change all collaborated to put an end to the milieu of the stewardess story. The circumstances of the classic portrayal of the stewardess had vanished, and an epoch in aviation fiction for girls had come to an end.[46]

Notes

1. Julie Wosk, *Women and the Machine: Representations from the Spinning Wheel to the Electronic Age* (Baltimore: Johns Hopkins University Press, 2001), 198. See also Maureen Honey, *Creating Rosie the Riveter: Class, Gender, and Propaganda during World War II* (Amherst: University of Massachusetts Press, 1984).

2. "Women in Steel," *Life* 15 (9 August 1943): 74; Mary Anderson, "16,000,000 Women at Work," *New York Times Magazine*, 18 July 1943, SM 18.

3. Nancy Woloch, *Women and the American Experience: A Concise History,* 2nd ed. (Boston: McGraw-Hill, 2002), 321-322; Deborah G. Douglas, *American Women and Flight since 1940* (Lexington: University Press of Kentucky, 2004), 53.

4. Douglas, *American Women and Flight since 1940,* 67-79. David K. Vaughan's "The War and the WAC: Bernadine Bailey's 'Youngest WAC' Series," *Dime Novel Roundup* 68 (December 1999): 217-223, examines one of the few series to deal with women in the 1940s military.

5. Molly Merryman, *Clipped Wings: The Rise and Fall of the Women Airforce Service Pilots (WASPs) of World War II* (New York: New York University Press, 1998), 3; Douglas, *American Women and Flight since 1940,* 67, 76-79; "WAAC: U.S. Women Troop to Enlist in Army's First All-Female Force", *Life* 12 (8 June 1942): 26.

6. Ernestine Evans, "The Sky is No Limit," *Independent Woman* 21 (November 1942): 326, 328; Robert Bellaire, "She Teaches the Army to Fly Blind," *Woman's*

Home Companion 71 (April 1944): 29, 74-75; Margot Roberts, "You Can't Keep Them Down," *Woman's Home Companion* 71 (June 1944): 19, 91.

7. "Women Will Form a Ferry Command," *New York Times*, 11 September 1942, 26; "Will Bear the Name Wafs," *New York Times*, 11 September 1942, 26; Sarah Byrn Rickman, *Nancy Love and the WASP Ferry Pilots of World War II* (Denton: University of North Texas Press, 2008), 49-58, 140-141, 160-163.

8. Doris L. Rich, *Jackie Cochran: Pilot in the Fastest Lane* (Gainesville: University Press of Florida, 2007), 11-21, 24-26.

9. Ibid., 43-49, 50-52, 54-56, 70-74; Jesse Harrison Mason, "On the Up and Up!" *National Aeronautics* 15 (December 1937): 31; "Jacqueline Cochran," *U.S. Air Services* 23 (January 1938): 25. "Unlimited" in Cochran's first record refers to the aircraft used; any class of ship using any form of powerplant would be eligible to compete.

10. Frederick Graham, "First Lady of the Air Lanes," *New York Times Magazine*, 25 September 1938, 130; "Miss Cochran Gets Air Trophy Again," *New York Times*, 16 June 1939, 14; "Jacqueline Cochran Flies Bomber To Britain for Service With R.A.F.," *New York Times*, 21 June 1941, 5; Elizabeth R. Valentine, "No. 1 Woman Flier," *New York Times Magazine*, 13 July 1941, 11; Rich, *Jackie Cochran*, 176-177, 214.

11. Rich, *Jackie Cochran*, 99-100; "Named To Direct Women's Air Work," *New York Times*, 15 September 1942, 26; Merryman, *Clipped Wings*, 18.

12. "Miss Cochran Put In High Air Post," *New York Times*, 6 July 1943, 18; Merryman, *Clipped Wings*, 7; "Wasp Statistics," http://www.pbs.org/wgbh/amex/flygirls/filmmore/reference/primary/wasprecord01.html (accessed 26 April 2008). See also Ann Darr, "The Women Who Flew – but Kept Silent," *New York Times Magazine*, 7 May 1995, 70-71.

13. "Wasp Statistics"; Ann B. Carr, *A Wasp Among Eagles: A Woman Military Test Pilot in World War II* (Washington, DC: Smithsonian Institution Press, 1999), 98-102.

14. Barbara Selby, "The Fifinellas," *Flying* 33 (July 1943): 166-167; "Girl Pilots," *Life* 15 (19 July 1943): 73-81; John Stuart, "The WASP," *Flying* (January 1944): 73-74, 148, 163; Marjorie Kumler, "They've Done It Again," *Ladies' Home Journal* 61 (March 1944): 28-29, 167-169; "Battle of the Sexes," *Time* 43 (8 May 1944): 68, 71; "Unnecessary and Undesirable," *Time* 43 (29 May 1944): 66.

15. "Home by Christmas," *Time* 44 (16 October 1944): 68-69. Chapters 5 and 6 of Merryman, *Clipped Wings*, 75-130, give a detailed account of the congressional and media collaboration leading up to the WASP's disbanding.

16. Douglas, *American Women and Flight since 1940*, 107; Anderson, "16,000,000 Women at Work," 18-19, 29; "Soldiers and Civilians," *Life* 17 (25 September 1944): 36.

17. Sheila Tobias and Lisa Anderson, "Whatever Happened to Rosie the Riveter?" *Ms.* 1 (June 1973): 93-94; "Industries in U.S. Replacing Women," *New York Times*, 19 February 1946, 27-28; Honey, *Creating Rosie the Riveter*, 5; Frieda S. Miller, "What's Become of Rosie the Riveter?" *New York Times Magazine*, 5 May 1946, 11.

18. For the Boeing 307, see Davies, *Airlines of the United States Since 1914*, 205-206. Davies' Chapter 13, "Postwar Domestic Boom" (324-335), discusses the coming of larger-capacity, long-range craft.

19. Kathleen M. Barry, *Femininity in Flight: A History of Flight Attendants* (Durham: Duke University Press, 2007), 51.

20. Elisabeth Lansing, *Nancy Naylor, Visiting Nurse* (New York: Thomas Y. Crowell, 1947), 228. Jim, like Mr. Naylor before him, takes for granted that the man of the family's wishes will take precedence over all others.

21. Elisabeth Hubbard Lansing, *Sky Service* (New York: Thomas Y. Crowell, 1939), 12, 14, 69-70, 283.

22. Ibid., 77; Lansing, *Nancy Naylor: Visiting Nurse*, 77, 66.

23. Lansing, *Sky Service*, 55; Elisabeth Lansing, *Nancy Naylor: Air Pilot* (New York: Thomas Y. Crowell, 1941), 29; Elisabeth Lansing, *Nancy Naylor Flies South* (New York: Thomas Y. Crowell, 1943), 21. Emphasis added.

24. Lansing, *Sky Service*, 14; Lansing, *Nancy Naylor Flies South*, 18, 206.

25. Elisabeth Lansing, *Nancy Naylor: Captain of Flight Nurses* (New York: Thomas Y. Crowell, 1946), 167; Lansing, *Nancy Naylor: Air Pilot*, 18-19.

26. Lansing, *Nancy Naylor: Visiting Nurse*, 236, 241.

27. For the Gibson attribution, see J. Randolph Cox, *Man of Magic & Mystery: A Guide to the Work of Walter B. Gibson* (Metuchen, NJ: Scarecrow Press, 1988), 52-53.

28. Julie Tatham, *Behind the White Veil* (New York: Grosset & Dunlap, 1951), 2, 129. See also Barry, *Femininity in Flight*, 51; Bobbie Ann Mason, *The Girl Sleuth: A Feminist Guide* (Old Westbury, NY: Feminist Press, 1975), 111-112; and Ilana Nash, *American Sweethearts: Teenage Girls in Twentieth-Century Popular Culture* (Bloomington: Indiana University Press, 2006), 184. For Nancy Drew, see Melanie Rehak, *Girl Sleuth: Nancy Drew and the Women Who Created Her* (Orlando, FL: Harcourt Inc., 2005), especially p. 270.

29. Helen Wells, *Silver Wings for Vicki* (New York: Grosset & Dunlap, 1947), 133; Helen Wells, *Peril Over the Airport* (New York: Grosset & Dunlap, 1953), 2-3.

30. Wells, *Peril Over the Airport*, 8-9, 116. "Fliers" is Wells' spelling, although the WFA used "Flyers." This passage is the only reference to the WASP occurring in any of the series.

31. Wells, *Silver Wings for Vicki*, 19, 22, 1, 55-56, 81.

32. Ibid., 57, 63, 61-62.

33. Helen Wells, *The Secret of Magnolia Manor* (New York: Grosset & Dunlap, 1949), 68-69; Julie Tatham, *Behind the White Veil* (New York: Grosset & Dunlap, 1951), 2.

34. Davies, *Airlines of the United States Since 1914,* 379-380, 511. See also Bowers, *Boeing Aircraft Since 1916,* 314-318, 356-358; Margaret Hill, *Senior Hostess* (Boston: Little, Brown, 1958), 44-45; Garvey and Fisher, *Age of Flight,* 161.

35. Margaret Hill, *Goal in the Sky* (Boston: Little, Brown, 1953), 64-66.

36. Ibid., 43; Margaret Hill, *Hostess in the Sky* (Boston: Little, Brown, 1955), 222-225.

37. Hill, *Goal in the Sky,* 72; Hill, *Hostess in the Sky,* 217, 233-234.

38. For the coming of the "swinging stewardess" image and the airlines' sexualizing of the job, see Berry, *Femininity in Flight,* 174-186.

39. Hill, *Goal in the Sky,* 48, 154-155; Hill, *Hostess in the Sky,* 126-127.

40. Hill, *Goal in the Sky,* 110, 198; Arlie Russell Hochschild, *The Managed Heart: Commercialization of Human Feeling* (Berkeley: University of California Press, 1983), 103.

41. Hill, *Goal in the Sky,* 58; Hill, *Hostess in the Sky,* 126.

42. Hill, *Goal in the Sky,* 8, 20; Hill, *Hostess in the Sky,* 123.

43. Jeanette Lea, "We Don't Fly for Love," *Popular Aviation* 43 (September 1938): 24-25.

44. Joseph Kastner, "Joan Waltermire: Airline Stewardess," *Life* 10 (28 April 1941): 104-106; "Air Stewardesses Mark Anniversary," *Western Flying* 25 (October 1945): 62, 84.

45. Hochschild, *The Managed Heart,* 122-124.

46. Barry, *Femininity in Flight,* 174-209, relates the course of the "sexy stewardess" era and the women's backlash against it. Drew Whitelegg, *Working the Skies: The Fast-Paced, Disorienting World of the Flight Attendant* (New York: New York University Press, 2007), continues and extends Hochschild's analysis, detailing the many pressures working on the flight attendants of the 21st century. See also Johanna Omelia and Michael Waldock, *Come Fly With Us! A Global History of the Airline Stewardess* (Portland, OR: Collectors Press, 2003), 91.

CHAPTER 7

Epilogue

B y the time Vicki Barr retired her silver wings in 1964, the world was leaving her behind. Complex social changes were taking place, some affecting women and aviation, others women generally. All, however, foreshadowed fundamental changes taking place in the perception and fulfilling of women's roles in American society. Newly energized female activists raised challenges to the social and domestic assumptions that Vicki, Nancy Naylor, and their flying feminine forebears took for granted. Women and industry together increasingly addressed the issues of what work was "appropriate" for women and how that work was to be designated. Women pressed for new ways to engage themselves in aviation and flight, forcing a sweeping rethinking of the entire enterprise. Women of all ages and skills found themselves in the midst of swirling social ferment, and the several milieus embraced by the girls' aviation stories of the past quietly gave way to the new.

Among the early catalysts for change was Betty Friedan's *The Feminine Mystique* (1963). Drawing upon her own domestic experiences, her political activities, and her interviews with American women during the preceding decade, Friedan challenged the commonly held assumption that women were happiest and most satisfied when wholly involved with home and family. This assumption, the "mystique" of the title, was for her a limiting one rather than a liberating one. It forced women into a life for which they might or might not be suited, and it tacitly discouraged them from experimenting with other roles. American women, she said, "were taught to pity the neurotic, unfeminine, unhappy women who wanted to be poets or physicists or presidents." Particularly vulnerable were educated women (single *and* married) who might once have looked forward to a life-long career making full use of their skills and interests. The "mystique" directed women toward a life of all-absorbing domesticity, making "house-wife mothers . . . the model for all women," equating "femininity" only with housewifely conformity, and preventing them "from doing the work of which they are capable." This, in turn, denied society the benefits of their talents and denied such women the satisfaction of a productive career outside the home. As they spread, Friedan's views "energized national debate on gender roles and encouraged women to look at their own lives as a subject for social and political analysis." That energy and analysis contributed to what in the 1960s came to be known as the movement for Women's Liberation.[1]

The Feminine Mystique was complemented by other events, notably the Food and Drug Administration's approval, in May 1960, of *Enovid*—G.D. Searles' brand of estrogen and progesterone that was the first oral contraceptive. *Enovid,* popularly known as "The Pill," offered women a freedom they had previously lacked: the privilege of taking the initiative in matters of birth control and, more particularly, sexual activity in general. No longer were women necessarily subject to men's whims concerning sexual relations, and their recognition of the new freedom was immediate. A million and a quarter American women were using *Enovid* barely eighteen months after its release; the number reached well over two million by 1963. As "the Pill" became more available during the decade of the 1960s—its effects bolstered by court decisions striking down anti-contraception laws and affirming the right to privacy—women began an unprecedented reevaluation of personal rights and personal activity.[2] This, too, became part of the Women's Liberation movement, as conventional views of women came under scrutiny.

A second catalytic event occurred in April 1963. Eight stewardesses for American Airlines, frustrated by company resistance to relaxing a rule compelling retirement at age thirty-two, called a press conference. Since the end of World War II, the airlines had increasingly flaunted stewardesses' beauty among the elements making commercial air travel enjoyable. Obviously, the carriers tacitly maintained, older women would lack the necessary looks and charm. All eight of the women appeared at the conference glamorously clad in their best uniforms, asking, "Do I look like an old bag?" Four of the eight were well into their thirties, but observers could not differentiate the antiquated from the blooming, giving the lie to one of the industry's nominal reasons for enforced retirement. The women's action dealt with a single issue: the presumption that female attractiveness ended at age thirty-two. It was, however, but one of a number of incidents to come that called into question widely held assumptions affecting women in the airline workplace.[3]

The questioning took some time to develop. Stewardesses had been unionized since 1949, when the Airline Stewards and Stewardesses Association (ALSSA) absorbed the smaller Air Line Stewardesses Association (ALSA) and became the bargaining agent for close to three thousand workers. Union activity was initially low-key, addressing problems such as scheduling of duty tours, hours of flight-time, and training in safety procedures. A notable strike, however, occurred in 1958. Thirty-two stewardesses kept Lake Central Airlines grounded for eleven days, pressing for improved pay and working circumstances. Their action drew widespread attention as an early expression of women's militancy in seeking recognition in the workplace. The success of the strike heartened the cabin staffs of other airlines, and the stewardess's world quickly became a near-adversarial one. Companies could no longer blithely impose arbitrary standards upon the stewardess corps, and the women insisted upon a part in determining the nature of their work.[4]

The increasingly militant stewardesses got a powerful tool in July 1964 with the passing of the Civil Rights Act of 1964. The act in its original form was intended solely to protect racial and ethnic minorities, outlawing racial discrimination in voting and in the workplace. Its final form, however, was expanded to include discrimination according to sex. Title VII of the Civil Rights Act, the section dealing with sexual discrimination, became the foundation for a series of actions against the airlines, all having to do with the stewardess's role. Suddenly age, appearance, and marital status joined race as issues central to the stewardesses' cause. The next several years saw men and minority women hired as cabin crew, restrictions on age and marriage eliminated, the gender-neutral label "flight attendant" substituted for the all-feminine "stewardess," and increased industry recognition that working as a flight attendant could be a full-time career.[5]

Access to the commercial cockpit took longer to achieve. The Civil Rights Act of 1964 technically opened the door for women pilots, but the airlines resisted. Pilot qualification standards across the industry generally required a college degree, a commercial license with instrument rating, and better than a thousand hours' flying time, all requirements that relatively few women fliers could meet. Yet some could meet them, and their records, combined with federal pressure, ultimately compelled the carriers to hire women pilots. The first was Emily Warner, who began flying for Frontier Airlines in 1973, and the major carriers soon followed suit with comparable hires. The number of qualified applicants began to increase as more women entered the military, where the training and flying hours accumulated there gave them a head start on the industry requirements. Military service quickly became a recognized avenue to airline employment with pilots transferring to the airlines upon completing their military hitch. Even so, the number of women in the cockpit remained small; in 1978, only fifty women had pilot status. Once begun, however, women's access to the cockpit continued to grow, and the sex at last became a genuine part, albeit a small one, of commercial flight.[6]

June 1963 witnessed a third catalytic challenge to the conventional. On the 16th of the month, the Soviet Union launched *Vostok VI*—the sixth in its series of manned orbital space flights and the first to carry a woman. Valentina Tereshkova returned safely to Earth after three days in orbit, accompanied by days of publicity praising the progressivism of Soviet society. Tereshkova herself helped add to the acclaim. An accomplished sport parachutist, she went into space with comparatively little cosmonaut training, allowing the Soviet publicity machine to hail the versatility of the nation's women and their readiness for space travel. Press coverage around the world said little of the *Vostoks'* almost total automation, which made an on-board pilot redundant if not superfluous. It focused instead upon Tereshkova herself and quickly made her into an emblem of feminine modernity.[7]

The question that followed was immediate and obvious: Why had a Soviet woman preceded an American woman into space? Once asked, the question uncovered a long-standing and previously unchallenged practice. The National Aeronautics and Space Administration (NASA) and the United States Air Force routinely rejected women as astronaut candidates. Ironically, an unpublicized series of tests on female volunteers well before Tereshkova's flight had already established American women's physical ability to cope with space flight. One of the first volunteers was Ruth Nichols. Nichols, a veteran of the Powder Puff Derby and the second American woman to win a transport pilot's license, ended her autobiography, *Wings for Life* (1957), with the pledge, "Of one thing I am certain—when space ships take off, I shall be flying them." She quickly tried to make good on her pledge. In the autumn of 1959, at age fifty-three, she quietly—and successfully—underwent a series of "astronaut tests" at the Wright Air Development Center in Dayton, Ohio. She used her testing as an opportunity to press for an official program of testing women astronaut candidates, but nothing came of it.[8]

Other test programs quickly came to light. Geraldine ("Jerrie") Cobb, a record-setting woman flier with commercial certification and several years' ferry-pilot experience, underwent the Project Mercury physical tests in early 1960, becoming the first woman to pass the full battery of physical tests used for vetting male astronauts. Her success prompted Dr. W. Randolph Lovelace II, head of the Lovelace Foundation for Medical Education and Research and the physician overseeing astronaut testing, to expand the program. Funded in great part by Jacqueline Cochran, Lovelace instituted the Woman in Space Program in 1961, inviting twenty-five women pilots to participate in the same physical testing used by NASA. Nineteen accepted, and twelve passed. These twelve, along with Jerrie Cobb, were invited to take part in more advanced testing at the Naval Air Station in Pensacola, Florida, in September 1961. Naval authorities met resistance from NASA and suddenly withdrew their permission. The Woman in Space Program collapsed soon afterward.[9]

Valentina Tereshkova's flight once again brought women's interest in flight and space to the foreground, but to no avail. Nichols's and Cobb's test results and the findings of the Lovelace program notwithstanding, NASA refused to consider women astronauts until 1978, when Sally Ride, who held a Ph.D. in physics from Stanford University, was admitted to the program. Ride became the first American woman in space, flying as a mission specialist aboard the space shuttle in 1983. Eileen Collins, a lieutenant-colonel in the United States Air Force and an experienced test pilot, was admitted to astronaut training in 1990. In 1995, she became the first woman to *pilot* the space shuttle and in 1999, the first woman *commander* of a shuttle flight.

These breakthroughs were abetted by a series of congressional actions. Public Law 90-130 (1967) opened advanced military rank (i.e., higher than colonel) to women serving in the armed forces and removed restrictions on the number of female enlistees serving in the military. A subsequent act, Public Law 94-106 (1975), opened

Jerrie Cobb and a Project Mercury space capsule, 1963. National Air and Space Museum, Smithsonian Institution (SI 90-6836).

the service academies to women cadets. Still later restrictions, notably the prohibition on women's flying in combat zones, fell with the 1991 passage of the Kennedy-Roth Amendment.[10] Women finally had full access to a military career, were achieving nominal equality with men in the military cockpit, and were taking active part in the American space program.

By 1964, American women, fictional as well as real, had the elements necessary for a massive rethinking of women's role in domestic life and the workplace. The last remaining girls' aviation stories, the stewardess books, make no mention of them. Neither Friedan nor *Enovid* appears in the Vicki Barr stories. The books, like the other stewardess stories before them, presented an idealized, conventional view of young women in contemporary American society. The prospect of marriage, which would mean the end of their flight work, was the girls' desired goal; thus, the stewardess's work became a temporary pastime rather than a lifetime career. The books' heroines were happy, even proud, to embrace the modified domestic role their work imposed upon them and serve until age or romance called them away.

That romance, when it occurred, was inevitably chaste and almost always male-centered. There was no call for "the Pill." No author of the times would even hint at the possibility of a sexual relationship for her heroine, and the teenaged audience (or their parents) would very likely protest it should one appear. And, though the books' heroines enjoyed a singular degree of independence for the times, they uncomplainingly bowed to would-be fiancés' insistence that women's place was in the home. The independence conveyed in the pre-war stewardess books gave way to a willing if unconscious acceptance of socially imposed expectations. Whatever else their adventures might entail, the stewardess heroines, case histories for Betty Friedan, operated in a compartmentalized, sexless world that subliminally prepared them for the domesticated life to come.

Neither does the growing critique of "women's work" appear in the stewardess stories. None of the series makes mention of unionization, union activities, or matters of civil rights, even though Vicki Barr's and Beth Dean's chronicles overlap the era of unionization and Nancy Naylor's approach it. In the books' world-view, there was no need for such things. The books postulate paternalistic carriers that are as committed to the overall well-being of their

crews as they are to that of their passengers. Pilots and stewardesses alike have the ear of management, and management listens. The
stewardesses are young women happy in their work, satisfied to be
part of an all-embracing company and proud to carry its logo and
its values all over the world. At no point do the later books perceive
that their stories (Beth Dean's in particular) silently delineate the
very assumptions and policies that real-world stewardesses were
increasingly protesting. They do not acknowledge, perhaps do not
even recognize, the discrimination inherent in their exercise.

The stewardess stories complete the three shifting stages dis-
cernible in aviation fiction for American girls: *Reassurance,*
Reassessment, and *Resignation.* The "birdwomen" books prior to
World War I ride the crest of a wave of reform, offering a *reassuring*
message to their young readers. Aviation, that most modern of
developments, was available to women. It was liberating to women,
allowing them new opportunities to test and assert their abilities.
And it was equalizing to women, offering an arena of achievement
in which neither men nor women held a distinctive advantage. It
was, therefore, an activity well-suited to the era of the "New
Woman," a complement to her "enhanced sense of self, gender, and
mission."[11] The books bear this out, portraying Peggy Prescott and
Orissa Kane as willing and able to operate in a men's world by men's
rules and demonstrating their competence at every turning. Young
readers could do the same, the stories implied, and look forward to
a life of exhilarating growth as women and as citizens.

Reassessment of women's roles began after the First World War.
The unsettling effects of total war, the loosening of society's corset
strings, and Prohibition's stressing the tantalizing appeal of alcohol
came into play. Women across the nation benefitted from the energy
of the "flapper" era and the 1920 ratification of the Nineteenth
Amendment to the Constitution, giving them the vote. Thus,
American women found themselves faced with a host of sometimes
daunting social choices. These were enhanced by aviation, as
Amelia Earhart, Louise Thaden, Ruth Nichols, "Chubbie" Keith-

Miller, and other women pilots captured headline after headline and implicitly challenged men's domination of the air. The girls' books picked up on the women fliers' overt independence and their demonstrated competence, presenting them as appealing role models for the future. The chronicles of Susan Thompson, Roberta Langwell, Ruth Darrow, Jane Grant, Cleo Bowman, Linda Carlton, even of the Mapes twins and Dorothy Dixon show young women embracing aviation and making it part of their lives. Some, like Roberta and Linda, use it to make a living; the others find it a ready complement to their already progressive lives. All, however, take for granted that aviation will be a necessary part of their approaching adult lives and that those lives will be conducted in an atmosphere of personal independence.

Even so, reassessment was necessary. Eugene Vidal's efforts notwithstanding, airplanes were *not* going to be available to every person. The cost of their operation and upkeep took money, and would-be fliers, particularly during the Depression years, had to consider their finances. Nor was aviation going to provide all who sought it a career in the cockpit. The commercial cockpit of the 1930s was closed to women, and those women who could support themselves by free-lance flying were few and far between. A reasonable alternative, of course, was for women to work in aviation support roles—in sales, demonstrations, or administration. The work allowed them to fly on the side, but flying itself was secondary to their larger employment concerns. Women also had to meet new and at times arbitrary standards if they wished to fly. The happy-go-lucky flying of the birdwoman gave way to pilots' licenses, flight plans, and prescribed air routes. Here, too, women pilots had to reconsider how to reconcile this new complexity with their progressive desires. The girls' books give some examples, even as they explicate the changing world of flight; as in the real world, the tendency is for women in aviation to accept a secondary function. There still is a place in society for the woman pilot, but she must modify some of her hopes and ambitions. Wholesale liberation is not going to come from the skies.

The stewardess books of World War II and after represent the ultimate modification of those ambitions, as young women increasingly and subliminally *resigned* themselves to societal mores, a secondary kind of aviation career, and a far more extensive "career" as wife and mother. Jane Cameron, Peggy Wayne, Nancy Naylor, and Vicki Barr earn pilot's licenses. Even so, independent flying, initially so important to Jane, Peggy, and Nancy, figures less and less in the stewardesses' lives as the times change. Wartime regulations and the expansion of the airline industry bring even greater changes. Carol Rogers and Beth Dean have no aspirations to earn a license and are content to fly as cabin crew. Caddy Palmer doesn't fly at all in any regular sense—but all think of themselves as engaged in aviation.

Their desire for flight, however, is challenged by a new desire: men. Jim Taylor, Grant Lowrie, Whitey McIntyre, and Peter Harcourt offer all four of the wartime and postwar heroines the prospect of marriage. Each young woman must reconcile her dreams of flying, her dreams of domesticity, and her desire to follow her husband's wishes. That reconciliation *may* include the continuing of her career, but larger issues must first be settled. Carol Rogers and Caddy Palmer will perhaps seek a balance between career and marriage, at least for a time, but Nancy Naylor and Beth Dean are quick to relinquish career for home. The books demonstrate that, for them, the stewardess's life has become only an interlude, giving them income and busy work while they wait for the life they were meant to live, that of marriage and the home.

It is here the girls' aviation books stop. They themselves seem unable (or unwilling) to deal with the complexities of career versus marriage, and they hold out no particular future for young women in aviation as flight moves into the postwar era. And there they still stand. No new series has yet taken up the possibilities of the challenges and satisfactions that the commercial cockpit might bring a woman airline captain. None has striven to explore what military training and a subsequent career in the armed forces might hold for a woman pilot, be she in the air force or the navy. None has taken up the challenges of a woman astronaut's life, even though educational opportunities and a liberalizing of the limitations on military life have made such a career possible. One can only ask: "Why not?"

One answer may lie in forms of recreation. Prior to 1950 or thereabouts, young people read for entertainment. Now, however, television has superseded recreational reading. Its network-controlled offerings have no place for flying women or technically oriented career stories. (Cable television's *Battlestar Galactica* offers both female pilots and female career officers in principal roles, but its classification as science-fiction relegates it to minor status.) Another may lie in taste. The liberated world of the modern girl reader has fish other than aviation to fry. Girls' books follow the money. They now deal more with fantasy, romantic encounters, and feminine careers in the earth-bound marketplace, dramatizing the escapes and the excitements that may lie there. (The heroines of *Sex and the City*, whether existing in book, video, or film, find more than enough to satisfy themselves in the urban workplace, while the burgeoning of assertive heroines possessing mystical powers, whose doings populate fantasy trilogies, is a publishing phenomenon.)[12] Reality notwithstanding, publishers see no market for tales of Amy the Astronaut or Caitlin the Commercial Pilot.

Still another may lie in aviation itself. Few persons can afford personal aircraft; those who do own ships seem principally to be the ultra-wealthy or celebrities. Flying itself is increasingly hemmed in by crowded skies, strict air traffic control, and reams of federal safety regulations. Headlines no longer trumpet fliers' achievements, and fliers no longer speak eloquently of the wonder of flight. (A small exception exists in the instance of the *Apollo* astronauts. Their reactions to seeing Earth from the Moon invoke the old sense of wonder.) Aviation's inherent appeal has been overwhelmed by the expanding state, just as the dream of space flight has been overwhelmed by the bureaucracies of NASA and the military. Commercial flying has become "a job" for pilots and cabin attendants alike, with much of its glamor eroded by economics-dictated policies and practices. Most crucial is that flying has at last become commonplace for all. The democratizing and commercializing of air travel has eroded aviation's sense of wonder. Economic strains have stripped it of its luxury and security concerns have imposed another level of inconvenience upon passengers. Individuals now associate flight more with long airport lines, crowded aircraft, and travel delays than with exhilaration and freedom. For men as much as women, flying has become a chore.[13]

But there remains a glimmer of hope. The history of women in the United States, especially since 1963, shows an evolution as progressive as the history of the pre-World War I era and the energy continues. Sexism exists, to be sure, and discrimination persists. Yet American women of the twenty-first century lead lives far freer and far more liberated than those of their forebears. And, just as the girls' aviation books from 1910 through 1940 supported and fed the dream of aviation for their young readers, some children's interests —in toys and activities if not in books—may hint at a continuing belief in flight's liberating qualities. In 1965, two years following Valentina Tereshkova's orbital flight, the Mattel toy empire released "Astronaut Barbie," the doll's bubble helmet and form-fitting silver space suit at least as evocative of things to come as Harriet Quimby's purple flying togs.[14]

A small glimmer indeed, but nature may yet imitate art. Preceding "Astronaut Barbie" was 1964's "Flight Stewardess Barbie," with companion Ken as the pilot. Like her stewardess predecessor, "Astronaut Barbie" retains the doll's long legs, wasp waist, and ample bust, all sources of concern to feminist critics. But she at least hints at her participation in space exploration, in an active role, as a nominal equal of her male counterparts. Younger girls are now regular participants in "space camps;" older ones are increasingly making their presence felt in the scientific and engineering realms;

and a third of the incoming astronaut class of 2009, from whom the next American lunar explorers will be selected, will be women.[15] Girls' books may no longer convey the wonder of atmospheric flight, but the dream of its younger and even more progressive sibling, space flight, remains alive. Where there are men, there are women, and women are, and will be, a part of the exploratory world to come.

Notes

1. Betty Friedan, *The Feminine Mystique* (New York: W.W. Norton, 1963), 15-16, 43, 253; Nancy Woloch, *Women and the American Experience: A Concise History.* 2nd ed. (New York: McGraw-Hill, 2002), 347-349; Kathleen M. Barry, *Femininity in Flight: A History of Flight Attendants* (Durham: Duke University Press, 2007), 130.

2. "The Pill," http://www.pbs.org.wgbh/amex/pill/timeline/timeline2.html, accessed 1 October 2008; "U.S. Approves Pill For Birth Control," *New York Times,* 9 May 1960, 75; Woloch, *Women and the American Experience,* 356-358. See also Ilana Nash, *American Sweethearts: Teenage Girls in Twentieth-Century Popular Culture* (Bloomington: Indiana University Press, 2006), 182-183.

3. Barry, *Femininity in Flight,* 122-123.

4. Ibid., 61-86. See also Drew Whitelegg, *Working the Skies: the Fast-Paced, Disorienting World of the Flight Attendant* (New York: New York University Press, 2007), 57-61.

5. Barry, *Femininity in Flight,* 128-131; Deborah G. Douglas, *American Women and Flight Since 1940* (Lexington: University Press of Kentucky, 2004), 159-161.

6. Douglas, *American Women and Flight since 1940,* 176-178.

7. Walter A. McDougall, *The Heavens and the Earth: A Political History of the Space Age* (1985; repr., Baltimore: Johns Hopkins University Press, 1997), 243, 288.

8. Ruth Nichols, *Wings for Life* (Philadelphia: J.P. Lippincott, 1957), 314; Margaret A. Weitekamp, *Right Stuff, Wrong Sex: America's First Women in Space Program* (Baltimore: Johns Hopkins University Press, 2004), 69-71.

9. Weitekamp, *Right Stuff, Wrong Sex,* 76-77, 90-117. See also Doris L. Rich, *Jackie Cochran: Pilot in the Fastest Lane* (Gainesville: University Press of Florida, 2007), 206-209.

10. Douglas, *American Women and Flight since 1940*, 239-240, 168-169, 191-192, 233.

11. Woloch, *Women and the American Experience*, 180.

12. Neil Postman's *Amusing Ourselves to Death: Public Discourse in the Age of Show Business* (New York: Viking Penguin, 1985) is a classic examination of the shifting relationship between television and reading. Robert A. Heinlein, in *Expanded Universe* (1980; repr., New York: Ace Science Fiction, 1982), 545-553, offers early remarks critical of the growing American obsession with fantasy.

13. Harrison H. Schmitt, "A Trip to the Moon," in *Where Next, Columbus? The Future of Space Exploration,* ed. Valerie Neal, 49-57 (New York: Oxford University Press, 1994), 49-57; Elizabeth R. Moles and Norman L. Friedman, "The Airline Hostess: Realities of an Occupation With a Popular Cultural Image," *Journal of Popular Culture* 7 (Fall 1973): 310. See also Rick Marin, "When Flying Tourist Meant Going in Style," *New York Times*, 28 March 1999, 1, 6; and Corey Kilgannon, "When Flying Was Caviar," *New York Times*, 19 October 2003, 23.

14. Bettyann Holtzmann Kevles, *Almost Heaven: The Story of Women in Space* (Cambridge: MIT Press, 2006), 45.

15. Michael Cassutt, "Fly Us to the Moon," *Air & Space/Smithsonian* 23 (November 2008): 52-53..

Bibliography

1. Girls' Aviation Fiction

Anderson, Betty Baxter. *Peggy Wayne, Sky Girl: A Career Story for Older Girls.* New York: Cupples & Leon, 1941.

Bardwell, Harrison [Edith J. Craine]. *The Airplane Girl and the Mystery of Seal Islands.* 1931. Reprint, Lafayette, IN: Purdue University Press, 2003.

——— [Edith J. Craine]. *The Airplane Girl and the Mystery Ship.* 1931. Reprint, Lafayette, IN: Purdue University Press, 2003.

——— [Edith J. Craine]. *The Lurtiss Field Mystery.* 1930. Reprint, Lafayette, IN: Purdue University Press, 2003.

——— [Edith J. Craine]. *Roberta's Flying Courage.* 1930. Reprint, Lafayette, IN: Purdue University Press, 2003.

Burnham, Margaret. *The Girl Aviators on Golden Wings.* Chicago: M.A. Donohue, 1911.

———. *The Girl Aviators' Motor Butterfly.* Chicago: M.A. Donohue, 1912.

———. *The Girl Aviators and the Phantom Airship.* Chicago: M.A. Donohue, 1911.

———. *The Girl Aviators' Sky Cruise.* Chicago: M.A. Donohue, 1911.

Hill, Margaret. *Goal in the Sky.* Boston: Little, Brown, 1953.

———. *Hostess in the Sky.* Boston: Little, Brown, 1955.

———. *Senior Hostess.* Boston: Little, Brown, 1958.

Lansing, Elisabeth. *Nancy Naylor, Air Pilot.* New York: Thomas Y. Crowell, 1941.

———. *Nancy Naylor: Captain of Flight Nurses.* New York: Thomas Y. Crowell, 1946.

———. *Nancy Naylor Flies South.* New York: Thomas Y. Crowell, 1943.

———. *Nancy Naylor, Flight Nurse.* New York: Thomas Y. Crowell, 1944.

———. *Nancy Naylor, Visiting Nurse.* New York: Thomas Y. Crowell, 1947.

Lansing, Elisabeth Hubbard. *Sky Service.* New York: Thomas Y. Crowell, 1939.

Lavell, Edith. *Linda Carlton, Air Pilot.* Akron, OH: Saalfield Publishing Co., 1931.

———. *Linda Carlton's Hollywood Flight.* New York: A.L. Burt Co., 1933.

———. *Linda Carlton's Island Adventure.* Akron, OH: Saalfield Publishing Co., 1931.

———. *Linda Carlton's Ocean Flight.* Akron, OH: Saalfield Publishing Co., 1931.

———. *Linda Carlton's Perilous Summer.* New York: A.L. Burt Co., 1932.

Moyer, Bess. *Gypsies of the Air.* Chicago: Goldsmith Publishing Co., 1932.

———. *On Adventure Island.* Chicago: Goldsmith Co., 1932.

O'Malley, Patricia. *Airline Girl.* New York: Dodd, Mead, 1944.

———. *War Wings for Carol.* New York: Dodd, Mead, 1943.

———. *Wider Wings.* New York: Junior Literary Guild and Greystone Press, 1942.

———. *Winging Her Way.* New York: Dodd, Mead, 1946.

———. *Wings for Carol.* New York: Dodd, Mead, 1941.

Tatham, Julie. *Behind the White Veil.* New York: Grosset & Dunlap, 1951.

———. *The Clue of the Broken Blossom.* New York: Grosset & Dunlap, 1950.

Van Dyne, Edith [L. Frank Baum]. *The Flying Girl.* Chicago: Reilly & Britton, 1911.

——— [L. Frank Baum]. *The Flying Girl and Her Chum.* 1912. Reprint, Bloomfield, NJ: Hungry Tiger Press, 1997.

Verrill, Dorothy. *The Sky Girl.* New York: Century, 1930.

Wayne, Dorothy [Noel E. Sainsbury, Jr.]. *Dorothy Dixon and the Double Cousin.* Chicago: Goldsmith Co., 1933.

——— [Noel E. Sainsbury, Jr.]. *Dorothy Dixon and the Mystery Plane.* Chicago, Goldsmith Co., 1933.

——— [Noel E. Sainsbury, Jr.]. *Dorothy Dixon Solves the Conway Case.* Chicago: Goldsmith Co., 1933.

——— [Noel E. Sainsbury, Jr.]. *Dorothy Dixon Wins Her Wings.* Chicago: Goldsmith Co., 1933.

Wells, Helen. *The Ghost at the Waterfall.* New York: Grosset & Dunlap, 1956.

———. *Peril Over the Airport.* New York: Grosset & Dunlap, 1953.

———. *The Search for the Missing Twin.* New York: Grosset & Dunlap, 1954.

———. *The Secret of Magnolia Manor.* New York: Grosset & Dunlap, 1949.

———. *Silver Wings for Vicki.* New York: Grosset & Dunlap, 1947.

———. *Vicki Finds the Answer.* New York: Grosset & Dunlap, 1947.

Wells, Helen [Walter B. Gibson]. *The Brass Idol Mystery.* New York: Grosset & Dunlap, 1964.

Wheeler, Ruthe S. *Jane, Stewardess of the Airlines.* Chicago: Goldsmith Co., 1935.

Wirt, Mildred A. *Courageous Wings.* Philadelphia: Penn Publishing, 1937.

———. *Ruth Darrow in the Air Derby or, Recovering the Silver Trophy.* New York: Barse & Co., 1930.

———. *Ruth Darrow in the Coast Guard.* New York: Grosset & Dunlap, 1931.

———. *Ruth Darrow in the Fire Patrol or, Capturing the Redwood Thieves.* New York: Grosset & Dunlap, 1930.

———. *Ruth Darrow in Yucatan.* New York: Grosset & Dunlap, 1931.

———. *The Sky Racers.* Philadelphia: Penn Publishing, 1935.

2. Critical and Historical Studies

A. Books

Abel, Alan, and Drina Welch Abel. *Bellanca's Golden Age.* Golden Age of Aviation Series, vol. 4. Brawley, CA: Wind Canyon Books, 2004.

Allen, Richard Sanders. *Revolution in the Sky: The Lockheeds of Aviation's Golden Age.* Revised edition. Atglen, PA: Schiffer *Aviation* History, 1993.

Avery, Gillian. *Behold the Child: American Children and Their Books 1621-1922.* Baltimore: Johns Hopkins University Press, 1994.

Barry, Kathleen M. *Feminity in Flight: A History of Flight Attendants.* Durham, NC: Duke University Press, 2007.

Berg, A. Scott. *Lindbergh.* New York: G.P. Putnam's Sons, 1998.

Biddle, Wayne. *Barons of the Sky.* New York: Simon & Schuster, 1991.

Billman, Carol. *The Secret of the Stratemeyer Syndicate.* New York: Ungar Publishing Co., 1986.

Bilstein, Roger E. *Flight in America: From the Wrights to the Astronauts.* Revised edition. Baltimore: Johns Hopkins University Press, 1994.

Boase, Wendy. *The Sky's the Limit: Women Pioneers in Aviation.* New York: Macmillan, 1979.

Bowers, Peter M. *Boeing Aircraft Since 1916.* New York: Funk & Wagnalls, 1968.

Brooks, Peter W. *Cierva Autogiros: The Development of Rotary-Wing Flight.* Washington, DC: Smithsonian Institution Press, 1988.

Brooks-Pazmany, Kathleen. *United States Women in Aviation, 1919-1929.* Washington, DC: Smithsonian Institution Press, 1991.

Cadogan, Mary. *Women with Wings: Female Flyers in Fact and Fiction.* Chicago: Academy Chicago Publishers, 1993.

Campbell, D'Ann. *Women at War with America: Private Lives in a Patriotic Era.* Cambridge: Harvard University Press, 1984.

Carl, Ann B. *A WASP Among Eagles: A Woman Military Test Pilot in World War II.* Washington, DC: Smithsonian Institution Press, 1999.

Cawelti, John G. *Adventure, Mystery, and Romance: Formula Stories as Art and Popular Culture.* Chicago: University of Chicago Press, 1976.

Chafe, William H. *The Paradox of Change: American Women in the 20th Century.* New York: Oxford University Press, 1991.

Clarke, Deborah. *Driving Women: Fiction and Automobile Culture in Twentieth-Century America.* Baltimore: Johns Hopkins University Press, 2007.

Conway, Erik M. *Blind Landings: Low-Visibility Operations in American Aviation, 1918-1958.* Baltimore: Johns Hopkins University Press, 2006.

Corn, Joseph J. *The Winged Gospel: America's Romance with Aviation, 1900-1950.* New York: Oxford University Press, 1983.

Cott, Nancy F. *The Grounding of Modern Feminism.* New Haven: Yale University Press, 1987.

Cox, J. Randolph. *Man of Magic & Mystery: A Guide to the Work of Walter B. Gibson.* Metuchen, NJ: Scarecrow Press, 1988.

Crouch, Tom. *The Bishop's Boys: A Life of Wilbur and Orville Wright.* NY: W.W. Norton, 1989.

Crouch, Tom D. *Wings: A History of Aviation from Kites to the Space Age.* New York: W.W. Norton, 2003.

Curtiss, Glenn H., and Augustus Post. *The Curtiss Aviation Book.* New York: Frederick A. Stokes, 1912.

Davies, R.E.G. *Airlines of the United States Since 1914.* Washington, DC: Smithsonian Institution Press, 1998,

Dodge, Pryor. *The Bicycle.* Paris: Flammarion, 1996.

Douglas, Deborah G. *American Women and Flight since 1940.* Lexington: University Press of Kentucky, 2004.

Dunlap, George T. *The Fleeting Years: A Memoir.* New York: privately printed, 1937.

Earhart, Amelia. *20 Hrs., 40 Min.: Our Flight in the Friendship.* 1928. Reprint, Washington, DC: National Geographic Adventure Classics, 2003.

———. *The Fun of It: Random Records of My Own Flying and of Women in Aviation.* 1932. Reprint, Chicago: Academy Chicago Publishers, 1977.

———. *Last Flight.* Edited by George Palmer Putnam. New York: Harcourt, Brace, 1937.

Erisman, Fred. *Boys' Books, Boys' Dreams, and the Mystique of Flight.* Fort Worth: Texas Christian University Press, 2006.

Friedan, Betty. *The Feminine Mystique.* New York: W.W. Norton, 1963.

Gann, Ernest K. *Fate is the Hunter.* New York: Simon & Schuster, 1961.

Gannon, Susan R., Suzanne Rahn, and Ruth Anne Thompson, eds. *St. Nicholas and Mary Mapes Dodge: The Legacy of a Children's Magazine Editor, 1873-1905.* Jefferson, NC: McFarland & Co., 2004.

Garvey, William, and David Fisher. *The Age of Flight: A History of America's Pioneering Airline.* Greensboro, NC: Pace Communications, 2002.

Greenwald, Marilyn S. *The Secret of the Hardy Boys: Leslie McFarlane and the Stratemeyer Syndicate.* Athens: Ohio University Press, 2004.

Gunston, Bill, ed. *Aviation Year by Year.* New York: DK Publishing, 2001.

Gwynn-Jones, Terry. *Farther and Faster: Aviation's Adventuring Years, 1909-1939.* Washington, DC: Smithsonian Institution Press, 1991.

Hall, Ed Y. Harriet *Quimby: America's First Lady of the Air.* Spartanburg, SC: Honoribus Press, 1990.

Hallion, Richard P. *Legacy of Flight: The Guggenheim Contribution to American Aviation.* Seattle: University of Washington Press, 1977.

———. *Taking Flight: Inventing the Aerial Age from Antiquity through the First World War.* New York: Oxford University Press, 2003.

Heinlein, Robert A. *Expanded Universe.* 1980. Reprint, New York: Ace Science Fiction, 1982.

Hertog, Susan. *Anne Morrow Lindbergh: Her Life.* New York: Anchor Books, 1999.

Hochschild, Arlie Russell. *The Managed Heart: Commercialization of Human Feeling.* Berkeley: University of California Press, 1983.

Hodgson, Marion Stegeman. *Winning My Wings: A Woman Airforce Service Pilot in World War II.* Annapolis: Naval Institute Press, 1996.

Honey, Maureen. *Creating Rosie the Riveter: Class, Gender, and Propaganda During World War II.* Amherst: University of Massachusetts Press, 1984.

Ingells, Douglas J. *The Plane that Changed the World: A Biography of the DC-3.* Fallbrook, CA: Aero Publishers, 1966.

Jaros, Dean. *Heroes without Legacy: American Airwomen, 1912-1944.* Niwot: University Press of Colorado, 1993.

Jessen, Gene Nora. *Powder Puff Derby of 1929: The True Story of the First Women's Cross-Country Air Race.* Napierville, IL: Sourcebooks, 2002.

Johnson, Deidre, ed. *Stratemeyer Pseudonyms and Series Books.* Westport, CT: Greenwood Press, 1982.

Kelly, R. Gordon. *Mother Was a Lady: Self and Society in Selected American Children's Periodicals, 1865-1890.* Westport, CT: Greenwood Press, 1974.

Kern, Stephen. *The Culture of Time and Space 1880-1918.* Cambridge: Harvard University Press, 1983.

Kessler, Lauren. *The Happy Bottom Riding Club: The Life and Times of Pancho Barnes.* New York: Random House, 2000.

Kevles, Bettyann Holtzmann. *Almost Heaven: The Story of Women in Space.* Cambridge: MIT Press, 2006.

Lanes, Selma G. *Down the Rabbit Hole.* New York: Atheneum, 1971.

Leary, William M. *Aerial Pioneers: The U.S. Air Mail Service, 1918-1927.* Washington, DC: Smithsonian Institution Press, 1985.

LeBow, Eileen F. *Before Amelia: Women Pilots in the Early Days of Aviation.* Washington, DC: Brassey's, 2002.

Link, Arthur S., and William B. Catton. *American Epoch: A History of the United States Since the 1890's.* 3rd ed. New York: Alfred A. Knopf, 1967.

Lomax, Judy. *Women of the Air.* New York: Dodd, Mead, 1987.

Lougheed, Victor. *Aeroplane Designing for Amateurs.* Chicago: Reilly & Britton, 1912.

———. *Vehicles of the Air: A Popular Exposition of Modern Aeronautics with Working Drawings.* 3rd ed. Chicago: Reilly and Britton, 1911.

Lovell, Mary S. *The Sound of Wings: The Life of Amelia Earhart.* New York: St. Martin's Press, 1989.

Luckett, Perry D. *Charles A. Lindbergh: A Bio-Bibliography.* Westport, CT: Greenwood Press, 1986.

MacLeod, Anne Scott. *American Childhood: Essays on Children's Literature of the Nineteenth and Twentieth Centuries.* Athens: University of Georgia Press, 1994.

Mason, Bobbie Ann. *The Girl Sleuth: A Feminist Guide.* Old Westbury, NY: Feminist Press, 1975.

McDougall, Walter A. *The Heavens and the Earth: A Political History of the Space Age.* 1985. Reprint, Baltimore: Johns Hopkins University Press, 1997.

Merryman, Molly. *Clipped Wings: The Rise and Fall of the Women Airforce Service Pilots (WASPs) of World War II.* New York: New York University Press, 1998.

Meyer, Dickey [Dickey Chapelle]. *Girls at Work in Aviation.* Garden City: Doubleday, Doran & Co., 1943.

Moolman, Valerie. *Women Aloft.* Alexandria, VA: *Time-Life* Books, 1981.

Mott, Frank Luther. *A History of American Magazines, 1850-1865.* Cambridge: Harvard University Press, 1938.

Mowry, George E. *The Era of Theodore Roosevelt, 1900-1912.* New York: Harper & Bros., 1958.

Nash, Ilana. *American Sweethearts: Teenage Girls in Twentieth-Century Popular Culture.* Bloomington: Indiana University Press, 2006.

Nichols, Ruth. *Wings for Life.* Philadelphia: J.P. Lippincott, 1957.

Nye, Russel B. *The Unembarrassed Muse: The Popular Arts in America.* New York: Dial Press, 1970.

Oakes, Claudia M. *United States Women in Aviation Through World War I.* Smithsonian Studies in Air and Space, vol. 2. Washington, DC: Smithsonian Institution Press, 1978.

———. *United States Women in Aviation, 1930-1939.* Washington, DC: Smithsonian Institution Press, 1991.

Pisano, Dominick A. *To Fill the Skies with Pilots: The Civilian Pilot Training Program, 1939-1946.* 1993. Reprint, Washington, DC: Smithsonian Institution Press, 2001.

Postman, Neil. *Amusing Ourselves to Death: Public Discourse in the Age of Show Business.* New York: Viking Penguin, 1985.

Putnam, George Palmer. *Soaring Wings: A Biography of Amelia Earhart.* New York: Harcourt, Brace, 1939.

Rehak, Melanie. *Girl Sleuth: Nancy Drew and the Women Who Created Her.* Orlando, FL: Harcourt, 2005.

Rich, Doris L. *Amelia Earhart: A Biography.* Washington, DC: Smithsonian Institution Press, 1989.

———. *Jackie Cochran: Pilot in the Fastest Lane.* Gainesville: University Press of Florida, 2007.

———. *The Magnificent Moisants: Champions of Early Flight.* Washington, DC: Smithsonian Institution Press, 1998.

Rickman, Sarah Byrn. *Nancy Love and the WASP Ferry Pilots of World War II.* Denton: University of North Texas Press, 2008.

Robie, Bill. *For the Greatest Achievement.* Washington, DC: Smithsonian Institution Press, 1993.

Rogers, Katherine M. *L. Frank Baum: Creator of Oz.* New York: St. Martin's Press, 2002.

Roseberry, C.R. *Glenn Curtiss: Pioneer of Flight.* Syracuse, NY: Syracuse University Press, 1991.

Rosenberg, Barry, and Catherine Macaulay. *Mavericks of the Sky: The First Daring Pilots of the U.S. Air Mail.* New York: William Morrow, 2006.

Scanlon, Jennifer. *Inarticulate Longings: The Ladies' Home Journal, Gender, and the Promises of Consumer Culture.* New York: Routledge, 1995.

Schurman, Lydia Cushman, and Deidre Johnson. *Scorned Literature: Essays on the History and Criticism of Popular Mass-Produced Fiction in America.* Westport, CT: Greenwood Press, 2002.

Smith, Elinor. *Aviatrix.* New York: Harcourt Brace Jovanovich, 1981.

Stoneley, Peter. *Consumerism and American Girls' Literature 1860-1940.* Cambridge, UK: Cambridge University Press, 2003.

Studley, Lt. Barrett. *Practical Flight Training.* New York: Macmillan Co., 1928.

Taylor, Frank J. *High Horizons: Daredevil Flying Postmen to Modern Magic Carpet —the United Air Lines Story.* Revised Edition 1964. Reprint, New York: McGraw-Hill Book Co., 1964.

Thaden, Louise. *High, Wide, and Frightened.* 1938. Reprint, Fayetteville: University of Arkansas Press, 2004.

Trites, Roberta Seelinger. *Disturbing the Universe: Power and Repression in Adolescent Literature.* Iowa City: University of Iowa Press, 2000.

van der Linden, F. Robert. *Airlines & Air Mail: The Post Office and the Birth of the Commercial Aviation Industry.* Lexington: University Press of Kentucky, 2002.

———. *The Boeing 247: The First Modern Airliner.* Seattle: University of Washington Press, 1991.

Veca, Donna, and Skip Mazzio. *Just Plane Crazy: Biography of Bobbi Trout.* Santa Clara, CA: Osborne Publisher, 1987.

Verges, Marianne. *On Silver Wings: The Women Airforce Service Pilots of World War II, 1942-1944.* New York: Ballantine Books, 1991.

Ware, Susan. *Still Missing: Amelia Earhart and the Search for Modern Feminism.* New York: W.W. Norton, 1993.

Weitekamp, Margaret A. *Right Stuff, Wrong Sex: America's First Women in Space Program.* Baltimore: Johns Hopkins University Press, 2004.

Whitelegg, Drew. *Working the Skies: The Fast-Paced, Disorienting World of the Flight Attendant.* New York: New York University Press, 2007.

Wohl, Robert. *A Passion for Wings: Aviation and the Western Imagination, 1908-1918.* New Haven: Yale University Press, 1994.

———. *The Spectacle of Flight: Aviation and the Western Imagination, 1920-1950.* New Haven: Yale University Press, 2005.

Woloch, Nancy. *Women and the American Experience: A Concise History.* 2nd ed. New York: McGraw-Hill, 2002.

Wosk, Julie. *Women and the Machine: Representations from the Spinning Wheel to the Electronic Age.* Baltimore: Johns Hopkins University Press, 2001.

B. Historical and Critical Articles

"5,000 Seek 20 Jobs as Air Stewardesses." *New York Times,* 17 October 1939, 27.

"7 Enter Contest for Safety Plane." *New York Times,* 10 October 1927, 23.

"10,000 'Baby Planes' At $700 Proposed." *New York Times,* 9 November 1933, 23.

Adams, Mildred. "Woman Makes Good Her Claim for a Place in the Skies." *New York Times Magazine,* 7 June 1931, 6, 20.

"A.E." *Aviation* 36 (August 1937): 22.

Aeroplane Blue Print Company advertisement. *Scientific American* 103 (29 October 1910): 352.

"The Air Hostess Carries On." *New York Times,* 19 April 1936, XX: 12.

"Air Hostess Finds Life Adventurous." *New York Times,* 12 April 1936, N1-2.

"Airplane Altered by Miss Earhart." *New York Times,* 23 March 1937, 3.

"Air Stewardesses Mark Anniversary." *Western Flying* 25 (October 1945): 62, 84.

"Airwomen." *Time* 29 (8 March 1937): 48-49.

"All Aboard the Lindbergh Limited!" *Literary Digest* 100 (2 March 1929): 54, 56-58.

"AM 23-3: NK to GX." *Fortune* 19 (February 1939): 65-66, 112, 114.

"Amelia Earhart, Ardent Feminist." *Equal Rights,* 15 June 1937, 82.

"Amelia Earhart New Vice-President." *National Aeronautic Magazine* 9 (May 1931): 34.

"Amelia Scores Again...." *National Aeronautic Magazine,* June 1932, 5.

"Amelias Have Changed Since Thackeray's 'Vanity Fair'." *U.S. Air Services* 17 (June 1932): 13.

"An American Bird-Woman." *Dallas Morning News,* 21 January 1912, 2.

Ammick, Hugh. "The Fimmale Wing." *U.S. Air Services* 14 (November 1929): 35-37.

Anderson, Mary. "16,000,000 Million Women at Work." *New York Times Magazine,* 18 July 1943, 8-19, 29.

"Army May Use Women to Ferry New Airplanes." *New York Times,* 3 July 1941, 12.

Arrow Aircraft & Motors Corporation. "Common Stock Notification." *New York Times,* 15 April 1929, 43.

Arthur, Julietta K. "Airways to Earning." *Independent Woman* 19 (February 1940): 34-35, 55-56.

———. "Now You Can Learn to Fly." *Independent Woman* 19 (October 1940): 320-321, 336.

Associated Press. "World's Greatest Aviator In Battle to Save a Life." *Washington Post,* 25 April 1928, 4.

"Autogiro is Hailed as Family Machine." *New York Times,* 6 June 1931, 14.

"Automatic Stabilizing System of the Wright Brothers." *Scientific American Supplement* no. 1828 (14 January 1911): 20-21.

"Autour Du Beffroi de Bruges." *L'Aerophile* 8 (1 October 1910): 435.

"Battle of the Sexes." *Time* 43 (8 May 1944): 68, 71.

Bellaire, Robert. "She Teaches the Army to Fly Blind." *Woman's Home Companion* 71 (April 1944): 29, 74-75.

Bilstein, Roger E. "The Airplane, The Wrights, and the American Public." In *The Wright Brothers: Heirs of Prometheus,* edited by Richard P. Hallion, 39-51. Washington, DC: Smithsonian Institution Press, 1978.

"Boeing's New Model 247 Transport." *Aviation* 32 (April 1933): 124-126.

Boykin, Elizabeth MacRae. "Amelia Earhart at Home." *Better Homes & Gardens* 15 (February 1937): 46-47.

"Braniff Welds the Southwest." *National Aeronautics* 15 (July 1937): 10-11.

Brown, Margery. "Flying is Changing Women." *Pictorial Review* 31 (June 1930): 30, 108-109.

Byrd, Commander Richard E., U.S.N. "Our Transatlantic Flight." *Aero Digest* 11 (July 1927): 8-10, 12-14.

Campbell Wood, G.F. "The International Aviation Meet." *Aircraft* 1 (December 1910): 353-359.

Cassutt, Michael. "Fly Us to the Moon." *Air & Space/Smithsonian* 23 (November 2008): 48-53.

Chamberlain, Kathleen. "'Wise Censorship': Cultural Authority and the Scorning of Juvenile Series Books, 1890-1940." In *Scorned Literature: Essays on the History and Criticism of Popular Mass-Produced Fiction in America,* edited by Lydia Cushman Schurman and Deidre Johnson, 187-211. Westport, CT: Greenwood Press, 2002.

"Chamberlin Flies Bellanca Plane to Germany." *Aviation* 22 (13 June 1927): 1276-1277.

Cierva, Juan de la. "Landing in Your Back Yard." *Popular Aviation* 16 (May 1935): 235, 268.

———. "A New Way to Fly." *Saturday Evening Post* 202 (2 November 1929): 20-21, 180-82, 186.

"City Greets Miss Earhart; Girl Flier, Shy and Smiling, Shares Praise with Mates." *New York Times,* 7 July 1928, 1.

"Classified Advertising." *Aerial Age Weekly,* 22 August 1921, 577.

Cleveland, Reginald M. "Air Transport Becomes Luxurious." *Scientific American* 149 (December 1933): 264-265.

———. "Contact." *New York Times,* 28 May 1933, XX: 8.

———. "Flying in Comfort." *Scientific American* 149 (August 1933): 68-69.

———. "Interest in Tiny Planes." *New York Times,* 8 December 1935, XX9.

———. "A New Day for Private Flying." *New York Times,* 7 April 1935, X13.

Clover, Samuel Travers. "First Meet of the Man-Birds in America." *Outing Magazine* 55 (March 1910): 750-763.

Cochrane, Dorothy. "Erco 415-C Ercoupe." 27 July 2001. http://www.nasm.si.edi/research/aero/aircraft/erco415.htm (accessed 13n November 2007).

"College Fliers." *Airwoman* 2 (March 1935): 10-11.

Commager, Henry Steele. "When Majors Wrote for Minors." *Saturday Review* 35 (10 May 1952): 10-11, 44-46.

Courtney, W.B. "High-Flying Ladies." *Collier's* 90 (20 August 1932): 29-30, 45.

———. "Ladybird." *Collier's* 95 (30 March 1935): 16, 40, 43.

Crandall, Rick. "Early Juvenile Aviation Fiction." *Dime Novel Roundup* 49 (October 1980): 82-86.

Dane, Roger. "Midnight Suns of the Air Mail." *Aero Digest,* July 1925, 12-18.

Darr, Ann. "The Women Who Flew -- but Kept Silent." *New York Times Magazine,* 7 May 1995, 70-71.

Davis, Edwina (Bunny). "I Like My Job." *U.S. Air Services* 18 (June 1933): 24-25.

"DC-4." *Time* 31 (23 May 1938): 33-34, 36-38.

Dizer, John T. "The Early Days of Youthful Motoring." *Dime Novel Roundup* 73 (August 2004): 119-128.

Drake, Francis Vivian. "Air Stewardess." *Atlantic Monthly* 151 (February 1933): 185-193.

———. "Pegasus Express." *Atlantic Monthly* 149 (June 1932): 663-674.

Earhart, Amelia. "Amelia Earhart's Own Story of Her Flight Over Pacific." *New York Times*, 13 June 1935, 1.

———. "Clouds." *Cosmopolitan* 86 (April 1929): 86-87.

———. "The Flier's Own Story." *New York Times*, 9 April 1931, 3.

———. "Fly America First." *Cosmopolitan* 87 (October 1929): 80-81, 134-136.

———. "Flying is Fun!" *Cosmopolitan* 93 (August 1932): 38-39.

———. "Flying the Atlantic." *American Magazine* 114 (August 1932): 15-17, 72.

———. "Fought Rain, Fog and Snow All The Way." *New York Times*, 19 June 1928, 1.

———. "A Friendly Flight Across." *New York Times*, 19 July 1931, SM: 4, 23.

———. "Here is How Fannie Hurst Could Learn to Fly." *Cosmopolitan* 86 (January 1929): 56-57, 163-164.

———. "Is It Safe for You to Fly?" *Cosmopolitan* 86 (February 1929): 90-91, 148.

———. "The Man Who Tells the Flier: 'Go!'." *Cosmopolitan* 86 (May 1929): 78-79, 144, 146.

———. "Miss Earhart Foresees Planes de Luxe, Due to Women's Interest in Aviation." *New York Times*, 20 June 1928, 1.

———. "Miss Earhart's Adventure on the Floor of the Sea." *Cosmopolitan* 87 (November 1929): 45, 98, 100.

———. "Mother Reads as We Fly." *Cosmopolitan* 90 (January 1931): 17.

———. "Mrs. Lindbergh." *Cosmopolitan* 89 (July 1930): 78-79, 196-198.

———. "My Flight from Hawaii." *National Geographic Magazine* 67 (May 1935): 593-596, 605-609.

———. "Practical Pilot." *Airwoman* 1 (October 1934): 11.

———. "Shall You Let Your Daughter Fly?" *Cosmopolitan* 86 (March 1929): 88-89, 142-143.

———. "Try Flying Yourself." *Cosmopolitan* 85 (November 1928): 32-35, 158-159.

———. "What Miss Earhart Thinks When She's Flying." *Cosmopolitan* 85 (December 1928): 28-29, 195-196.

———. "Why Are Women Afraid to Fly?" *Cosmopolitan* 87 (July 1929): 70-71, 138, 140.

———. "Woman's Status in Aviation." *Sportsman Pilot* 1 (March 1929): 8-9, 36.

———. "Women and Courage." *Cosmopolitan* 93 (September 1932): 54-55, 147-148.

———. "Women's Influence on Air Transport Luxury." *Aeronautic Review* 8 (March 1930): 32-33.

————. "Women's Influence on *Aviation*." *Sportsman Pilot* 3 (April 1930): 15.

————. "Your Next Garage May House an Autogiro." *Cosmopolitan* 91 (August 1931): 58-59, 160-161.

"Electric Rudder Is Urged." *New York Times*, 8 November 1935, 25.

"English Aviators Feature Long Island Meet." *Fly Magazine* 4 (November 1911): 11-15

Erisman, Fred. "Flying Suffragettes: Margaret Burnham's 'Girl Aviators' Series." *Dime Novel Roundup* 76 (April 2007): 36-46.

————. "Why 'The Flying Girl' Crashed." *Baum Bugle* 50 (Spring 2006): 20-26.

Evans, Ernestine. "The Sky is No Limit." *Independent Woman* 21 (November 1942): 326-328, 346.

"The Fatal Aeroplane Accident at Boston." *Scientific American* 107 (13 July 1912): 27.

"Feminists Stirred Over Woman Flier." *New York Times*, 8 November 1935, 25.

Field, Charles K. "On the Wings of To-Day." *Sunset* 24 (March 1910): 245-252.

"First Woman Airline Co-Pilot Flies Plane From Capital to Detroit With 7 Passengers." *New York Times*, 1 January 1935, 22.

"Flying Supermen and Superwomen." *Literary Digest* 122 (14 November 1936): 22-23.

"For It Was Indeed He." *Fortune* 9 (April 1934): 86-89, 193-194, 204, 206, 208-209.

Freedman, Leo. "The Duties of an Air Hostess." *Popular Aviation* 12 (February 1933): 81-82, 124-125.

"French Aviatrice Here." *New York Times*, 24 September 1911, C5.

Furnas, J.C. "Mr. Milquetoast in the Sky." *Scribner's* 104 (September 1938): 7-11, 60-61.

"Giants of 1938." *Aviation* 37 (July 1938): 20-21, 30-33.

Ginger, Bonnie R. "Here's the Airgirl! A Talk With Harriet Quimby." *World Magazine*, 27 August 1911, 3.

"Girl Flier Thrilled by Motorcycle Ride." *New York Times*, 8 July 1928, 16.

"Girl Pilots." *Life* 15 (19 July 1943): 73-81.

"Glamor Girls of the Air." *Life* 45 (25 August 1958): 68-77.

"Glenn Curtiss Flies Over Aviation Park." *Los Angeles Times*, 10 January 1910, 1.

"Glenn Curtiss Wins the Scientific American Trophy." *Scientific American*, 14 January 1911, 29.

Gould, Bruce. "Daughter of the Skies." *American Magazine* 112 (July 1931): 78-79, 88, 90.

————. "Girls Have Wings, Too! How Elinor Smith, 17, Set an Endurance Record." *St. Nicholas*, June 1929, 631, 674.

Graham, Frederick. "Air Currents." *New York Times*, 23 June 1940, XX9.

———. "First Lady of the Air Lanes." *New York Times Magazine*, 25 September 1938, 11, 27.

———. "Winged Hostess." *New York Times Magazine,* 17 January 1940, 15, 17.

Graham, Frederick P. "Miss Cochran Wins Bendix Air Race: Close to Record." *New York Times*, 4 September 1938, 1, 3.

Haff, James E. "Bibliographia Pseudonymiana." *Baum Bugle* 18 (Spring 1974): 4-5.

Harriman, Margaret Case. "Ring Bell for Hostess." *Woman's Home Companion* 64 (December 1937): 12, 93, 96.

"The Harvard Aviation Meeting." *Scientific American* 103 (17 September 1910): 216-217, 227.

"Helen Richey Gets Post." *New York Times*, 14 December 1935, 13.

"Helene Dutrieu, Aviator, is Dead." *New York Times*, 28 June 1961, 35.

"Home by Christmas." *Time* 44 (16 October 1944): 68-69.

"Hoover Voices Nation's Pride; King Likely to Honor Flier." *New York Times*, 22 May 1932, 1.

"Hourly Air Service to Capital Planned." *New York Times*, 3 June 1930, 3.

"Industries In U.S. Replacing Women." *New York Times*, 19 February 1946, 27-28.

Inness, Sherrie A. "On the Road and In the Air: Gender and Technology in Girls' Automobile and Airplane Serials, 1909-1932." *Journal of Popular Culture* 30 (Fall 1996): 47-60.

"International Aviation Meet Advertisement." *Fly Magazine* 3 (October 1911): back cover.

"Jacqueline Cochran." *U.S. Air Services* 23 (January 1938): 24-28.

"Jacqueline Cochran Flies Bomber To Britain for Service With R.A.F." *New York Times*, 21 June 1941, 5.

"John J. Montgomery Falls to Death in Glider." *Fly Magazine,* December 1911, 19.

Johnson, Deidre. "From Abbott to Animorphs, from Godly Books to Goosebumps: The Nineteenth-Century Origins of Modern Series." In *Scorned Literature: Essays on the History and Criticism of Popular Mass-Produced Fiction in America,* edited by Lydia Cushman Schurman and Deidre Johnson, 147-165. Westport, CT: Greenwood Press, 2002.

Karant, Max. "Air-Sleepers On American Line." *Popular Aviation* 18 (January 1936): 25-26.

Kastner, Joseph. "Joan Waltermire: Airline Stewardess." *Life* 10 (28 April 1941): 102-04, 106, 108, 110, 112.

Kilgannon, Corey. "When Flying Was Caviar." *New York Times*, 19 October 2003, TR 23.

Kirkwood, Edith Brown. "With Milady of the Skies." *Aerial Age* 1 (June 1912): 5-6.

Klemin, Alexander. "An Airplane in Every Garage?" *Scribner's Magazine* 98 (September 1935): 179-182.

————. "The Evolution of the Private Plane." *Sportsman Pilot* 14 (15 July 1935): 11, 80, 82.

————. "Planes for Private Flying." *Scientific American* 140 (March 1929): 206-215.

Kline, Sherman J. "Development and Operation of the Safeway System." *Southern Aviation* 2 (15 October 1930): 13-17.

Krarup, Marius C. "A Chamber of Horrors: Wild Designs in Flying Machines." *Scientific American* 105 (14 October 1911): 338-339.

Kumler, Marjorie. "They've Done It Again." *Ladies' Home Journal* 61 (March 1944): 28-29, 167-169.

"Lady Monoplanist Arrives in City." *Dallas Morning News,* 20 March 1912, 6.

Law, Ruth. "Miss Law Tells of Her Record Flight; To Try Non-Stop New York Trip Next." *New York Times,* 20 November 1916, 1, 4.

[Lawrence, Josephine]. "The Newarker Whose Name Is Best Known." *Newark Sunday Call,* 9 December 1917, 1.

Lea, Jeanette. "We Don't Fly For Love." *Popular Aviation* 23 (September 1938): 24-26, 80.

LePage, W.L. "The Development of the Amphibian Airplane." *Aviation* 22 (25 April 1927): 828-832.

Lindbergh, Col. Charles A. "Aircraft for Private Owners And How to Choose One." *New York Times,* 25 November 1928, XX: 10.

————. "Lindbergh Writes of Aviation's Advance." *New York Times,* 26 August 1928, 1.

Lindbergh, Col. Chas. A. "Differing Types of Planes Now Built to Serve Special Uses." *New York Times,* 18 November 1928, XX: 12.

Lindbergh, Colonel Charles A. "Lindbergh Calls for Airways to Link Capitals of Continent." *New York Times,* 16 December 1927, 1, 2.

————. "Lindbergh Says His Mind Is Ablaze With Noise and an Ocean of Faces." *New York Times,* 14 June 1927, 1, 3.

"The Lockheed Cabin Monoplane." *Aero Digest* 11 (August 1927): 188, 190.

"Loening Cabin Amphibian." *Aviation* 24 (9 April 1928): 888, 902-906.

Loening, Grover Cleveland. "Automatic Stability of Aeroplanes." *Scientific American* 104 (13 May 1911): 470-471, 488.

Lurie, Alison. "Reading at Escape Velocity." *New York Times Book Review,* 17 May 1998, 51.

"Maitland and Hegenberger Fly to Hawaii." *Aviation* 23 (11 July 1927): 72-73.

Marin, Rick. "When Flying Tourist Meant Going in Style." *New York Times,* 28 March 1999, ST 1.

Martyn, T.J.C. "Women Fliers of the Uncharted Skies." *New York Times Magazine,* 10 August 1930, 7, 22.

Mathiews, Franklin K. "Blowing Out the Boy's Brains." *The Outlook,* 11 November 1914, 652-654.

Mazet, Harold S. "Pro Patria et Gloria." *Sportsman Pilot* 6 (August 1931): 30-31, 54.

McIntyre, O.O. "I Want You to Meet a Real American Girl." *Cosmopolitan* 85 (November 1928): 21.

McLaughlin, George F. "United States' Airplanes and Engines." *Aero Digest,* May 1927, 402-407.

Miller, Frieda S. "What's Become of Rosie the Riveter?" *New York Times Magazine,* 5 May 1946, 11, 47-48.

Mingos, Howard. "The Ladies Take the Air." *Ladies' Home Journal* 44 (May 1928): 3-4, 159-160.

"Miss Cochran Gets Air Trophy Again." *New York Times,* 16 June 1939, 14.

"Miss Cochran Put In High Air Post." *New York Times,* 6 July 1943, 18.

"Miss Earhart Answers Some Questions About Flying." *Cosmopolitan* 85 (December 1928): 30-31.

"Miss Earhart Backs Flier." *New York Times,* 8 November 1935, 25.

"Miss Earhart Pilots Passenger in Autogiro." *New York Times,* 20 December 1930, 3.

"Miss Quimby Flies English Channel." *New York Times,* 17 April 1912, 15.

"Miss Stinson Ready to Bring Aerial Mail." *New York Times,* 12 May 1918, 4.

Mitchell, Brigadier-General William. "The Automobile of the Air." *Woman's Home Companion* 59 (May 1932): 18-19, 126.

Molson, Francis J. "American Technological Fiction for Youth: 1900-1940." In *Young Adult Science Fiction,* edited by C.W. Sullivan III, 7-20. Westport, CT: Greenwood Press, 1999.

National Air and Space Museum, Smithsonian Institution. "Arrow Sport A2-60." http://www.nasm.si.edu/research/aero/aircraft/arrowsport (accessed 9 November 2007).

National Air and Space Museum, Smithsonian Institution. "Beech C17L Staggerwing." http://www.nasm.si.edu/research/aero/aircraft/beech.htm (accessed 23 November 2007).

"National Movement to Popularize Aeronautics to Be Launched by the Aero Club of America." *Aerial Age Weekly* 11 (19 April 1920): 179-180.

"Navy Sale of Seaplanes." *Aerial Age Weekly* 11 (19 April 1920): 175.

"New Books for the Aeronautical Library." *Fly Magazine* 4 (April 1912): 26.

Newton, Byron R. "Amelia and Her Chariot—A Thrilling Fairy Story as Our Grandmothers Would Have Told It." *U.S. Air Services* 17 (June 1932): 11-12.

Nichols, Ruth. "Behind the Ballyhoo." *American Magazine* 43 (March 1932): 78-80.

———. "The Sportsman Flies His Plane." *National Aeronautic Review,* April 1930, 33-36.

Nichols, Ruth R. "*Aviation* for You and for Me." *Ladies' Home Journal* 46 (May 1929): 9, 159, 161.

————. "Flying for Sport." *Ladies' Home Journal* 46 (September 1929): 12, 213-214.

Ninety-Nines. http://www.centennialofflight.gov/essay/ Explorers_Record_Setters_and_Daredevils/99s/ (accessed 27 August 2007).

"Notes of the Los Angeles Aviation Meet." *Fly Magazine* 4 (March 1912): 8-9.

O'Malley, Patricia. "Women With Wings." *Senior Scholastic* 42 (19-24 April 1943): 23-24.

Omlie, Phoebe Fairgrave. "Women in the Air Races." *Aero Digest* 17 (October 1930): 40-42.

Our Washington Correspondent. "The First Flight of the Wright Aeroplane at Fort Myer." *Scientific American* 99 (12 September 1908): 169.

Ovington, Earle. "The Airplane and Autogiro Compared." *Popular Aviation*, November 1931, 36.

Owen, Russell. "Adventure Rides with the U.S. Air Mail." *New York Times*, 10 June 1928, 10-11.

Patterson, Alicia. "I Want to Be a Transport Pilot." *Liberty*, 7 September 1929, 18-20, 22, 24.

"A Plane for the Sportsman." *Sportsman Pilot* 6 (August 1931): 39, 50.

Poole, Barbara E. "Requiem for the WASP." *Flying* 35 (December 1944): 55-56, 146, 148.

"President Hears Plea for Women's Rights; Amelia Earhart Cites Equality in the Air." *New York Times*, 23 September 1932, 1.

Price, Clair. "Amy Johnson Wings Her Way to Fame." *New York Times Magazine*, 1 June 1930, 4, 19.

————. "England's Air Heroine Talks of Fear." *New York Times Magazine*, 15 January 1933, 7, 17.

Purcell, Capt. Charles W. "What I Think About Women! A Rip-Snorting Opinion of Women's Place in Aviation." *Popular Aviation* 8 (April 1931): 15-16, 54.

"Putting Luxury in the Air." *Literary Digest* 112 (9 January 1932): 34.

"'Queen Helen' of Air." *Literary Digest* 120 (26 October 1935): 34-35.

Quimby, Harriet. "American Bird Women: Aviation as a Feminine Sport." *Good Housekeeping Magazine* 55 (September 1912): 315-316.

————. "The Dangers of Flying and How to Avoid Them." *Leslie's Illustrated Weekly*, 31 August 1911, 248-249.

————. "Exploring Air Lanes." *Leslie's Illustrated Weekly*, 22 June 1911, 703, 715.

————. "Flyers and Flying." *Leslie's Illustrated Weekly*, 27 June 1912, 725, 735.

————. "How a Woman Learns to Fly." *Leslie's Illustrated Weekly*, 17 August 1911, 181, 191.

————. "How a Woman Learns to Fly." *Leslie's Illustrated Weekly,* 25 May 1911, 602-603.

————. "How I Made My First Big Flight Abroad." *Fly Magazine* 4 (June 1912): 8-10.

————. "How I Won My Aviator's License." *Leslie's Illustrated Weekly,* 24 August 1911, 207, 221.

————. "New Things in the Aviation World." *Leslie's Illustrated Weekly,* 6 June 1912, 647.

"The Quimby Monument Fund." *Fly Magazine* 4 (September 1912): 16.

Railey, Capt. Hilton H. "Miss Earhart Held Victim of 'Career'." *New York Times,* 11 September 1938, 49.

Roberts, Margot. "You Can't Keep Them Down." *Woman's Home Companion* 71 (June 1944): 19, 91.

Rogers, Bogart. "Flying the Mail." *Cosmopolitan* 92 (March/April/May/June 1932): 24-27, 156-159; 80-83, 190, 192; 62-63, 159-162; 74-77, 148-149.

"Ruth Law Lands Here from Chicago in Record Flight." *New York Times,* 21 November 1916, 1, 3.

"Sainsbury, Noel Everingham, Jr." In *Who Was Who in America,* vol. 7, 498. Chicago: Marquis Who's Who, 1981.

"Says Man's Strength Is Needed." *New York Times,* 8 November 1935, 25.

Schmitt, Harrison H. "A Trip to the Moon." In *Where Next, Columbus? The Future of Space Exploration,* edited by Valerie Neal, 41-75. New York: Oxford University Press, 1994.

Selby, Barbara. "The Fifinellas." *Flying* 33 (July 1943): 76,   78, 166-167.

Semple, Elizabeth Anna. "Harriet Quimby, America's First Woman Aviator." *Overland Monthly* 58 (December 1911): 525-532.

"The Service is Excellent as the Stewardess Profession Grows Up." *Airwoman* 2 (August 1935): 10-11.

Shaffer, Cleve T. "The Los Angeles Aviation Meet." *Scientific American Supplement* 69 (5 February 1910): 90-91.

"Shall America Take the Lead in Aeronautics?" *Scientific American* 98 (29 February 1908): 138.

Sharples, Lawrence P. "The Pilots of Pylon." *Sportsman Pilot* 7 (April 1932): 30-31, 44.

"Sick and Tired of Ocean Flights." *Literary Digest* 114 (13 August 1932): 30.

"Skylounge Luxury." *National Aeronautics* 15 (February 1937): 22-23.

"Sleepers: New Douglas Ships Have More Lift, Space, Comfort." *Newsweek* 8 (4 July 1936): 25.

Smith, Helen Huntington. "New Woman [Elinor Smith]." *New Yorker* 6 (10 May 1930): 28-31.

"The Society's Special Medal Awarded to Amelia Earhart." *National Geographic Magazine* 62 (September 1932): 358-367.

Soderbergh, Peter A. "Edward Stratemeyer and the Juvenile Ethic, 1894-1930." *International Review of History and Political Science* 11 (February 1974): 61-71.

———. "The Great Book War: Edward Stratemeyer and the Boy Scouts of America, 1910-1930." *New Jersey History* 91 (Winter 1973): 235-248.

"Soldiers and Civilians." *Life* 17 (25 September 1944): 36.

Spencer, G.K. "Pioneer Women of Aviation." *Sportsman Pilot* 3 (May 1930): 16-17, 49.

"Sportsmen in Aviation Assembled." *Sportsman Pilot* 7 (April 1932): 22-25, 49-50.

"Stewardess Claims Job Becomes Chore." *Dallas Morning News,* 18 August 1961, 4.

Stuart, John. "The WASP." *Flying* 34 (January 1944): 73-74, 148, 163.

"Student, Worker as Well as a Flier." *New York Times,* 4 June 1928, 2.

"Tact and Heroism on U.S. Air-Lines." *Literary Digest* 121 (18 April 1936): 6.

Tarbell, Ida M. "Flying —A Dream Come True." *Flying* 2 (November 1913): 20-22.

"Termination of the Rheims Aviation Meeting." *Scientific American* 101 (11 September 1909): 180-181.

"Thaden, Louise McPhetridge." In Document File CT-141000-01. Washington, DC: Smithsonian Institution.

"This Month's Cover." *U.S. Air Services* 19 (June 1934): 32-33.

Thomas, Joan. "What About That Hostess Job?" *Popular Aviation,* May 1933, 290, 333, 338.

Thornley, Betty D. "Madame, the Aeroplane Waits." *Vogue,* 15 June 1920, 35-38, 108, 110.

"Timeline 1951-1990." The Pill.
http://www.pbs.org/ wgbh/amex/pill/timeline/timeline2.html
(accessed 1 October 2008).

Tobias, Sheila, and Lisa Anderson. "Whatever Happened to Rosie the Riveter?" *Ms.* 1 (June 1973): 92-94.

Toombs, Alfred. "Flight Nurse." *Woman's Home Companion* 70 (December 1944): 36, 117-118.

"The Tri-Motored Ford Air Transport." *Aero Digest* 10 (June 1927): 582.

"Two Women Fliers Hail Achievement." *New York Times,* 22 May 1932, 36.

"Unnecessary and Undesirable?" *Time* 43 (29 May 1944): 66.

"U.S. Approves Pill For Birth Control." *New York Times,* 9 May 1960, 75.

Van Zandt, Lieut. J. Parker. "On the Trail of the Air Mail." *National Geographic Magazine* 49 (January 1926): 1-61.

Vaughan, David K. "Girl Fliers in a World of Guys: Three 1930s Girls' Aviation Series." *Dime Novel Roundup* 68 (February 1999): 16-27.

———. "Technology and American Values: Juvenile Aviation Adventure Series of the 1930s." *Journal of Popular Literature* 1 (Spring/Summer 1985): 102-116.

———. "The War and the WAC: Bernadine Bailey's 'Youngest WAC' Series." *Dime Novel Roundup* 68 (December 1999): 217-223.

"Vidal Seeks Bids on 'Flivver' Planes." *New York Times,* 27 May 1934, 10.

Vultee, Gerard F. "20 Miles Faster." *Western Flying* 5 (March 1929): 38-39.

"WAAC: U.S. Women Troop to Enlist in Army's First All-Female Force." *Life* 12 (8 June 1942): 26-27.

Ward, John William. "The Meaning of Lindbergh's Flight." *American Quarterly* 10 (Spring 1958): 3-16.

"WASP Statistics." http://www.pbs.org/wgbh/amex/flygirls/ filmmore/ reference/primary/wasprecord01.html (accessed 26 April 2008).

"Wilbur Wright's Trial Flights in France." *Aeronautics* 1 (September 1908): 66-67.

"Will Bear the Name Wafs." *New York Times,* 11 September 1942, 26.

Wines, James P. "The 48 Hr. Coast to Coast Air-Rail Service of Transcontinental Air Transport." *Aviation* 27 (6 July 1929): 26-29.

"A Woman Hops the Atlantic." *Literary Digest* 97 (30 June 1928): 8-9.

"Woman in Trousers Daring Aviator." *New York Times,* 11 May 1911, 6.

"Woman to Be Co-Pilot." *New York Times,* 4 June 1928, 1.

"Woman to Drive Auto to Frisco." *New York Times,* 15 May 1910, S: 4.

"Woman's Monoplane Wrecked and Burned." *Dallas Morning News,* 15 April 1912, 1.

"Women Are Held Back, Miss Earhart Finds." *New York Times,* 30 July 1929, 26.

"Women Auto Drivers in Endurance Run." *New York Times,* 31 October 1909, S: 4.

"Women Aviators to Race." *New York Times,* 18 September 1911, 7.

"Women for War Flying." *New York Times,* 11 August 1940, 114.

"Women in Steel." *Life* 15 (9 August 1943): 74-81.

"The Women's Air Derby." *Literary Digest* 102 (7 September 1929): 9.

"Women Take to the Air." *U.S. Air Services* 15 (May 1930): 44-45.

"Women Will Form a Ferry Command." *New York Times,* 11 September 1942, 26.

Woodhouse, Henry. "Pioneer Women of the Air." *Flying* 2 (June 1913): 22-25, 32.

"The World Awheel." *Munsey's Magazine* 15 (May 1896): 131-159.

"Would Bar Sea Hop by Amelia Earhart." *New York Times,* 30 December 1934, 15.

"The Wright Aeroplane and Its Fabled Performances." *Scientific American* 94 (13 January 1906): 40.

"The Wright Aeroplane and Its Performances." *Scientific American* 94 (7 April 1906): 291-292.

"The Wright and Voisin (Farman) Flying Machines Compared." *Scientific American* 100 (9 January 1909): 18-19.

Wright, Orville, and Wilbur Wright. "The Wright Brothers Aeroplane." *The Century Magazine* 76 (September 1908): 641-650.

Index

Page numbers in italics refer to illustrations and photographs.

ISBN 978-0-87565-397-6

From Birdwomen to Skygirls: American Girls' Aviation Stories
ISBN 978-0-87565-397-6
Cloth. $29.95.